HUGH GLASS

by

Bruce Bradley

Hugh Glass
by Bruce Bradley

Monarch Press
P.O. Box 708
Calistoga, CA 94515

First Monarch Press printing of this edition: 1999
Most recent printing indicated by the first digit below:
1   2   3   4   5   6   7   8   9   10

Library of Congress Catalog Number: 98-92276

ISBN 0-96690905-0-2

Printed in Canada

I would like to thank everyone who helped me in the development of this book, including: Jim Pryts, of Pryts Photo Services, for all the computer imaging work that was done on the cover. Deanna Gosset, for all those hours of typing. JoAnn Barberi, for all her help and support. My Mother and my sister, Dianna, for their support. John Le Bourgeois, of M.A.P.O.M. -for his animal tracking class at Kule Loklo, Pt. Reyes, CA. I would also like to thank Don Landers and Mark Murphy of Honeywell and Todd, and my friend Philip Claypool—for introducing me to them. Most of all, I would like to offer a very special thanks to Charles Lee Todd, for the incredible artwork that he did for the cover of this book.

THANKS TO YOU ALL!

For JoAnn, who once said,
"Why Don't You?"

Dear Reader,

When I first began researching the story of Hugh Glass, more than seven years ago, I had no idea where or how long it would take me, or how little I actually knew about this great continent of ours and the people and conditions that once existed here. I knew, or thought I knew, about indians and buffalo. Having grown up in Alaska, I knew about bears. If anyone had told me that here were once canibals living in this country, or that a well-known plains tribe once practiced human sacrifice, I wouldn't have believed them. I knew that, later on in the nineteenth century, buffalo hunters had driven that great animal to the edge of extinction, but I never conceived the extent of that butchery. At the time that this story takes place, there were two great herds that roamed the plains, numbering more than twenty-five million strong.

Because of the lack of historical documentation, I had to re-create much of the early part of this book. I've tried to be as accurate as possible and any liberties I have taken were merely to keep the story moving. The events that take place in the latter part of the book—which I consider to be the most fantastic—have been well documented. Anyone who wants to take the time can check them out. I am including a bibliography at the end of the book which may help in that search. I'll also include short biographies of some of the people found within these pages.

Writing this book has been a wonderfully educational experience for me. I hope reading it will be the same for you.

Bruce Bradley
-October 1995

"In point of adventure, dangers and narrow escapes; and capacity for endurance, and the sufferings which befell him, this man (Hugh Glass) was pre-eminent. He was bold, daring, reckless and eccentric to a high degree; but was, nevertheless, a man of great talents, and intellectual as well as bodily power."

George C. Yount
(1794-1865)
The Chronicles of George C. Yount

PART ONE

"One man who allso tore nearly all to peases by a White Bear and was left by the way without any gun who afterwards recover'd"

—Daniel T. Potts
(of the Rocky Mountain Fur Co.)
—— The DTP Letters

CHAPTER ONE

MAY, 1817—

The sea had always been good to him. There was no time in his memory when he had not been near the sea or on the sea, or had not loved the sea. From his first voyage—working as cabin boy on a trip that took him around the world—he had known the sea would be his life.

In a way, he and the great waters were alike. He was quiet and deep as they were quiet and deep, and as they had their wild, tempestuous times, so had he. He respected the sea but had no fear of her. He knew her harsh realities. Many times danger braced him, but rarely had he felt uneasy when on the deck of a ship.

The sea. Always the sea. The sea challenged him and worked him, tried him and bled him and cleansed him. He saw the water not so much as a liquid but as a solid, living thing, a thing that exemplified all that was noble within him. It renewed him with its endless energy and made him strong in ways both spiritual and physical. The sea was pure and it was clean. The sea was life. To be upon the sea and a part of the sea, was all he ever asked.

All of that would change, soon.

The old brig shuddered and moaned with each ball that struck her. Sometimes she bawled in unresisting protest, slowly dying an undignified death. Only meters away the other ship, the *Madalaine*, continued to pummel her mercilessly. The artillerists aboard the *Madalaine* were incredibly accurate. Their cannonballs struck the brig with each discharge, yet none hit the ship below the water line, where it would cause her to take on water. Unable to return the constant barrage of cannon fire, the men of the ship, *Gallant*, huddled deep within her bowels and waited for the shelling to stop.

Most of the men were quiet. They waited, not wishing to show the fear they felt. Some prayed. Three men were wounded. Two of these lay moaning quietly while others tended them. The third man, a sailor named Connors, couldn't contain his pain. Others held him down, but still he thrashed about, screaming incoherently. The hold was rank with the smell of sweat and fear, which was overlaid with the more familiar odors of tar and canvas. A lantern had been hung from an overhead beam, but the unsteady motion of the ship—not only from the sea but from the continuous pummeling of cannonballs—caused the lantern to dance wildly about, creating shadows and adding to the confusion. One of the men took it down and held it, so that the light would be steady.

The captain of the *Gallant* had been killed in the first moments of the attack. The first mate was a man named Hugh Glass. A highly capable man, Glass had been a sailor for twenty-four out of his thirty-seven years. He had been educated at sea, both in books and in sailing, and was comfortable in almost any emergency.

Except this one. Glass had been a merchant seaman his entire life. His only experience with fighting had been in his earlier, wilder days. Physically, he was up to the challenge. He was a little taller than most men of his time and powerfully built, with a look in his gray eyes that often stopped confrontations before they began. But he had no experience with leading men into battle, and now he must do so.

The *Gallant* shuddered violently as three cannonballs struck her at once.

"Good Christ!" one of the men yelled. "Are they *never* going to cease?"

"They'll stop soon," Glass told the man. "They'll have to, if they're to get anything for their troubles!"

Glass thought briefly about his family. His wife, Sarah, had divorced him two years earlier, in favor of a young banker. Hugh had seen neither her, nor their two boys, since that time. He'd written to the boys once, and had meant to do so again. Somehow, he had never gotten around to it.

He steadied himself as another ball struck the ship. Looking through the gloom at the faces of his men, a sudden anger engulfed him. They didn't deserve this, none of them. They were not fighting men, just plain, honest sailors. A *few* of them would take their toll—Clint Hastings, it was said, was good with his fists, and was one of the strongest men Hugh Glass had ever met. Bill Snider was another who would hold his own. Tall and pious, Tom Halpern had been a volunteer at the Battle of New Orleans, and if Glass knew Halpern, the man would have enough righteous indignation inside him to take on half the pirate crew when they came aboard. Most of the men, though, were ordinary working men—seamen, who sweated and toiled, and whose families depended on their incomes for support and who suffered their absences while they were away. They would be no match for the experienced killers who were waiting to board the *Gallant*.

Glass continued to study the men. Many were nearly sick with fear. They needed something to bolster them. He wanted to tell them everything would be fine, but he knew it would be a lie and so would they.

He noticed that Connors was no longer screaming.

"Did he faint?" he asked one of the men.

"No sir," the man answered. "Mr. Connors has died."

Glass nodded to the man. Under his breath he swore, "*DAMN!*"

The men were waiting. They needed him to say *something*. Anything.

"Men!" he began. "Listen up! There are some things I want to say!" He looked around at them. "We all know what's waiting for us once those cannons stop! I wish I could tell you that this will all turn out well enough, but we know better! Those men out there—no matter what happens or what they might try to tell you—" he stopped as two cannonballs struck the decks above, rocking the ship. "—No matter what they say, they want no witnesses! Their creed is, *Dead men tell no tales!*"

"*None* of us will probably ever leave these waters, and that's the truth of it! When they come aboard, we have to fight them! If they even try to talk to us, it will be a trick, so fight! Fight as though you've nothing to lose! Don't fight for the *Gallant*, or her cargo! Fight for yourselves and for each other! Fight as though it were your wives and daughters you are protecting! Do not try to fight fair—fight to win! Remember that as long as life remains, there is hope!"

"If we, each of us, tries to kill at least one or two *them* before they take us down, some of us may yet live to see another day!"

His words seemed to help a little, but Hugh Glass knew that once the fighting started, it would be pretty much a one-sided battle.

The shelling continued only a few minutes more. Then, abruptly, it stopped. Hesitating a moment to be certain the shelling was through, Glass started up the ladder.

"Come on, men!" he shouted. "We'll catch them as they come aboard!"

CHAPTER TWO

HE WAS stunned by the sight that greeted him. This ship, which had been his home for the past two and a half years, would never sail out of these waters. Whole sections of the main deck had been destroyed by cannon fire, leaving gaping holes that looked down into the decks below. The masts were down. Sailcloth and lines, pieces of broken decking and rail and all manner of debris lay everywhere about. Looking to port, he saw that the *Madalaine* was uncomfortably close, with lines already attaching her to the *Gallant*. One man had already managed to bridge the distance between the two ships. He climbed up onto the deck of the *Gallant* only a half-dozen steps away from Hugh Glass, and came at Glass in a rush. With a pistol he'd taken from the armory, Glass took aim and fired. The pirate made a clutching motion toward his chest and fell backward into the sea.

Ducking behind a section of railing that, miraculously, had not been destroyed, Glass began to reload the pistol. His hands were shaking badly. After a few moments he threw the pistol in disgust and drew his sword.

He didn't have long to wait. The two ships came together with a dull *thud*. The pirates swarmed over onto the *Gallant* and attacked. The crew of the merchant ship fought back, holding their ground. Hugh Glass had only a moment to observe them, but what he saw made him proud. The men fought with spirit and determination. Then Glass himself was too busy to watch what was going on around him.

He had never thought of himself as a violent man, a fighting man, but now something seemed to burst within him. He watched old Johnnie, the cook, go down under a pirate's blade, and an anger engulfed him that was impossible to contain. Time seemed to slow down for him, making the movements of those around him slow and awkward. He was relentless, tireless, filled with an energy born of pure rage. He threw himself into the midst of the pirates, slashing and killing. What he lacked in skill, he made up for with frenzied wrath and violence. For a time, he was unstoppable.....

Clint Hastings thought he was going to be sick. He stood, sword in hand, dazed and queasy, staring down at the man he'd just killed. Momentarily stunned, he was very aware of how slippery the handle of his sword was, because of his own sweaty palm, and quite aware of the bile that had risen in his throat, but was only vaguely aware of the violence that was going on around him. Clint had taken down many a man before, in bar fights and street brawls, but he'd never killed a man before. This was the first time.

The man hadn't died gracefully. He came on, fast and strong, leaving Clint little room or time to react, but Clint had always had good reflexes. When the pirate rushed him, Clint managed to sidestep. Without ever having been trained in swordplay, he performed the most basic of moves—parry and thrust—and ran the pirate through. Blood and entrails spilled out onto the deck. The pirate fell onto his side, kicking and convulsing until the life went out of him. Clint watched, feeling sick inside and somehow apart from the carnage that was going on around him.

The pirate died. Clint continued to stare at him for a minute, then looked around. Across the deck from him, about a dozen steps away, Clint's best friend was in trouble.

At twenty-five, Jeffrey Molloy was a year younger than Clint. He was good-natured, as most good sailors are, and had a wit that often made him the life of the ship. Whenever he and Clint went together on shore leave, women sought them out. They liked Jeffrey for his boyish charm, Clint for his bulging muscles. The two of them made a good team.....

Jeffrey was doing a fair job of defending himself, considering the pirate that faced him was larger and very dedicated, and had a good deal more skill with a sword. Using both hands on his own sword, Jeffrey managed to parry the pirate's blows, never managing to strike back. He was slowly being forced backward, toward a spot where the main mast had fallen at an angle and blocked his way. When he reached it he would be trapped and the pirate would clearly have the advantage.

Clint headed toward them, but his progress was slowed by the incredible amount of debris that covered the deck. He was still trying to get to them when he saw Jeffrey trip on some rigging and fall backward, losing his sword. Moving quickly, the pirate stepped over him. Unable to get near enough to help his friend, Clint watched as the pirate placed his blade against Jeffrey's chest and drove it home.

The pirate moved off. Working his way over the debris to where he could move freely, Clint ran to where his friend lay bleeding. Jeffrey had a bewildered look about him. Clint knelt down next to his friend.

"Clint!" Jeffrey choked. "I lost me sword! I—he....." His eyes glazed over and he died.

Feeling suddenly lost, Clint stood. Woodenly, he rubbed his forehead.

"Oh, Christ in Heaven, Jeffrey," he said.

He looked around. A heated battle was raging up near the bowsprit. The pirate that had just murdered Jeffrey was moving to join it. Clint went after him.

As he drew near, Clint realized that it was the Chief Mate, Mr. Glass, and Tom Halpern who were at the middle of it. Six of the pirates were trying to take them down, but were having no success in getting to them. Looking at Glass, Clint was stunned. In the year that Clint had served aboard the *Gallant,* he had never seen the Mate riled, much less violent. Now he was like a madman. None of the pirates could get near him.

The pirate that had killed Jeffrey was moving carefully, picking his way along what was left of the rail, toward the two men. Clint looked around. A few feet away from him, amidst the debris, was an iron loop that had been broken free from the mast by cannon fire. The loop was about three inches in diameter and was mostly intact. Sweeping it up, Clint threw it at the pirate.

The missile struck the man squarely in the back. The pirate took two quick steps forward, catching his balance and howling in pain. Then, roaring in anger, he turned and charged back across the clutter that lay over the deck of the ship.

Clint waited. When the pirate was six feet away, Clint let out a yell and stepped forward to meet him, at the same time striking downward with his sword. The pirate raised his own sword to block the blow, but Clint's downward strike contained such force that it knocked the sword from the pirate's hand. Before the man could recover, Clint took hold of his shirt, pulling him in close. With the blade of his sword against the pirate's jugular, he said:

"This is for Jeffrey, you son-of-a-bitch!"

He cut the pirate's throat.

Hugh Glass was in trouble. After fighting for what seemed like hours, he was beginning to tire. The man he was fighting seemed unfatigued, as though he had just arrived.

The man was enormous. He was several inches taller than Glass, and powerfully built. For nearly a quarter hour they had fought back and forth along the deck of the ship, neither gaining a clear advantage. Glass was fired by rage and hatred. The pirate was stronger and a skilled swordsman. In the beginning, they had seemed an equal match, but now Glass began to feel exhaustion creeping in. He continued to fight on, as determined as ever, but he was beginning to grow tired.

The pirate seemed to sense his fatigue. With a series of powerful, unrelenting blows, he began forcing Glass backward, never letting Hugh recover from one blow before the next was struck.

The handle of Hugh's sword had become slippery. His arm ached with each blow he countered and he could feel the painful vibration up into his shoulder and into the middle of his back. The pirate rained blow after blow upon him, striking with such ferocity that Glass expected his own sword to break each time the pirate struck. He continued to move backward, looking for an opening to strike back. No opening appeared. Suddenly, Glass lost his footing and fell against a section of the deckhouse. Seeing an opportunity, the pirate moved in to make the kill. Just as he struck, the two ships came together and he was thrown slightly off balance. Hugh felt the blade tear through his shirt and graze across his ribs. With a downward slice of his own sword, Glass half-severed the pirate's head from his shoulders. Not for the first time in Hugh Glass' life, the sea itself had saved him.

Then it seemed otherwise. A very small, wiry man stepped up. From less than six feet away, he pointed a pistol at Hugh's face, and fired.

CHAPTER THREE

HE AWOKE without comprehension, in blackness and in pain. For several minutes he lay very still, trying to remember what had happened and hoping the pounding in his head would cease. *What on earth had he been drinking?*

Then he remembered. He sat up much too quickly and the pain became nausea. Gagging, he fell back again.

"You all right, Captain?" A voice from the darkness. Hugh recognized it as Tom Halpern.

"I'm....not the captain," he said thickly.

"You are now, sir," —Clint Hastings' voice. "The captain's dead. We're all agreed—those of us that are left—you're in charge, for whatever it's worth."

"How many...." he swallowed, "....how many are left?"

"Only six, sir, counting you. Are you all right?"

"I feel like dog's leavings. I can't see a blessed thing. Are we in the hold?"

"Aye, sir," Hastings said. "They've blacked out the light. You aren't blind."

"What happened?"

"They got us, sir. They sank the *Gallant*. We put up a good fight, though. A couple of us thought you were gonna lick 'em all single-handed, 'til one of 'em bounced a pistol ball off your skull. Then it all just stopped, and we were surrounded."

"Who's left?"

"You and me, Potter, Sanders, Tyler, and Tom Halpern. McBride and Newlan were alive, but they were wounded. Soon as they dropped their weapons the pirates murdered them, because they couldn't work. Hacked 'em to pieces."

"They *will* be punished," Tom Halpern again. "The Lord, God, will punish them!"

"If they killed Newlan and McBride because they couldn't work," Hugh asked Hastings, "then why am I still alive?"

"They knew you'd come 'round, sooner or later. You killed someone named Tully. None of them could believe it. I think they want to take your measure before they let you die. I don't know what they have planned. They used those of us who were able-bodied to move the cargo off the *Gallant* and onto this hell-bucket. When we were done they made us watch while they sent her to the bottom."

"They blew her up, Captain," Halpern added, speaking softly, "blew her to Hades. There *will* be a reckoning, you can be certain of it!"

Glass started to protest the use of the title again, then gave up. The men wanted a leader, someone they could rally around. He was the logical choice.

"How long ago did they sink her?" he asked at length.

"A day, I think," Hastings told him. "It's hard to tell down here in the dark. From the amount of time and the noise topside, a day seems right."

They were silent for awhile as each man pondered what the coming hours—or minutes—might hold for them. At any moment they might be taken out and put to death, or put to work, as the pirates saw fit to do. They were being kept alive for something. Slave labor seemed likely.

In the closeness of the hold the heat was suffocating, the smell intolerable. The constant pounding in his head and the odor of unwashed, bloodied bodies brought waves of nausea to Hugh Glass, but he managed to choke it back.

It was impossible to tell the passage of time. In darkness, minutes can seem as hours, hours can be days. Twice the pirates lowered food and water to them. At first Hugh took only some of the water. The second time, he was feeling a little better and managed to eat a little food.

He could not believe the number of cuts he had sustained. He remembered getting nicked a *few* times during the fight, but now it seemed as though every inch of skin on his chest, arms, back, and legs had a small gash on it. Where the skin had begun to knit back together, it pulled at every movement. There was no way to tell if any of these were infected. Only time would tell if that were the case.

During this time, the men spoke often of their families. Tom Halpern, pious and stern, had no family. He spent the hours quoting the Bible and praying. Always devout, with a shock of gray near the middle of his forehead, Halpern seemed less than suited for a sailors life. Hugh Glass had often wondered that Halpern had not become a preacher. The man had a temper, but for someone who spouted Hellfire and brimstone, that didn't really seem like much of a drawback. There was something in his voice now that Glass found vaguely disturbing, but the men seemed to find Halpern's words comforting, so he said nothing.

He wasn't aware just when it happened, but the pounding in his head ceased, even though his lacerated skin continued to pull painfully whenever he moved. At least it was something.

He awoke suddenly, sore and confused. Bright, painful light flooded the hold. It took Hugh a moment to remember where he was. An unfamiliar voice, deep and gravelly, yelled down at them.

"All right, you men! Up on deck!"

Slowly, their aching bodies making it hard to move, the six men hauled themselves up onto the deck of the *Madalaine*. It was midmorning. The air and the sea were still, with just the hint of a breeze coming from the south. The brightness of the sun hurt the men's eyes, but the light breeze and the fresh air felt so good to them that they hardly noticed. A dozen men stood around them, all well-armed. Even the cabin boy had a pistol in his belt. Hugh recognized the small, wiry man who had shot him. The man stood several feet away, leaning against the mast, regarding Hugh with something that, to Hugh, seemed more than contempt.

One man among them stood out. He was better dressed than the others and strikingly handsome, with eyes and hair that were both black. More than that, there was a quality about him that was somehow instantly magnetic. It astounded Hugh Glass that, although they were strangers and enemies, he felt a sudden liking for the man.

"Well, Captain," gravel-voice said, "this bunch is certainly ripe enough!"

The rest of the pirates laughed. Hugh looked at his comrades. They were, indeed, a sight. All of them, including Hugh, were covered with filth and dried blood. Hugh was glad that the breeze carried the scent away from him.

Something about Tom Halpern bothered him. Always devoutly religious and very proud, the man shook visibly. It wasn't fear that caused this. Halpern's eyes burned with hatred. He looked insane.

"You men of the *Gallant!*" It was the man with the black hair. "I am Captain Michele Renoux—master of the *Madalaine* and third in command of Jean Lafitte's privateers! You men have been sentenced to die.!" Renoux spoke the words simply, in a voice accustomed to English but definitely French. The men next to Hugh looked from one to another in shock. Hugh kept his own eyes on Renoux. *There's more*, he thought. There has to be more. *They didn't keep us alive this long for nothing.*

"It is a shame to lose such brave men," Renoux continued, "but that is how it must be. You men are our enemies, and our enemies cannot be allowed to live.

Still, you fought well against us. Your efforts....cost the lives of many of my men. That leaves us shorthanded, which means more work for the rest of my crew, and my crew....." he looked around the ship at the faces of his men,".....would rather drink rum than work."

The pirates all laughed in agreement.

"At *their* request," Renoux went on, "I am prepared to offer you one chance to live. You must relinquish your former loyalties. You will swear complete obedience and loyalty to this ship and Jean Lafitte, as well as to me, Michele Renoux. You must do this if you would live. Decide now."

Hugh Glass thought for only a moment. He looked at his comrades, all of whom seemed to be in shock.

"Well lads," he said quietly, "it seems we're caught betwixt the deep blue sea....and the devil. Remember, where there's life, there's hope."

Tom Halpern threw him a sharp look.

"You would consider it?" he said angrily. "You would sign with this.....*offal*? After watching them butcher men you worked and toiled and laughed with for two years? Good men? Men who looked up to *you*? Good God—!"

"I would consider staying alive," Hugh told him, "and I would advise you to do the same!"

"ENOUGH!" Renoux stopped them. "Decide."

"I'll take life," Hugh said solemnly.

"*I'll take death!*" Halpern fairly spat the words at him. He continued to glare at Hugh as, one by one, the other men made their choices. Three of them chose, like Tom Halpern, to die rather than to sign aboard with the pirates. Only one other man, Clint Hastings, chose as Hugh did, to live.

"Very well," Renoux said at length, "You have made your choices. You and you," he indicated Hugh and Clint, "stand over there. You will see what you have saved yourselves from."

Following his directions, the two men moved over to the port railing. For the first time Hugh noticed the ship's cook. He was up near the front of the ship throwing chum—buckets of fishheads, blood, and entrails—over the side. Glancing out at the water Hugh counted the dorsal fins of almost a dozen sharks, some of them quite large.

The other four men, those who had refused to join the crew of the *Madalaine*, were taken aside. Each man had his arms bound tightly behind him. Together, they were led up to the railing, near where the cook had been throwing chum into the water. The gangplank had been stretched out over the side and secured, waiting. The first man to be led to it was a powerfully built seaman named Potter. When he saw the sharks, panic spread over his features.

"If you have any last words," Renoux told him, "speak them quickly."

Potter's eyes were wide with fear.

"I-I changed my mind," he said. "I'll join up! I'll do anythin' you want, just don't put me out there with those man eaters!"

Renoux gave him a tired look.

"I will have to ask my crew," the pirate said. Then, turning to the others, he spoke loudly. "Men? What shall it be? We have here a man who, minutes ago, was bravely ready to die rather than to become one of us and live the life we lead. Now...." he looked at Potter, "he pisses his breeches and begs us to let him join. What do you say?"

The pirates all looked at each other with amused interest. In unison they turned back and yelled, "NAY-Y-Y!"

"Very well," Renoux said, turning back to Potter. "You have heard the verdict. You made the choice. Go now and be eaten."

Potter was in shock. Several of the pirates moved toward him, intending to lift him onto the plank. Suddenly he came alive with the determination that they would not put him into the water. His arms bound behind him, the sailor could only kick and bite at his assailants, but this he did ferociously. Instinctively, Hugh started forward to help his shipmate.

"I don't think you'd be wantin' to do that, mate!" a voice next to him said. Hugh turned to see the small, wiry man, the one who had shot him. The man spoke the words quietly, but his pistol resting an inch from Hugh's ear made the message plain enough.

"Don't think I could miss you a second time," the man said. "Not at this range."

Seething, Hugh sighed with disgust and stepped back.

Potter, meanwhile, had managed to injure two of the pirates in a way that might have an effect on their future generations, and had shattered the kneecap of another. The pirates who were watching from the sidelines thought this was great sport. They roared with hilarity at the damage Potter inflicted upon their friends.

When, in the end, Potter was hauled still-kicking onto the gangplank, the man whose knee he had ruined limped forward. With his cutlass, the man gave Potter a wicked slash on his thigh.

"There!" he said angrily. "That'll give the beasties somethin' to lick at!"

Using poles, the pirates slowly forced Potter out to the end of the gangplank. Potter was silent now, his concentration focused on pushing against the poles and maintaining his balance. When he was at the end, he desperately tried pleading once more.

"Please!" he yelled. "*Don't!* I'll do anythin'! *ANYTHIN'*! I'll—-!"

Then he was off the end of the plank. He went into the water screaming and came up again, spitting and screaming incoherently. His panicked, awkward kicking drew the sharks quickly to him. Hugh tried to look away.

"Watch!" the wiry man ordered. "The captain wants you to see!"

Hugh glared at the man for several seconds before, sickened, he turned back to look at the water. He was in time to see Potter pulled under the surface, still very much alive. The sharks, driven to a frenzy by the chum, came at him from all sides. Potter continued to kick at them until finally one of the sharks managed to get his head into its mouth. The body of the man gave one final, convulsive kick. Then it went limp.

"He was a good man," Hugh heard himself say.

"Aye!" the small man agreed. "And you see what happens to good men aboard this ship! Good men fall, here. Bad ones rise." He pushed the pistol hard against Hugh's ear. "I hope you're a good man," the pirate told him.

With the feeling that all of his senses had gone dead inside him, Hugh continued to watch as the other three men were brought forward, all to fight for the last moments of their life. His mind scarcely registered what he saw. Instead, he saw Potter working hard on the deck of the *Gallant*, sweating heavily from exertion. Then he saw him in the quiet times, in the evening, smoking his pipe and talking of his home and family. Potter *had* been a good man—too good for the end he'd been given. They all were.

Only Tom Halpern refused to play the game the pirates had devised. When his turn came, he walked with dignity to the gangplank and allowed himself to be lifted up. Hugh would remember this later, in the hundreds of times his mind would replay the scene. For the moment, though, his mind was still far away.

"HUGH GLASS!"

At the sound of his name, Hugh's head snapped up and he came back to the present.

"*MISTER GLASS!*"

The crew went suddenly still.

Halpern stood upon the gangplank, glaring at Hugh. When he spoke again, his words were barely more than a whisper, but there was vehement menace in them that made them seem loud.

"Life....you have chosen," he began, "....and life you have. But on my *soul*, as *God is in Heaven*, it will not be an easy life. You will know pain and suffering and hardship of every sort. You will *NEVER* know peace. And when you *do* die, you will die *bloody*. Remember these words. They are the last words of a dying man, the last I will ever speak!"

The words were like a physical force. Hugh felt them strike somewhere in his midsection and impact there. In his numbed, guilt-ridden state, they seemed as weapons. He had no defense against them.

Having finished his say, Tom Halpern took two long strides and leapt off the end of the gangplank. He went into the water and never rose again to the surface.

The crew of the *Madalaine* had suddenly become quiet. Hugh could hear them muttering amongst themselves.

"....not a good sign," said one.

"Dead man's words...." another mumbled. Hugh didn't care. It didn't matter what they thought, and he no longer cared what happened to him.

When it was over, Renoux walked over to where the last two remaining members of the crew of the *Gallant* stood. He gave Hugh an appraising look.

"Well!" he said at length, still regarding Hugh. "That was certainly a curse that took, wasn't it!"

CHAPTER FOUR

THE TIDE rose and broke within him, but failed to cleanse or free him. He felt it rise again, swelling inside him until he thought he would burst from a quiet, unspeakable despair. Day after day he labored, working himself to exhaustion in an attempt to wash away the darkness that had come into his life. Nothing helped. No amount of hard work or exertion purged him. It seemed that a murkiness had entered his soul and, soiling it, remained there.

In time, he would come to know himself a murderer. The fact that he had little choice in his crimes would do nothing to exonerate him.

The port of Campeche was located on Galveston Island, just off the coast of Texas. It was an unwelcoming place, heavily fortified against attack, either by sea or from the mainland. Most of the structures were tents, and only a couple of the buildings were constructed of lumber. Lafitte's *Maison Rouge* was one, the *Bucket O' Blood*, another. Hugh sat in a corner of the tavern drinking a "flip", a drink made from beer, brandy, and sugar. He was mildly drunk. Outside, a hot, hard rain pelted the island. Inside, it was sweltering.

More than anyone Hugh Glass had ever met, Renoux was a puzzle. Intensely charismatic, the Frenchman could have been anything he wanted. He would have risen to the top of any profession he chose. A man of tremendous ability, he was dynamic, with a magnetism that rivaled Lafitte himself. He could have been a great statesman, a leader...

14

But he had chosen a darker, more violent role for himself. In time, Hugh Glass grew to hate him for it.

"You're one of the men from the *Madalaine.*"

Hugh came up with a start. He had been deep within himself, where he seemed to spend most of his time, these days. Charlotte Travers, the owner of the *Bucket O' Blood*, stood a few feet away. She was a tall woman, big-busted, with bright red hair. A handsome woman.

It hadn't been a question.

"I am," Hugh said simply.

"Mind if I sit down?"

"It's your place," he told her. Hugh had no craving for company.

Charlotte nodded to the bartender, then sat down across from Hugh. The bartender brought them drinks. Hugh started to pay. Charlotte Travers stopped him.

"On the house," she told him. Hugh eyed her suspiciously. He had been with the pirates for less than six months, but that was more than enough time to learn that nothing in Campeche ever came free.

"It's all right," she reassured. "It's good business to buy customers a drink now and then. Besides, I want to get a good look at the man who took down Patrick Tully."

Hugh said nothing. He'd heard the name several times over the past months. It was the name of the huge pirate he had killed aboard the *Gallant*, just before he'd been shot.

Charlotte Travers continued to regard him. Hugh said nothing to her. Finally, she downed her drink and stood up.

"Watch out for yourself, Hugh Glass," she told him. "When you killed Tully, you made yourself a very dangerous enemy. If you drop your guard, Weasel will kill you."

Hugh thanked her for the drink.

Weasel—Henry Weissel—was the small, wiry man that shot Hugh and put an end to the fighting aboard the *Gallant*. Hugh had seen the man watching him as he worked, taking his measure. Weasel had tried to kill him and had missed. Hugh had the feeling he would try again. Charlotte Travers' words came as no surprise. The surprise was that she had bothered to warn him at all.

He finished his drink and went outside, nodding to Charlotte and the bartender as he made his exit. Outside, he stood in the dark and let the rain beat down upon him. Campeche was a dismal place, not because of locale—the setting was beautiful. The inhabitants made it ugly. All the worst attributes of humanity thrived here. Lafitte had given these men a license for pettiness, treachery, cruelty, and murder. Like pestilence, they prospered.

Hugh shook himself, trying to eliminate the dark feelings and thoughts. It didn't work. They clung to him. He looked out in the direction of the mainland, unable to see it through the rain.

I could always swim for it, he thought.

He doubted he would get very far. Not that the mainland was that far away, for it wasn't. What was *on* the mainland was what he would have to worry about. Over a thousand miles of wilderness lay between here and St. Louis, all of it crawling with indians. The Karankawas were the closest, and they kept a constant eye on Campeche. Hugh had heard that many tribes of indians practiced cannibalism, for ceremonial purposes. The Karankawas were different. As Cobb, the gravel-voiced Third Mate put it, "They like *long* pork!" They ate human flesh simply because they enjoyed it.

That was a big deterrent. Shortly after setting up their base here, the pirates had sent a party of men over to the mainland to hunt for game. After several days, when they didn't return, a second party was sent to look for them. They managed to find and rescue only one man from the hunting party. The party had been captured by the Karankawas shortly after leaving the island. The indians had taken the men from the hunting party, one by one, and had killed them and eaten them, until only one man remained. He had been, literally, only hours away from the roasting pit, when the others arrived to save him. No, as much as Hugh Glass hated the pirates, life with them was still preferable to ending his days as part of a Karankawa feast.

He wondered again why Charlotte Travers had bothered to warn him about Weasel. Women had the worst of it in Campeche. Stolen from every strata of society, they were brought here, many as slaves, to serve the needs of the men. Only Charlotte Travers had come willingly. Hugh had heard that she'd left a successful business in New Orleans to come here and set up shop, catering to Lafitte's men. In Hugh's mind, that made her more suspect than those she served.

From inside the tavern came the sound of laughter. Hugh decided to walk back through the rain, to find out when a boat would be heading back to the ship. Rain suited this place, he thought. He doubted that all the rain in the world could wash it clean.

CHAPTER FIVE

THE SHIP was a Spanish merchant. She sat low in the water, a half-mile off their weather beam, growing closer by the moment.

Aboard the *Madalaine*, excitement was high. The crew looked forward eagerly, anticipating what treasures they might find aboard her. Hugh gave thanks to the fact that it was not an American ship. According to their license, Renoux was well within his rights to attack. Not that it made the idea any more appealing to Hugh, but he dreaded the day that Renoux attacked a ship that Hugh was familiar with. He hoped he would never be forced to go against men whom he had once called friend.

The ship grew closer. Hugh felt his anxiety grow.

Bad things happen, he told himself, *you accept them and go on*. Here was a bad thing, about to happen. He could think of no way to prevent it. Hugh had seen what the pirates could and would do. That his own government condoned and even promoted those actions disgusted him.

For a moment he toyed with the idea of going below and setting a charge in the hold of the *Madalaine* and blowing her to Hell before they could attack the Spaniard. The odds were he would be killed in the blast, but it would save the lives of many innocent men...

Hugh discarded the idea when he saw that Weasel was watching him.

Renoux was flying the Venezuelan flag, under which his privateering charter was held. Hugh could see the concerned looks of the crew of the Spanish ship. He felt for them. He managed to stifle his feelings, knowing he would soon enough be aboard that ship, and that he would probably have to kill some of those men or be killed himself.

Their looks of concern turned to panic when the shelling began.

The ship was the *Dona Elena*. In her hold were spices and coffee, cotton, tobacco—and gold. The crew of the *Madalaine* were overjoyed at their luck. Apparently, the *Dona Elena* had been provided with a Spanish naval escort, but had become separated from it in a storm a few days earlier and had not yet found their way back together. The threat of discovery by a Spanish warship only heightened the excitement of Renoux and his men, and this was taken to even greater heights by the discovery of passengers.

Hugh had taken a bad cut on his arm, which was beginning to throb. Clint was dressing it for him. They stood to one side as the prisoners were brought on board.

Sometimes, in the case of Spanish ships, the passengers were held for ransom due to their wealth or position, but only on rare occasions. Hugh immediately knew that would not be the case here. The pirates had made a good haul. There was no need to risk trouble by sparing them.

The passengers consisted of a middle-aged man, his wife, and their young daughter, whom Hugh judged to be no more than twelve or thirteen. It would have been better for them, Hugh thought, if they had been killed outright during the heat of the battle. Especially the girl.

Moving the cargo from the Spanish ship onto the *Madalaine* took hours. When it was finished Hugh's back ached and his injured arm was nearly useless to him. Fires were set aboard the *Dona Elena*, and a charge set in her hold. The charge went off with a loud WHUMPHH! The *Dona Elena* split in two. In moments, she slipped beneath the waves.

Hugh looked at the passengers. The Spaniard was a frail man. He sat to one side, hands on his knees, staring at nothing. His fine clothes were soiled and disheveled. He looked broken. His wife, Hugh guessed, must have been the power in this family.

Had been.

Taking a deep breath, the man stood suddenly. Proudly, he walked over to Renoux.

"You!" he said. "*Capitan!*" He spoke imperiously, addressing Renoux in a tone obviously reserved for underlings. Renoux smiled.

"Yes?"

"I want to know what you intend to do with us!"

"That remains to be seen," Renoux told him. "We…"

The Spaniard made the mistake of reaching inside his coat. Before he could withdraw his hand the muzzles of two pistols were thrust into his face and the tip of Renoux's sword was at his throat.

"I, er…" the man gulped. "I have a dispatch, for the King of Spain. It is important that it reaches its destination. You will be paid handsomely if…"

Renoux smiled again.

"Your dispatch isn't going to make it," he said. Renoux drew back to strike.

The move surprised Hugh, then he realized it was only for show. Hugh had watched Renoux in battle. Renoux was all grace, total economy of movement. To kill the Spaniard he had only to thrust forward a couple of inches.

"*NO!*" It was the Spaniards wife. Renoux stopped. Smiling, he turned to her.

"No?" he said. "No? And why not?" He turned back to the woman's husband. "You," he said, "are everything I hate in this world. With your pompous ways and your superior attitude—you think that you are better than others because of an accident of your birth. You are *nothing!* You take from others; walk over them with nothing less than contempt as you go through life. Yet, for you, the slightest prick of your finger is a monumental concern. You see, I know you all too well. I was brought up with your kind—and trod upon by them. You do not deserve life. As far as I am concerned, you are feces…" he leaned forward with the blade.

"*PLEASE!*" It was the woman again. "Please…" She came forward, pleading. She really was an attractive woman; big, dark eyes; black hair that was just beginning to show gray at the temples; a good figure. If she was given to excesses, they didn't show.

"Please," she repeated. "I will do anything you want. *Anything.* Just spare my husband and my daughter. Please…there must be something. Do not harm them."

Renoux hesitated for a moment.

"Very well," he told the woman. "We will go to my cabin and discuss it." Then he gave the Spaniard a big, knowing smile. The Spaniard looked angrily away. Renoux nodded to Cobb, the Third Mate, then he and the woman disappeared below. Cobb and four others immediately took hold of the Spaniard. Without ceremony they led him to the port railing, cut his throat, and threw him over the side. The girl, meanwhile, was taken forward and stripped. The rest of the crew, with the exception of Hugh, Clint, and a couple of others, all took turns at her.

Hugh never saw the woman again. The girl, ravaged again and again by the crew, went into a kind of shock. Three weeks after the sinking of the *Dona Elena*, she died of pneumonia.

The morning after the sinking of the *Dona Elena*, the chief mate called, "All Hands!" Hugh was puzzled by this. Aboard a ship there were two watches, starboard and port, or larboard. Normally, only one of the watches was on duty at a time, while the other rested below decks. As a rule, "All Hands!" was only called if foul weather occurred, or if a special meeting was to be held, for disciplinary action or whatever. Aboard a pirate vessel, discipline was extraordinarily lax, so the call was rarely made for that reason. The reason for this call was made clear soon enough. Four men had been lost in capturing the *Dona Elena*—three from the larboard watch and one from starboard. To balance this out, one man had to be taken from starboard and transferred to the other watch. The Mate chose Clint. Thereafter, Hugh saw little of his friend, as they were on opposite sides of the clock.

CHAPTER SIX

THE SEA ROSE and fell, ever changeless. The days rolled one into another into another, each the same as the next and the last. Occasionally, there was a storm, but Hugh had faced many storms.

For the first time in his life, Hugh found himself thinking about his own death, wondering about it. Moreover, he found himself wondering that it already overtaken him.

How can it be, he wondered, *that a man can so despise the moments and facts and even the mundane matters of his life, and still continue? When every breath drawn is heavy with loathing and despair, every bite of food concentrated with anger, guilt and shame, sorrow and pain—how can it be that disease and tragedy are not consumed as well?* Yet day after day he went on, nor was his condition weakened or physically reduced by it in any way.

The little girl died, he thought, *yet I live on. I am surrounded by evil. I bathe in it and eat with it and sleep with it, and still live on. If anything, I am stronger than before... What am I? What sort of being thrives on iniquity?*

"You're like Moses in the desert."

"Hunh?" The words startled Hugh and brought him out of himself. He'd been sanding a section of deck, then varnishing, unaware of his own labor and sweat, or the smell of sawdust, or the varnish that stuck to his fingers where the brush had slipped.

"You're like Moses." It was Billings, the carpenter. Hugh had seen the old man at work many times but had paid him little mind.

20

"The sea and this ship are your desert," Billings continued. "You think they should kill you, but the work only makes you stronger."

Hugh eyed him for a moment, then went back to sanding.

"What do you know about it?" he said sullenly.

"More'n you think. I been watchin' you, all these last months since you joined up. You're a troubled man. You did what you had to do—you stayed alive. Now you're a-thinkin' you deserve to be dead because of it. I've seen it afore. Believe me, Hugh Glass, many a day will come and go before you take your last breath. You think you're the only man ever didn't want to become a pirate?"

Hugh looked up at him.

"No," he said "I don't. But some men take to it a little easier than others."

"Aye, they do. Some men take to this life right well. Some never will. Stop whipping yourself. If a big Spaniard puts her mark on us tomorrow, you'll be hung right along with the rest of us, conscience or no."

The old man moved off. Hugh watched him go. Moses, huh? Moses would never have stood by and watched that little girl face brutality and rape day after day, until it finally killed her.

Hugh had.

He had...

If Clint harbored any such feelings of guilt, he managed to bury them under the simple fact that he had no choice in the matter. The men he and Hugh killed were, in truth, dead men already, for pirates seldom attacked when there was even a slight chance of losing. As for the girl, he could not have saved her and probably would have gotten killed, had he tried.

As far as Hugh was concerned, Clint felt concern for his former Chief Mate. Clint had served under him for a year and a half, and had always known Hugh Glass to be a good, even-tempered man, not given to moods, self-pity, or fits of guilt. There was no question in Clint's mind that they had done the right thing in staying alive. In his opinion, Tom Halpern and the others had been foolish in choosing to die as they did. Had they stayed alive, the six of them might even have found a way to one day take control of the *Madalaine*.

Clint knew the effect that Tom Halpern's words had upon Hugh, and he earnestly hoped that Hugh recovered from them soon.

It was wrong to think or speak ill of the dead, but Clint had always thought that Tom Halpern was a little too pompous for his—or anyone else's—good. Halpern had proved him right.

CHAPTER SEVEN

"BLACK AS A POCKET" the saying was. The decks of the *Madalaine* were awash with brackish green water. The bilge pumps, which pumped water from the bowels of the ship, and which took four men to operate, had been constantly at work for two days. There was no sign of letup. The crew of the small brig, able to sleep only in two-hour shifts, were at the point of exhaustion from wet and cold, and from the amount of work required to keep them afloat.

Hugh was just returning from his two hour "break" in the foc'sle. He was hardly rested, nearly as wet under his oilskins as he had been upon entering. He had been a sailor all his life, though. He knew he could expect no better. He had seen many storms, some worse than this.

The Chief Mate, Peatman, was at the weather-rail. Hugh smiled at that. He had wondered how long Renoux would last there. The Frenchman had stood at that post for more than thirty-hours—a respectable stint for any sea captain. He was probably in his cabin now, dead to the world and deservedly so.

"LAND HO!" The call came from somewhere amidships. Hugh looked to the starboard side and saw nothing but blackness. When he looked to port he saw a rocky coastline, looming dangerously close.

The crew looked at Peatman and waited. The man stood, holding onto the weather rail, rocking with the ship. His mouth was open, but no words came out.

Hugh looked back at the coastline. He had no idea what body of land this was, or how far the reefs might extend, or how shallow it might be here. At any moment the *Madalaine* could be upon them lurching and screaming with the sound of timbers crushing against rock, spelling doom for them all.

Peatman wasn't moving.

We don't have time for this, Hugh thought.

The rocks seemed closer by the second. Peatman's mouth had begun to move, as though he were trying to speak, only no words were coming out.

"The *Hell* with that!" Hugh said out loud. Then, turning, he began shouting orders to the crew.

"DROP THE MAINSAIL!" He managed to scream above the storm. Two men, anxious for orders, sprang quickly aloft. Hugh turned to the helmsman. "Haul into the wind!" he shouted. "We have to sail the hell away from this—*IF* there's still time!" He looked back at Peatman, who stood holding the rail and looking down at the deck, rain dripping from his beard. Lightning flashed. Slowly, the *Madalaine* began to come about, moving away from the rocks.

The storm lasted one more day, then subsided as quickly as it had come upon them.

Having been tossed and twisted and turned in every conceivable way, the *Madalaine* had taken a terrific beating in the storm. As the weather cleared, repairs began. Hugh was at work driving oakum—a tarred rope that was forced between the decking with the use of a mallet and caulking iron—while another man followed behind and finished the job by pouring molten tar into the cracks, sealing them. In storms as violent as the one that had just passed, most of the oakum was forced out from between the planks, causing the decks to leak.

A shadow fell across Hugh's work. He looked up and saw Peatman. The First Mate looked troubled.

"The Cap'n wants to see you," Peatman said, "and I—I wanted to thank you. That other day, during the storm..."

"Forget it," Hugh shrugged.

"I can't. It shoulda been me shoutin' those orders... Somethin' happened. I saw them rocks, and my insides...I just went weak. Nothin' like that ever happened to me before."

Hugh watched him for a moment.

"I think," he told Peatman, "that every man has his own, private fear, whether we're aware of it or not. If we're lucky, we never have to face it. Stop whipping yourself. You'll do better next time."

Peatman nodded. Brushing himself off, Hugh went to see Renoux.

A sailor's life aboard ship is always austere. He has his trunk and a bed. He gets his meals, but the fare is often less than desirable, and quite often monotonous. For the Captain it is different. His quarters are spacious and well-fitted. The food he receives is always better than that of the crew. The advantages of rank are never denied.

Renoux's cabin was like other Captain's cabins he had seen. The furnishing were a little finer—silk curtains, gold place settings, tiny, delicate gold chains holding the curtains in place—but it was a good deal less ornate than Hugh might have expected. Renoux was a wealthy man, many times over.

Renoux offered him brandy—something that would never happen aboard a regular merchant ship. Hugh thought for a moment, then accepted.

"It seems," Renoux said in crisp English, "that I owe you my ship." He handed the brandy to Hugh in a crystal aperitif.

Hugh accepted the drink and said nothing.

Renoux watched him for a moment. Then, breathing with disgust, he said, "I get the feeling that you disapprove of me."

Hugh remained silent. Noting his reticence, Renoux tried to reassure him.

"It's all right for you to speak freely. There will be no repercussion. I want you to tell me what you think."

"Why?" Hugh asked him. "Why should it matter what I think?"

Renoux thought for a moment.

"I've been watching you," he said. "You are a very capable man. If anything should happen to Mr. Peatman, I would like you to take over as First Mate."

"No."

Renoux looked at him with surprise.

"No?"

"No," Hugh repeated. "I've been at sea my whole life, but I was an honest sailor. *This…*" He gestured, indicating the ship. "You are right to think that I don't approve of you, Captain. What is there, here, that I could possibly approve of?"

Renoux's face became red. He held his temper.

"Isn't that a little pompous?" he said. "After all, you *are* a member of this crew. You, too, have been a party to all that we have done."

"Not exactly," Hugh told him. "I've not been a party to everything, and what I've done, I've done under the threat of death."

Renoux was silent for a moment, thinking. Finally, exhaling with exasperation, he spoke again. He didn't look at Hugh, though, but away from him.

"You know," he said quietly, "the world is filled with beasts, and man is one of them. We think because we can reason and build churches and schools and courtrooms that we are different, but we are not. In my life I have seen that the ones who sit in judgment are seldom different from those whom they would condemn." He looked up at Hugh. "The ocean is full of fishes and it is full of sharks. The strong eat the weak. That is the way it has always been and that is the way it will always be. The world of men is no different. The big fishes eat the little fishes. It is no accident that you and I both serve aboard this ship. We are more alike than you suppose."

The two men were silent again. Hugh drank the last of the brandy, placing the glass on the edge of Renoux's desk.

"I don't think so, Captain," he said.

Renoux glared at him.

"You really are a fool! Very well, then, go back to your work. If you decide that you want to do better for yourself, let me know!"

CHAPTER EIGHT

THE PIRATES were doing a booming trade. Two more ships fell before them. Hugh and Clint had now been pirates for nearly fifteen months.

Little by little, the grief had finally left him. Guilt still lingered and haunted him, but his temperament was on an even keel again. Still, Hugh Glass would never be quite the same man he was before the sinking of the *Gallant*. As long as he lived, he would never quite feel clean.

Physically, he was as strong as ever. Never at sea for too long a time, the pirates lived well. They had no place they had to be, no schedules to keep, except for day to day maintenance that was required for keeping the *Madalaine* ship-shape. Into this Hugh threw himself, knowing that the more he concentrated on his work, the less time he would have to give to those around him.

Clint had become quite popular with the pirates. Although he avoided taking part in their more unsavory practices, he had twice let himself get maneuvered into bare-knuckle boxing bouts in Campeche, fighting men from other ships. Clint won both bouts easily. Many of the men from the *Madalaine* made money off those fights, and if ever there was a community where money could buy friends, this was it.

Fifteen months. More than a year. An impossibly long time in an intolerable situation. Hugh still believed, as he always had, that as long as there was life, hope remained, but that hope grew dimmer and fainter and further away with every day that passed. As time went on, he became more than aware that his escape from piracy would come, most likely, from a pistol ball, or at the end of a sword, or with his neck in a hangman's noose.

Well, it's God's will, he thought. If there still *was* a God. Hugh wasn't sure just *what* he believed anymore, at least as far as religion was concerned.

It seemed that Campeche had been waiting for them. Something was in the air, and the excitement could be felt a mile off shore. Four ships lay in the channel between Galveston Island and the mainland. They were the *Jupiter*—Lafitte's own ship, the *Success*, the *Tonnere*, and the *Ciel Blue*. Hugh knew little enough about these ships. The master of the *Success* was a man named Gambio—Gamby, he was called. Gamby was rumored to be quite ruthless and ambitious, but that was all Hugh had heard.

As soon as they dropped anchor, preparations were made for Renoux and a party of six men to go ashore. Most of the rest of the crew would be allowed to go later, but first arrangements had to be made to off-load the cargo from the last ship they had scuttled.

Among those to go ashore in the first shore party were Clint and a young sailor named Willie Brandt. Brandt had grown up a pirate. Indeed, his father had been one of Lafitte's original Baratarians, from Grand Terre Isle in Barataria Bay, near New Orleans. Despite his origins, he and Clint had become good friends. He had a disarming way about him and made no bones about who or what he was.

"I be a pirate!" he told Clint. "I was born a pirate, an' I been a pirate me whole life. I takes me a pirate's liberties. A freer man never walked the earth or sailed the sea. When me time comes, let people say, "There was Willie Brandt. He lived an' died under the Jolly Roger, an' a happier man there never was!""

Clint couldn't help but like Willie. The two of them had been thrown together as watch-mates when Clint and Hugh had been separated. In a way it was a relief for Clint, after so many months with Hugh as his only friend. Where Hugh was older, Willie was around Clint's age. As Hugh was brooding, morose, and full of guilt, Willie was fun and full of devilishness. Willie *reveled* in being a pirate. In spite of the occasional violence (which he took as part of the job) he was essentially sweet natured, though he had been around enough to let no man tread on him.

The *Madalaine* dropped anchor about a half-mile out into the channel. The landing party rowed themselves ashore, pulling the boat high up on the beach, where they left it.

Taking two men to accompany him, Renoux set off for *Maison Rouge*—Lafitte's gaudy, crimson painted "palace". One man was left to stay with the boat. That left Clint, Willie, and another man, Camden, all free. Renoux told them to be back at the boat within two hours, and not to get too drunk. They immediately headed for Charlotte Travers' *Bucket O' Blood*.

Campeche hadn't changed much. It was late in the day, and the smell of roasting meat mingled with the smoke from cooking fires, following the three men as they walked. Here and there a crude wooden shack had been built. Mostly, though, Campeche was still tents.

With five ships in port, Campeche was bustling. Excitement was everywhere. The slight dizziness that Clint felt from coming onto land after being so long at sea, seemed to add to it.

The *Bucket O' Blood* was crowded with men—and women—that Clint had never seen before. Ordering three "flips", the men began to make their way around the room. Men from every ship in the channel were there. Willie seemed to know all of them He stopped to talk to one of the few men that Clint knew, off the *Ciel Blue*, name Jacques Bouchard. Another man interrupted them.

"So I hear the *Madalaine* thinks she has a boxer!" the man said.

"Aye! That we do," Willie answered him. He glanced at Clint "A might good one!"

"Hah! Aboard the *Success* is a man named Simon Johnson. Now *there* is a man who can box!"

Willie winked at Clint.

"I've got four gold doubloons 'says our man can beat him!" Willie told the man.

And so it began. Clint watched the interest spread around the room. He watched with mixed feelings. Many men and women were betting on him. People he didn't know.

Many more, he noticed, were betting against him.

He knew nothing about the man they were setting him against. Simon Johnson might be a giant, or he might be a short, powerful man with arms like tree trunks. It would have been hard to say which he would prefer to go against. A giant would have the advantage of reach, but Clint had known short men who were just as powerful, maybe more so. Such men seemed almost impossible to hurt, while their own blows would put a mule to shame.

"You're not betting?"

Clint started at the question, then started again. The most incredibly beautiful woman was addressing him. She had big, soft brown eyes, dark hair—very long and curly, and a smile that absolutely dazzled him. Clint could only stare.

"You're not going to bet?" the woman repeated. She cocked her head to one side. Somehow, it made her even more beautiful.

"Um…uh…no…" Clint stammered.

"Too bad," she told him. "I was hoping to make a bet with you. I hear Hastings is good. I hear he's *very* good!"

With a shrug, she turned and disappeared into the crowd, leaving Clint to wonder just what had happened to him.

A short while later, when they returned to meet Captain Renoux, Willie was all smiles. He had a good heat on. He had total confidence in Clint and had made many bets, all of which he expected to win.

Clint said little. The interchange with that extraordinary woman had been so brief, so fleeting. He had the feeling that he'd been presented with an incredible opportunity, and had failed to act. What was it he had said to her? "Um…uh…no…?"

Good God.

When news of the boxing match reached Renoux, he immediately ordered Clint to remain on shore—and to remain sober. The captain of the *Success* was an old rival of Renoux's. Renoux was determined not to allow any advantage to him. Clint was to remain on shore and get his land legs.

"It is important that you win this fight," Renoux told him. "More than you know."

Willie Brandt was ordered to stay on shore with Clint, and to keep him out of trouble. The following day that order was rescinded and Hugh was given the job. Unconscious and reeking of rum, Willie was carried back to the *Madalaine*.

CHAPTER NINE

ESTELLE LEMIUX first met Jean Lafitte when she was thirteen. At fifteen, she secretly became the mistress of his number one captain, Dominic You. That relationship lasted for three years. At eighteen, she had gone back to Charlotte Travers, wiser in the ways of the world than most women, or men, ever get to be. Now, at twenty-two, she had a good deal of gold to go with that wisdom, but it would do her little good as long as she was stuck at Campeche.

One more favor, Charlotte had told her. One more favor, and then she would be given passage back to New Orleans. Estelle wondered if it could be true. Estelle *needed* it to be true.

Appraising herself in her buffet mirror, she thought of Charlotte. Charlotte had never been the beauty that Estelle was now, but when Estelle was eleven she had thought Charlotte to be the most beautiful woman in the world. Most of that beauty was gone now. There was a puffiness about Charlotte's features that told of the life she led, and a hardness had begun to creep into her looks that Estelle thought was less than attractive.

And it will be exactly the same for me, she thought, *if I remain here.*

She had to get back to civilization. If she could just get herself to a city again, say, to St. Louis or even New York, she would have the means now to buy her way into society. Then, she had only to meet the right man and her future would be set.

Having grown up a whore to pirates, playing the part of the perfect, doting wife would be easy.

It was a nice change for both of them. Hugh, who had never seen Clint box, was actually looking forward to the event.

There was little enough for him to do. Clint knew far better than he how to prepare for the match, although with only three days to get ready, there wasn't much to be done except to rest. Too much exercise now would work against him. In the morning they ran on the beach, but only for a short distance, to get warmed up. Then the two men rigged a heavy canvas bag, filling it with sand and hanging it from the limb of a tree. On this Clint practiced his punches. When they learned that the time of the fight was moved from three days to five, both men were relieved.

By now the whole island had gotten involved. Betting was high on both sides, and it soon became evident that there was more to this even that either Clint or Hugh might have guessed.

For several years prior to receiving his own ship, Michele Renoux had sailed as first mate with Dominique You. You had been and would always be, Lafitte's favorite lieutenant. Shorter of stature than Lafitte, yet broad shouldered and strong, Dominique was incredibly good natured and loved to play practical jokes. His bravery, as well as his skill as an artillerist, were legendary. At the battle of New Orleans, Andrew Jackson said of Dominique's skill and daring, "If I were ordered to storm the gates of Hell, with Captain Dominique as my lieutenant, I would have no misgivings of the result!"

After that famous battle, with a full pardon, Dominique chose to retire and live a "respectable" life. Already well-liked by Lafitte, Michele Renoux was promoted to the rank of Captain, inheriting Dominique You's ship and crew.

He inherited an enemy as well.

Gambi—Captain Gambio—had been a rival of Dominique You since the day Dominique arrived at the island of Grand Terre in Barataria Bay. Indeed, Gambi had been in Barataria long before Jean and Pierre Lafitte were. When Jean Lafitte took control and organized the smuggling trade, Gambi went along, only because it meant better trafficking and more profits. Quarrelsome, easily the most treacherous and bloodthirsty of all Lafitte's captains, he was not disposed to taking orders from anyone. Once, he had tried to have Jean Lafitte killed, but that had ended with Jean killing the man who had been sent to do the job. Gambi remained a member of Lafitte's band because it offered the best way to dispose of the contraband he obtained, but he always resented Jean and anyone who was close to him. When Dominique was gone, Gambi passed that hatred on to Michele Renoux.

Gambi was the master of the *Success*.

That, then, was the reason that this fight was so important to Renoux. If Clint lost, it would mean a loss of face.

Personally, Hugh couldn't have cared less. He wanted Clint to win for no other reason than Clint Hastings was his friend.

It was early on the morning of the second day. Hugh was sitting on the beach, his feet ankle deep in the sand. For the first time in over a year, he felt good. There was a high fog, but it was warm and the air was still. He closed his eyes and listened to the waves break over the beach. In the distance, in town, someone was cooking bacon. The smell of it made him hungry.

He wiggled his toes, buried beneath the sand. It was good to be on land again. *I could live on land,* he thought. I *could leave the sea, and still be happy*.

The thought startled him. In the twenty-six years he had been at sea, it had never occurred to Hugh to return to land.

Opening his eyes, he was startled again to see a woman walking past him. The woman was exceptionally beautiful and was dressed provocatively in a long, flimsy white dress that, Hugh thought, would be more appropriate for evening.

Trouble, he thought to himself. This woman is trouble.

He watched her walk down the beach. Beautiful women were not an uncommon sight in Campeche. Something about this one was different. In Campeche, women were slaves, either outright or almost, or they were wives and were kept on a very short leash. This woman was none of those. There was an air of independence about her that was out of place here. Hugh would have bet money that she belonged to no one.

He watched her disappear down the beach.

Clint was running hard along the beach. Naked to the waist and barefoot, he ran at the water's edge. Sweat poured from him. His breath came in great, rasping gulps. He felt clean.

He was surprised at the enjoyment he was getting from this—from all of it. The excitement, the buildup, the exercise, the preferential treatment—everything about the fight made him feel good.

More than anything, though, it was the anticipation of the fight itself that excited him. Clint had never lost a fight, and the thought of losing really was not real for him. The *idea* existed for him, but only in an abstract way, like imagining some catastrophic event. Actually, Clint had been witness to a few catastrophic events, but he had still never lost a fight.

He stopped running and walked for awhile. Five days was not enough time to do any major physical conditioning, and if he pushed it too hard he was likely to do himself more harm than good. Better to take it easy and get lots of rest.

He wondered about his opponent. Simon Johnson was a free man of color who served under Gambi, who was said to be the most murderous of all Lafitte's captains. He was said to be tall, nearly a giant. And like Clint, Johnson had never lost a fight. Well, at the very least, the two of them should give the others a good show.

Far down the beach he could see someone walking in his direction. A woman. As she grew closer, Clint suddenly stopped walking.

It was the woman from the *Bucket O' Blood,* the one who had spoken to him and then disappeared. If anything, she was even more beautiful than he remembered.

And here he was, about to meet her again, shirtless, covered with sweat and smelling like a horse.

Clint looked at the water. He had an impulse to run and dive in, wash himself off, and them come back to this same spot to wait for her. It was too late for that. The woman was too close.

He watched her approach. When she was ten feet away she greeted him.

"Hello," she said. She stopped just before him and gave him a shy smile. "I'm Estelle."

"H-Hello," he stammered. "I'm Clint Hastings."

"I know who you are, Clint," she told him. Her voice had a throatiness to it that he liked, somehow. Looking out at the water, she said, "I was thinking of going for a swim. Would you like to join me, Clint?"

"Yes," he managed to answer. "I think that would do me good."

"Wonderful!" She turned from him and, without another word, began to strip, right there in front of him. In a moment she was wearing nothing but pantelettes, which came to just below her knees, and a corset. Then, smiling at him over her shoulder, she ran down the beach and into the water. Feeling suddenly intoxicated, Clint watched her go, then followed. In his mind he could hear Willie Brandt's voice: "I be a pirate. I was born a pirate an' I been a pirate me whole life. I takes me a pirate's liberties…"

As he entered the water, Clint made up his mind that he would have this woman today, right there, before they left the beach.

And he did.

The smell of frying bacon had been drifting down from town for quite some time, causing Hugh's stomach to growl at him. He decided that Clint had been off running long enough. It was time to collect him and go get some breakfast.

He started walking down the beach. About an eighth of a mile away, the woman in white was coming back toward him. Far beyond her, Hugh could see Clint sitting in the sand, looking out to sea and occasionally glancing at her as she moved away from him.

As she passed by Hugh she looked up at him and smiled. Her hair was wet. She was *incredibly* beautiful, even more so than he had first thought. Something about the *way* she smiled puzzled him.

Like a canary, he thought, *that just ate the cat.*

CHAPTER TEN

IT WAS THE night before the fight—and Clint was nowhere to be found. Hugh fought to remain calm as he searched for his friend. A tight, anxious feeling in the pit of his stomach told him something was wrong.

There was an air of celebration throughout Campeche, as there always was when so many ships converged to the town at once. This time the feeling was even stronger. There was expectation throughout the settlement. Everyone knew of the upcoming fight. Almost everyone had bets laid down.

More than that, some of the men had returned from a hunting party on the mainland and had captured a Karankawa squaw. Quite a few of the pirates were intent on having sport with her. Hugh could hear their comments as he searched through the town for Clint.

"Careful, George," one man was saying. "Remember that she's a cannibal!"

"That's right," another added, "she might bite it off!"

"Hell, I heard that Karankawa women had teeth in their cunnies!"

"I can tell you for a fact," a fourth man said, "that they do not."

And so it went. Wherever Hugh looked, talk was the same. Much of it was spoken in French, but it didn't matter. After a year and a half with Lafitte's pirates he understood French almost as well as English.

At one time, their talk of what they planned to do with the woman might have disgusted him, but the time he'd spent with these men had dulled his sensitivities somewhat.

To each man his own fancy, he thought, *but leave me out of it.*

Anyway, Hugh knew pirates to be capable of much worse things than rape.

For two days Clint had been able to think of only one thing, and that one thing was Estelle Lemiux. The fight was forgotten. Since that morning on the beach, Clint had been in a daze.

Estelle. Estelle. Her name rang like a bell. Clint was not just a boxer, but a poet as well...

At least he felt like one. He felt giddy inside. Just the thought of her intoxicated him.

As if the wine wasn't enough.

It had amazed him that, two days before, when they were at the beach, she hadn't fought him. They had gone into the water together, had splashed around a bit, and then he had simply taken hold of her and kissed her. At first she went limp, then she began to respond to him. A moment later she pulled him up onto the beach, pulled off his breeches, and took him inside her. When they were done she dressed, touched him once on the cheek, and walked off in the direction she had come from, all without so much as a word.

Clint wondered if he would ever see her again. It amazed and flattered him even further when she contacted him and wanted to get together once more.

Pirates lead lives that are different from other men. Pirate women did, too.

Clint had said nothing to Hugh about the encounter on the beach. If Hugh guessed what had happened, he also said nothing. Nor was Hugh aware of the small Negro boy that had brought word from Estelle—and an invitation for this, their second meeting. Earlier, when Hugh left to get word from the ship, Clint had slipped away. They met behind Charlotte Travers' place, where Estelle had been waiting for him. She had packed a picnic lunch and knew of a spot, about a mile from town, where they could be alone.

Earlier, Estelle had added honeysuckle to her bath water. The scent of it kept drifting to Clint as they walked, driving him half-crazy with desire for her. As soon as they arrived at the spot she had picked, they made love again, this time on a blanket and not in the surf. Then she had opened the wine she brought while Clint built a small fire.

Estelle was the most beautiful woman Clint had ever met and she affected him in a way no other woman ever had. She apologized to him for her un-ladylike forwardness:

"The lives we lead," she told him, "so full of danger! Anything can happen at any time! Ordinary people have the time for courtship games and formalities. We do not."

The made love a second time, this time much more slowly and creatively. They drank nearly a whole bottle of wine in the process. The wine had a slight off-flavor, but Clint was far too preoccupied to notice.

"Estelle, Estelle, I'm under your spell..." was the last thing he remembered saying to her.

Hugh had now been looking for Clint for more than two hours. He'd gone back to the makeshift cabin twice, hoping to find him there, but found no indication that the younger man had returned. Hugh was now quite certain that something was wrong.

For the fifth time, he went into the *Bucket O' Blood* and looked around. A half-dozen sailors from the *Madalaine* were there, but no Clint Hastings. Willie Brandt was at the bar, his arms around two of Charlotte's "girls". Willie's long blond hair was hanging loose and there was a half-emptied bottle of rum in his hand. At Hugh's approach, Willie gave a broad grin.

"Hugh Glass, you old sogerer!" he shouted. "Come have a drink with me an' the girls here!"

"Another time, Willie," Hugh told him, looking around the room. "We need to talk."

Willie looked at him for a moment. Then he sighed.

"Damn!"Willie swore. "Well girls, it looks like you're gonna have to excuse me for a bit." He turned to the woman on his right. "Ellie, don't you go off with any-body else, now. I want you for the night!" He slipped her a gold coin, adding, "Put that on account!"

Ellie gave him a lewd smile and slipped the coin into her bodice. Willie led Hugh over to a corner where they could talk undisturbed.

"All right," he said, "what is it?"

"It's Clint. He's missing. I think something's happened to him."

Willie looked at him.

"Aw, he's prob'ly just off somewhere, makin' the double-backed beast."

"Maybe. I think there's more to it than that. The fight is tomorrow night, Willie."

"That's right, it is. Well, you got any ideas?"

"Only one. Do you know a young woman, about twenty—long dark, curly hair. Dark eyes?"

"I know a few like that."

"This woman's different. She's extremely beautiful, and…she has an air about her. She's independent."

"That sounds like Estelle…" Willie thought for a moment. "Estelle belongs to Charlotte. If they're involved, you're prob'ly right. It's trouble." He looked around the room and spied Charlotte. She was talking to one of the men off the *Success* and looking toward Willie and Hugh.

"Uh-oh," he said. "I think we'd better get out of here."

The two men headed for the door. A tall, muscular sailor stood in the doorway with his arms folded in front of him. Without breaking stride Willie kicked him in the groin. The man doubled over, and Willie pushed him out of the way. Then he and Hugh walked out into the night.

"I'll prob'ly have to answer for that later," Willie said, looking back. "Right now we have to figure out what Estelle has done with our boy, if she hasn't just kilt him outright!"

"Would she do that?"

"Estelle? Prob'ly not, but that was one of Gambi's men at the door, and I saw one of Gambi's boys talkin' with Charlotte. If they're all in it together, anything's possible." He thought for a minute, then said, "No, they prob'ly wouldn't kill. That'd be too easy. More as like they'd make it so Clint would be in no shape to fight, so Gambi's boy Johnson would have an easy win. That'd make more sense. There's a lot of gold ridin' on this fight. More'n that. It's a matter of honor. If Johnson wins—or wins too easy, it'll make the Cap'n look bad."

Hugh grunted. He could care less about Renoux's "honor", or his gold. Hugh's only concern was his friend.

"So where do we look for Clint?" Hugh asked.

"I'm thinkin' on it," Willie told him. He was quiet for a time. Hugh did his best not to seem impatient.

"Okay." Willie said finally. "It makes sense that they wouldn't keep him in town—someone might see 'em. I don't *think* they'd take him to the *Success*—that'd be too obvious. That means they got him here, on the island, but not in town."

"Fine. Where?"

"I'm thinkin'! I'm thinkin'! Okay, there's a small beach, just about a mile out of town. It sits down in a hollow, like, so they could have a fire an' no one would see it. They could be down there just havin' a picnic, makin' the beast on the beach—and Gambi's boys could just happen to drop in an' bust him up some. Knowin' Estelle, she have him so side-tracked that Clint'd never know they were there until it was too late, an' then wouldn't never believe she set him up."

"So where is this beach?"

"Come on."

Willie led the way, back past the last of the makeshift cabin-tents that made up the town of Campeche. It was a rag-tag setup if ever Hugh had seen one. Then, he would have expected no better. These people were not craftsmen, they were killers.

Once away from the town, it became nearly too dark to see. Willie led them, weaving just a little, but doing a pretty fair job for a man who'd been interrupted in his night of fun.

After twenty minutes of walking in the dark, Hugh detected a faint whiff of woodsmoke. A few minutes later they cleared a small rise. The hill fell away and there, on the beach, two figures lay sprawled and unmoving. The fire next to them had all but gone out.

Without waiting to see if it was safe, Hugh rushed down onto the beach. Willie, ever suspectful of a trap, waited above. When he was certain that no one lurked nearby, he followed Hugh down onto the beach.

Both Clint and the girl were unconscious. Hugh made a quick inspection. One of the bottles of wine was untouched. The other was nearly gone. Pouring a little into one of the cups, Hugh smelled it. Then he took a small taste. *Laudanum,* he thought, *or some other opiate!*

"The wine is laced," he told Willie. "Come on, we have to get them back to the ship. I'll take Clint, you take the girl."

"The girl?" Willie responded. "Why don't we just cut her throat an' leave her here? She's the one 'at did this!"

Noting the knife already in Willie's hand, Hugh thought quickly. "Renoux may have some questions for her," he said.

Satisfied, Willie put his knife away and reached for Estelle.

Later, back aboard the *Madalaine*, the ship's cook prepared a brew, which he and Hugh fed to Clint. Without fully regaining consciousness, Clint spent the night vomiting his insides out. Estelle, they decided could sleep it off for herself.

The following morning, just before dawn, the Karankawas attacked Campeche. They hit the settlement hard and fast, and caused some damage. The pirates recovered quickly and retaliated. Jean Lafitte himself went out to fight them, backed by two pieces of artillery.

The fighting was long and bitter, lasting most of the day. When it was finally over, more than thirty indians had been killed, and nearly half that many pirates. Others were missing and were never found.

Among those missing was the man that Clint was supposed to fight, Simon Johnson. Questions were raised about this: How could any man as big and as powerful and as *visible* as Simon Johnson have been taken by the cannibal tribe—with no one aware of it. Johnson was an enormous man, standing head and shoulders over the tallest of the pirates. No one seemed to know the answer to that.

Willie Brandt knew, but Willie wasn't talking to anyone.

CHAPTER ELEVEN

TIME, IT WAS said, heals all wounds. There were days, when the sea was calm and the air was warm and the work was light, when Hugh could get lost in what he was doing and almost, *almost* forget. It was like he was an ordinary seaman again, serving aboard a common seagoing merchant, without responsibilities, long before he had made Third or Second Mate. Long, long before he had set foot aboard the *Gallant*. Balmy days.

Today was like that. Hugh was picking oakum, which had been forced from between the decking during storms and from the normal movement of the ship. He was in a thoughtful mood.

They had been out for three weeks. Life had taken on the regularity of the sea, unbroken except by changes in the weather, which had been fair for many days. Despite himself, Hugh had begun to actually like some of the crew—Willie Brandt for one. In spite of his piratical nature, Willie was thoroughly likable. Another was Ganz, the cook, and Billings, the carpenter. And Peatman, the Chief Mate, rather than being threatened by Hugh's skill as a sailor, actually treated him with a sort of respect. All in all, it wasn't too bad.

The fight with the Karankawas became known as, "The Battle of the Three Trees", and was counted among Lafitte's many victories. Hugh and Clint had missed it—Clint because he was still recovering from the drugged wine, Hugh because he had spent the entire night before looking after him. Even so, he had been surprised when Renoux told him not to go.

"There are over seven-hundred men in that camp," Renoux explained. "If they can't handle the indians, one more won't help. Besides, most of my crew is there.

If they all get killed I'll need you to help sail the *Madalaine*."

Late in the afternoon the girl, Estelle, had come up on deck, looking ragged. The natural roll of the ship was too much for her. She vomited again and again over the side, all the while decrying her innocence. Renoux let her live. Apparently, she and Lafitte had once been on intimate terms. It had been years earlier, but Jean Lafitte still considered Estelle Lemiux to be his friend. Since there was no real harm done—the fight was called because Simon Johnson was missing —this was enough for Renoux.

The night after "The Battle of the Three Trees", a huge celebration was held, with Jean Lafitte himself in attendance. This was a rare thing. Lafitte rarely left his gaudy fortress, *La Maison Rouge*, for anything.

Hugh and Clint missed it all, both being restricted to the ship—Clint for irresponsible behavior; Hugh for not watching him close enough.

Staying on board hadn't bothered Hugh, but Clint, who was finally feeling better, was glum.

"Think of it," he told Hugh, "this might have been the only chance we'll get to see the great and legendary Lafitte, and we missed it!"

Hugh laughed and took a pull at his pipe.

Since that time things had mellowed somewhat for Hugh. His attitude had softened somehow—probably something to do with "pulling together in a crisis". He'd seen it happen again and again on other ships. Hugh had been in many crisis situations while aboard the *Madalaine*, but none of them ever made him feel closer to the rest of the crew, except for Clint. This was the first time that he'd had to rely on any of the others.

Hugh thought once more about Willie Brandt. Willie was a true professional pirate, if ever there was one. He was everyone's best friend, and genuinely so. He begrudged no one anything, yet was nobody's fool. Best friends though you might be, if Practicality demanded it, Willie would slit your throat as quickly and dispassionately as another man might clean a fish. Still, Hugh had come to like him.

"ALL HANDS! *SAIL HO!*"

Hugh started at the call. Sudden concern filled him, which grew in intensity as he looked aft to starboard and, far in the distance, made out the sail of a ship.

She was a fat Portuguese merchant, loaded down and all alone. She was in full sail and moving gracefully along. As for speed and armament, she could never hope to be a match for the *Madalaine*. Hugh felt a sudden, odd impulse to go back to picking oakum and pretend the ship wasn't there, that the *Madalaine* was just another merchant ship plying her trade, that the men around him were nothing more than honest, ordinary seamen...

Oh, that's grand, he thought bitterly. *Really grand! They're NICE men. Killing, torturing, raping, and stealing are just things that they happen to do for a living. It's nothing personal...*

He looked around. As usual, Weasel was watching him. Hatred for the irritating little man suddenly filled him. After they had sunk the *Dona Elena*, Weasel had been foremost in taking his pleasure at the girl's expense. Hugh had the unreasoning urge to run over and strangle the little man and throw his body into the sea.

The last thing he remembered, just before the cannon fire began, was hearing Tom Halpern's voice:

"...and you will *NEVER* know peace!"

None of their victims ever had a chance, really. This was mostly due to the fact that no one among them knew quite what to expect. None of them knew what was coming. They always cooperated, hoping for mercy that was never, ever shown. If there was one law that was absolute among the pirates, it was to kill everyone who wasn't a pirate. And no one among the pirates, including Renoux, ever seemed to care what traumas and horrors were visited upon the prisoners before death finally came to them.

The fight had been extremely one-sided. Only one of the pirates had been killed. The deck of the Portuguese ship, slippery with blood earlier, had now become sticky. Wherever anyone walked it made a wet, smacking noise. The sound made Hugh sick to his stomach. He was glad there was a light wind. It carried the scent of recent butchery away from him. Absently, he remembered that it had been, before the attack, a balmy day.

They had taken four prisoners—two priests and an elderly couple. The priests, having made their protests in the name of God, were now being quietly stoic. The old woman had tried, with stately dignity, to hold her composure, but it had given way and now she was sobbing quietly. The old man was trying to comfort her. Hugh tried not to listen, but it didn't work. He could feel the old man's hopelessness and despair and shame over having failed to protect his wife, and it enraged him.

The image of the young girl from the *Dona Elena* came back to him, her eyes vacant and dull, her hair and clothes a mess from constant abuse. He saw her mother and father and at least a dozen others, all of whom faced humiliation, shame, and torture before being put to death, but mostly he saw the girl. She had been so young and pretty—in the end she had been nothing but a lifeless, smelly, rag of a girl, with no will or intelligence to respond to anything or anyone. Still they had kept at her, until she wasted away and died of pneumonia.

Hugh looked down at his hands. He was holding his pistol. Vaguely, he remembered discharging it into a young sailor who had come at Hugh in an effort to defend his ship. Now it was loaded again. Hugh didn't remember reloading it.

"Now's time for some fun!" Hugh heard someone say.

"Aye, yer right!" Hugh recognized the second voice—a man named Mahoney. "She ain't much to look at, but after three weeks at sea, I'd bugger me own grandmother!"

"Hell, she probably *is* yer grandmother!"

Laughter. Hugh felt strangely tired and lethargic. Earlier, he'd been full of good feelings and the camaraderie of brotherhood. What had he been thinking? If there was such a thing as *evil* in this world, it was here, in these men. The concepts of mercy and kindness and love were alien to them.

The men had worked themselves up. Three of them moved in, separating the old man from his wife. When the old man saw what they were about to do with her, he tried to fight them. His efforts were weak. Mahoney gutted him and pushed him down onto the deck, where he would die watching the pirates rape his wife.

"Diego!" the old woman cried plaintively, trying to go to him. The men pushed her back and began to strip her.

Hugh took a deep breath, held it for a moment, then let it out.

"I don't think so," he said out loud. Then he walked forward. Pushing his way through the men to where the old woman was, he raised the pistol and shot her in the heart.

The pirates jumped away, startled. Hugh looked at Diego, the old woman's husband. The old man seemed to nod to him, then he put his head down on the deck and died.

Turning, Hugh started away. One of the pirates struck him. Then, suddenly, several of them converged on him at once, hitting and kicking him. Hugh tried to fight back, landing some good blows, but he'd been caught off balance. The others had the advantage.

More of the pirates joined in, kicking at him when they could get close enough. In a way, this helped Hugh—there were too many of them and they all got in each other's way. Then something seemed to well up inside him. He managed to get his feet under him.

Somewhere in front of him, Hugh caught a glint of sunlight on the blade of a sword. Then there was a pistol shot.

Everything stopped.

For a moment no one moved. A pirate named De Lour lay dead on the deck, sword in hand. A few feet away Clint stood, holding a pistol.

A sudden flash of light on Hugh's left caused him to pull sideways, to the right. Weasel's sword nicked Hugh's scalp and bit deep into the mast, just behind him. Before Weasel could recover Hugh moved in, pulled his knife, and thrust it into the little man's throat. Weasel's eyes grew wide. He clutched his throat, trying to stop the flow of blood. His mouth began to work, but no sound came out. Then he fell face forward onto the deck.

"*ENOUGH!*" It was Renoux's voice. The Frenchman pushed through the crowd of men that surrounded Hugh. Eyes blazing with fury, he looked at Hugh, then at the bodies that lay strewn upon the deck, then back at Hugh.

"Just *WHAT* has happened here?" he demanded. "What?"

"I killed one of the prisoners," Hugh said flatly. "They didn't like it."

"We was just havin' some fun, Cap'n, like we always do," Mahoney broke in, "an' he goes an' *shoots* the bitch!"

"And now," Renoux put a hand for silence, "two of my men are dead. Do you realize," he was looking at Hugh again, "that is twice the number of men we lost in the taking of this vessel?"

Hugh said nothing.

"Very well," Renoux said tiredly. He looked around at the others. "Bring me the other prisoners."

The two priests were brought forward. By now Clint had moved forward too, so that he stood next to Hugh.

When the two priests stood before them, Renoux spoke again.

"I need two loaded pistols," he said to the crowd of men. "Quickly! We have wasted enough time on this!"

Two pistols emerged from the crowd. Renoux handed on of them to Hugh.

"There!" Renoux told him. "Since you like to kill prisoners, kill this one." He pointed at one of the priests.

Hugh looked at the priest. The man was trembling with fear, but the look in his eyes showed that he had accepted his fate. Strangely, Hugh felt nothing toward the man, just a small sympathy. Not enough to kill him.

"No," he said to Renoux.

"I'm giving you a direct order," Renoux insisted. "Kill him!"

Hugh shook his head.

Renoux took the pistol from him and handed it to Clint.

"You!" he said to Clint. "You were part of this. You kill the prisoner."

Clint refused.

"Kill him!" Renoux demanded.

Clint dropped the pistol onto the deck and stood, looking at nothing.

"Have it your way," Renoux said, seething. Then, to the others, he said, "These two men have disobeyed a direct order from their Captain! They are to be taken back to the *Madalaine* and locked in the hold until we return to Campeche! There, they will be tried by Jean Lafitte himself and will be hung for refusing to obey!" He turned back to Clint and Hugh. "I would hang you right here and now, but Jean insists on reserving that privilege for himself!"

CHAPTER TWELVE

THEY REMAINED locked in the hold for three days, after which they were allowed up on deck to work. At night they were returned to the hold. This was as much for their own protection as punishment. Pirates were a strange and unpredictable breed. They might have already forgotten the incident aboard the Portuguese ship, or some of them might be holding a grudge. In the grip of sleep, a man's throat is an easy target for a skilled blade.

Neither Clint nor Hugh were particularly concerned about the prospect of being hanged. In a sense, they had both looked at death too many times and had come away unscathed to take it too seriously.

"Look at it this way," Hugh told Clint. "You're finally going to get to meet Lafitte!"

As for shooting the old Portuguese woman, Hugh found himself not so easily removed. He'd had no time to think about it when it happened, but in the darkness of the hold the scene replayed itself again and again. Despite the heat, she'd been wearing a long-sleeved, black dress, with gray stripes running the length of it and white ruffles at the sleeves and at the neck. Her hair was up, in a bun. Something about her reminded Hugh of his own grandmother.....

She had been very frightened, for herself as well as for her husband. Three of the pirates had surrounded her. One man held her while another was ripping back her dress. She didn't resist.

She saw Hugh approach her. At the sight of the pistol her eyes grew wide. He pulled the trigger from less than two feet away. Shock registered on her face and then she fell...

Hugh was certain that shooting the old woman was the best thing he could do, the most merciful. It didn't completely stop him from being plagued by guilt over it.

Accepting guilt seemed to have become his pastime.

Campeche hadn't changed. It was still there, at Galveston Island, waiting. There were no crowds, though, waiting and eager to set up a new fight for Clint, no beautiful women to seduce him. There was only a gibbet.

"Don't worry," Hugh told him, "they'll enjoy your performance just as much there as in the ring. This is a very loyal audience."

The thought didn't seem to cheer Clint much.

Renoux had gone ashore and returned, and now most of the crew were gone. Only a few hapless crew members remained aboard for security. The *Madalaine* lay at anchor in the channel between Galveston Island and the mainland, about a half-mile from shore. Hugh and Clint were in her hold. Hugh was lying on some burlap bags that were filled with coffee beans. The beans molded around him, creating a very comfortable bed. The roll of the ship and the gentle lapping of waves against the hull relaxed him, and he dozed...

It was Christmas again. Sarah was at the stove, cooking chicken and dumplings. She was a good cook. The smell warmed him. Their two boys, Wes and Phil, were in front of the hearth, playing with the toy carts Hugh had built for them. Hugh was at the kitchen table, repairing a stool. Something about Sarah bothered him. She was quiet and withdrawn, a little sad. Hugh knew why she was that way— he was getting ready to go to sea again. Still, it made him feel anxious.

There was a knock at the door. It was a loud knock, strong and unhurried. Someone in authority. Hugh got up to answer it. No one was there. Concerned, he closed the door and sat down.

As soon as he sat down, the knock came again. Hugh looked at the door. It was illogical, but Hugh had a strange feeling that something terrible was out there.

Again the knock, this time louder and more insistent. Hugh opened the door. Again, nothing. What was going on? Worried, he closed the door.

Once more the knock came. Hugh was starting to feel afraid. Carefully, he opened the door. Nothing.

Cautiously, he stepped outside. Something was wrong. His yard was gone. So were the houses that sat next to his. No lights shown anywhere. In fact, the whole town was gone. Hugh was standing in a wooded area, next to a stream. It was beautiful here, *really* beautiful, but for some reason Hugh was more afraid than he could ever remember being.

Hugh turned to go back inside, but his house was gone.

He sat up, choking and gasping for breath.

"Are you all right?" Clint's voice. They were in the dark of the hold, aboard the *Madalaine*. Despite the heat, Hugh was bathed in an icy sweat.

"Are you all right?" Clint repeated.

"I-we...the dream. It was just a dream..." Suddenly he stood up. "We have to get out of here!"

"Hah! Not much chance of that. We're locked in."

"I don't care. We have to find a way out. We have to escape."

"And where will we escape to? We're a mile from land. If we managed to get off the *Madalaine* and swim to shore without being eaten by sharks, we'd like as not end up in a Karankawa stew. No thanks. I prefer to take my chances here."

"Then you'll die. Lafitte isn't going to show us any mercy. We killed two of our own crew members and refused a direct order from our Captain. He'll make an example of us."

Clint thought about that.

"Well, I suppose you're right," he said finally, "but it doesn't change the fact that we're still locked in here."

"True, but if we're looking, an opportunity may present itself."

And so they waited. An hour later the hatch opened and the diffused light of dusk flooded in.

"Ahoy, mates!" It was Willie Brandt. "Come on up. Cap'n wants to see you!"

Renoux was quite cool and formal with them at first. He told them their trial was to be held the next day and that, most likely, they would be hanged the following morning.

"Do you have anything you want to say?" he asked them.

Clint looked at Hugh. Hugh shrugged.

"Not really," Hugh told him.

Renoux was silent for a moment. Finally, he looked at Hugh.

"You were never one of us," he said accusingly. "Never. This one," he indicated Clint, "this one we might have turned, but not you. Never you." Renoux sighed with exasperation. "Why could you not just kill the prisoners? Why did you have to defy me? You didn't save them—you knew they would die anyway. Why? The two priests died that very night!"

Hugh didn't answer.

"Very well," Renoux said after a minute. He looked tired. "Tomorrow you will be taken to Campeche. You will never leave. You men, both of you, have served well aboard this ship, at least until now. Tonight, you will have the freedom of the ship. If you try to *leave* the ship, you will be shot. There is nowhere for you to go. If you made it to shore, the Karankawas would get you. There is no help for you anywhere within a thousand miles."

Gradually, even the noise from the island quieted down. Silent as shadows, the two men slipped over the side of the *Madalaine* and into the water. It was not an exceptionally long swim and the water was warm. God willing, they would make it.

As they moved away from the ship, Hugh heard a familiar voice call out softly.

"Luck, brothers!"

It was Willie. There would be Hell to pay for all of them if anyone heard him, but the ship remained silent. Hugh and Clint continued to swim toward the mainland uninterrupted.

HughGlass

They came ashore at high tide. Pausing for only a moment to catch their breath, the two men moved inland. Hugh took one last look at the sea before starting out, and wondered if he would ever set foot on the deck of a ship again.

CHAPTER THIRTEEN

ON THE evening of the fourth day, Hugh suddenly realized he was a free man again.

They had been traveling at night, sleeping during the day, and staying in the water to avoid leaving any tracks. Earlier that evening, they had finally left Galveston Bay and had moved into a river that would take them north—and through Karankawa territory. They had been pushing a tree limb as they went. Ahead of them, Hugh noticed three other logs moving in their direction.

"I think we need to get out of the water," he told Clint. The younger man agreed. Both of them had seen alligators before. Both men knew that to stay in the water meant death.

"Damn!" Clint swore good naturedly, climbing onto the riverbank. "Seems wherever we go here, something wants to eat us!"

"Yes," Hugh agreed, grinning, "but think of it! You'd be dying a free man!"

"Aye! I probably taste better this way." Clint looked around. "Snakes, alligators, indians... I don't think the odds are greatly in our favor."

Hugh grunted. "I don't know if this is the time to tell you this," he said, "but the odds have not been in our favor for almost two years now. Come on, let's keep moving."

Traveling by land, they were able to make good time. They stayed near the river, following it upstream as it wound northward. They had eaten little since they left the ship. The day before they had found a berry bush. Neither of them knew if the berries were edible. Starving, they had taken a chance, but it was much too early in the year. The berries were sour. Still, Hugh wished he had some now. It felt

47

as though his stomach were gnawing on his backbone.

At sunup they stopped, found a place to hide for the day, and slept.

Hugh awoke in mid-afternoon. It was hot. His body was sore from sleeping on the ground. His stomach ached from hunger.

Clint was already awake. He sat looking out at the water, thinking. When he saw that Hugh was awake he nodded.

"I've counted three snakes and two alligators," he told Hugh.

"How long?"

"About an hour."

"What kind of snakes?"

"I don't know. I think one was a copperhead."

They were silent for awhile. Finally, Clint spoke again.

"These moccasins were a good idea," he said.

Hugh nodded.

"Hartley had them in his store in Campeche. He had eight pair. I bought two for ten cents apiece. Figured if we ever decided to swim for it we wouldn't want to drag shoes along."

"You were right."

They were silent again. Hugh had begun to doze when he heard Clint ask, "Do you think we'll make it?"

"I don't know," Hugh answered without opening his eyes. "We've made it this far."

A moment later Clint said, "I don't think I'm going to make it."

Hugh opened his eyes again.

"I don't know," Clint continued. "I have this creepy feeling. I've never felt this way before."

"You've just been watching snakes too long," Hugh said and closed his eyes again.

"Maybe," Clint acknowledged. "Maybe."

Hugh woke again just before sundown. Clint was sleeping. Moving carefully, Hugh worked his way down to the water's edge to get a drink. He drank quickly, feeling exposed. Then he headed back toward the clump of trees that had been their refuge. He had taken only a few steps when he saw a dark, slender form sliding through the grass ahead of him.

Clint's right, he thought. *There are a lot of snakes here.*

Looking around, he sighted a large stick, about four feet long, with a crook at one end. The stick was about two inches thick. Snapping it up, he ran to where the snake was and hit it.

That proved to be a mistake. Immediately, the snake struck at him. Using the stick like he would a sword, Hugh managed to parry the strike, knocking the snake's head away when it was only an inch away from biting his foot. The snake withdrew, coiling to strike again, hissing at him. For the first time, Hugh saw the snow-white interior of the reptile's mouth.

So, he thought. *You're a cotton-mouth!*

The snake struck again, missing. As it tried to withdraw, Hugh struck it on the head with the stick. Then he struck it five more time, in rapid succession.

That night, before setting out, they decided to risk, and managed to create a small fire.

Night after night they continued northward, following the river. When the river began to angle to the west they struck out across the desert-like plain. They were in luck. Before they had traveled half the evening they crossed a small stream, which they were able to follow north until it opened into a lake. Hugh couldn't believe the amount of game they encountered. Though novices at hunting, with no weapons save for rocks and an unseasoned bow that Clint made, they managed to feed themselves pretty well.

Night after night they traveled. Their plan was to head north and slightly east, then go due east until they came to the Missouri River. Then they could follow the river south until they came again to civilization, which would most likely be St. Louis. Hugh thought it would take them three to four weeks to get to that city, but he was wrong.

It would take him almost four years.

CHAPTER FOURTEEN

GRADUALLY, THE terrain had changed. What had been desert-like plain gave way to rolling prairie, with tall grass and wildflowers that seemed to stretch on endlessly. After awhile, though, even this changed, and the two men found themselves in heavily wooded hills. For three weeks they traveled north. Twice, roving groups of indians came within a stone's throw of where Clint and Hugh lay hiding. Both times the indians passed them by. There was no way for either Clint or Hugh to know what indians these were, or if they were friendly or hostile. The safest thing was to assume that any indians they met would be hostile and, as such, try to avoid them. Yet, as each night passed and they found themselves bedding down for the day, safe and unharmed, the two men found it impossible not to breathe a little easier.

"One more week," Hugh told Clint as they settled in for the day. "One more week and we'll be out of this—if not back to St. Louis. If we start moving east tonight, we should cut across the Missouri in a couple of days. Then all we have to do is build a raft and let the water take us to a town."

"It almost seems too good too be true," Clint sighed. "A normal life again! It's too bad that we'll be arriving in St. Louis without any money. It'd be grand to live it up!"

"Aye, but we should be able to arrange something. First thing, we'll contact the shipping office and let them know what happened to the *Gallant*—*and* to us! They should send us some money, even if it isn't much. Then, with them behind us, we'll contact the government, tell them what's been happening in Campeche, and then the Navy can go and blast the bastards to Hell!"

"What if they don't believe us?" Clint said. "What if they charge *us* with piracy?"

"Oh, there will probably be an inquest, but with both of us backing each other up, it should be all right. What other choice did we have?"

"That's true, I suppose…" Clint's voice trailed off and he was quiet for a moment. "You know," he said finally, "it's too bad—we never *did* get to meet Lafitte!"

Hugh laughed out loud.

"Go to sleep," he said.

It seemed as though he'd just fallen asleep. Something poked Hugh hard in the ribs. He rolled over, sluggishly at first, then faster as his mind cleared. He sat up quickly.

The two men were not alone.

There were six of them, indians, the like of whom Hugh had never seen. Three were on horseback and three were on their feet, standing over Clint and Hugh while their horses waited nearby. The indians were frightening to look at. Their faces were painted completely over in shades of red, yellow, white, and black. Two of them wore their hair long and loose. The others had shaved their heads, leaving only a narrow strip that ran from the brow back, over the center of their heads, Mohawk style. They had laced feathers into this narrow strip of hair, giving the indians a bird-like appearance. One of the two who were mounted wore what looked like a wolf skin across his shoulders. The others were all naked from the waist up. Their bodies and scalps were painted the same as their faces. Each man wore a necklace that was different from those of the others. Hugh noticed that the mounted Indian with the wolf robe wore a necklace made from huge claws, which could only have come from a great bear.

The men on the ground all carried painted shields. Two of them carried lances. One held a sort of stone ax. The indians who were mounted all carried rifles.

The indian closest to Hugh jabbed his lance threateningly and spoke in a language that was unfamiliar to the two white men. Clint glanced quickly at Hugh.

"I think," Hugh said carefully, "that he wants us to stand."

Slowly, keeping their eyes on the indians, the two white men got to their feet. As they did, they managed to edge closer together.

"I heard somewhere," Hugh said quietly, "that the only thing indians respect is strength and courage, so be strong."

"I'll try," Clint told him.

That brought an involuntary smile—probably from nervousness—to Hugh's lips. Clint was one of the strongest men Hugh had ever met.

The indian with the lance didn't see the smile. He was walking a slow circle around the two men, examining them. The indian with the stone ax did. He came forward quickly, yelling at Hugh. Without warning, he jammed the head of the ax into Hugh's midsection. Hugh doubled over, coughing, but managed to straighten up with a big smile for the man who had struck him. The indian glared back.

"I don't think he likes you, Hugh." Clint said.

The indian moved over to Clint. Glaring, he spoke softly to Clint, his words heavy with malice. Striking suddenly, he hit Clint in the stomach with the stone ax, just as he had done with Hugh a moment earlier. Expecting the blow, Clint tightened the muscles in his stomach. To Hugh, Clint seemed not to feel the blow at all. In a blur of speed Clint reached out and, grabbing the head of the ax in one hand, stiff-armed the indian in the chest. The blow caught the indian off guard and knocked him completely off his feet. The man landed a few feet away in the dirt, in a sitting position. Recovering quickly, the indian jumped to his feet, pulling a knife from his belt. Before he could move toward Clint a sharp word from the man in the wolf robe stopped him. The man with the knife hesitated for a moment, then put the knife away.

Clint now held the ax. Taking it in both hands, he broke the ax across his knee and threw it down in front of the indian he had knocked down.

None of the other indians had moved. The indian with the lance, who had been circling the two white men when the commotion started, now walked around and stood in front of Clint. He looked Clint over and gave him a slight nod of approval.

"Well," Hugh said quietly, "it looks like we got their attention."

The indians began talking amongst themselves. The man with the lance pointed at the moccasins on the white men's feet. They seemed curious about these. At the same time they found Clint's bow and arrows somewhat humorous.

Abruptly, wolf-robe decided it was time to go. One of the indians came forward with a rope. He pointed at Clint, then crossed his arms together at the wrists, indicating what he wanted Clint to do.

"What do you think?" Clint asked Hugh, continuing to stare at the indian, but not complying. "Do we go along, or fight?"

"Well, considering that they've got three rifles trained on us, we may as well see what they want."

Reluctantly, they allowed their arms to be bound in front of them. Then, mounting their horses, the indians led them away in single file. The rider of the second horse led Hugh, by means of a rope that was tied to Hugh's bound arms. The rider of the fourth horse led Clint in the same way.

Traveling north and west, they moved at a pace that was hard on the two men who were afoot. Fortunately, three weeks of walking had toughened them and they were able to keep up. The terrain didn't help them. It was all rolling hills, sometimes grassy, but often covered with rocks, brush, and small trees, places that were difficult for the men being pulled along behind.

It was late afternoon before they stopped. The hours of keeping up with the horses had left Hugh at the point of exhaustion. The last two hours of walking-running had left an unending stitch in his side. When the horses stopped, he literally fell to his knees. Behind him, Clint did the same.

Their respite didn't last long. The indians, wanting to set up camp for the night, soon came and collected the two white men and led them to a nearby stream, allowing them to drink for the first time since waking them up. Then, after checking the bonds on their wrists, the indians bound the white men's feet as well, and set about making their camp for the night.

Hugh was too tired from keeping up with the horses to care about running away. Moments after being left alone, he fell asleep.

He awoke to the smell of roasting meat. Hunger gnawed at him, but it was overshadowed by the ache in his wrists and ankles, and by the frustrating closeness that being bound gave him. Clint was no better off. Any attempts at finding relief by stretching or straining at their bonds only increased their discomfort.

From the position he lay in, Hugh could see the camp. There was a fire, with what looked like an antelope roasting over it. Three of the indians lounged nearby, talking softly, while a fourth lay on his back, near the fire. The man on his back was thumping rhythmically on his chest and humming a low, sad-sounding song. The other two indians did not seem to be around.

Presently, one of the indians rose and turned the antelope. He spoke to one of the others, who rose and went to the stream for water. When he came back, the "cook" cut off a large piece off of the roast and motioned toward the two white men. The second indian then brought food and water to Hugh. Grunting from pain, Hugh managed to work himself into a sitting position and accepted it. The indian then did the same for Clint.

Throughout it all, the indian on his back kept thumping his chest and humming, stopping only for a short time to feed himself before he returned to his music. Despite himself, Hugh found the indian's music strangely comforting. He wondered who these people were and what they intended for him and for Clint. They weren't Karankawas. Hugh was certain they had left Karankawa territory far behind. Otherwise, he would never have given in and allowed himself to be tied up by them, no matter how many rifles they had.

These indians could have been from any other tribe. Hugh's knowledge of indians had been limited to what he had been able to read about them while at sea. This far west, he doubted that they would be friendly to white men, although they must have traded with them—they had rifles.

Aside from being tied, and from being forced to keep up, Hugh and Clint had not been treated badly.

Not yet, anyhow.

Late into the night he had the dream again. Sarah was at the stove, cooking chicken and dumplings. Wes and Phil were in front of the hearth, playing with the toy carts Hugh had made for them. Despite it being Christmas, there was a sadness about Sarah that bothered Hugh, a distance. It made him feel anxious...

There was a knock at the door. Hugh answered it but there was no one there. Concerned, he closed the door.

Again the knock. Hugh opened the door. Again, nothing. Worried, he closed the door.

Once more the knock came. Hugh was starting to feel really afraid. He opened the door.

No one was there. Cautiously, he stepped outside.

From out of nowhere, an enormous beast came at him, all teeth and claws and massive brute strength, rending and tearing at him. Hugh tried to get away, but it bore down on him, getting him into it's huge jaws, crushing him, tearing at him with it's claws, tearing and tearing...

He awoke in complete panic, unable to move his arms or legs. The indian with the wolfskin robe stood over him, watching, the necklace of bear claws dangling from around his neck.

Those were the claws...

CHAPTER FIFTEEN

THE TWO MEN spent a restless, uncomfortable night, restricted by their bonds. They were awake before the indians. When they were finally allowed to get up and move around, and to relieve themselves, the freedom of movement was almost painful.

The second day was much the same as the first. They continued traveling west throughout the day, stopping late in the afternoon to set up camp for the night. The next day was the same, and the day after that. They passed herds of elk and deer, none of which seemed frightened of them. The indians took what they needed and kept moving. Hugh began to lose track of the days...

The indians treatment of them was rough, but not particularly cruel. They were fed when the indians ate, were given water when they needed it, and in general, shared the same conditions as their captors. As far as Hugh could tell, the man that Clint had knocked down held no ill will toward them.

One afternoon, while the sun was still high in the sky, they began to pass by what looked to Hugh to be signs of civilization. There were no roads, only trails, but they began to pass through areas that had been cultivated. Small, numerous patches of vegetable gardens sprang up around them. As yet, they saw no people, though. This went on for three or four miles. Then they passed a group of indian women who were working in one of the patches. The women ran over and began chattering excitedly to the men on horseback, checking out the two white men who trailed along behind as they did. Then the group continued on their way. An hour later they entered the indian village.

It was an interesting sight, and not at all what Hugh Glass would have expected. The village had a wooden palisade around it, about fifteen feet high. They entered through a gate, though no one seemed to be on guard.

The indians lived in earthen domes. Each dome was about fifty feet across and fifteen-to-twenty feet high. There were about forty or fifty of the domes, all grouped together without any particular pattern. Each dome had an entrance that extended roughly ten feet from the front. Hugh found it interesting that all the entrances faced the same direction, and this was east. As they entered the village, people began to exit the domes, coming out to greet them. Within moments after their arrival, they were surrounded by several hundred men, women, and children, and at least that many dogs.

The warrior with the wolf-skin robe and the bear claw necklace came back and, drawing a knife, cut their bonds, freeing their hands for the first time in days. The increased circulation caused Hugh's hands to tingle, almost painfully.

A group of twenty or thirty children had gathered to stare at the two white men. A young girl, about eight years old, brought forward a bowl of water and handed it to Hugh. Hugh accepted, strangely touched.

"Thank you," he told her.

The little girl smiled and went to get some water for Clint.

Wolf-robe came back and motioned for Hugh and Clint to follow. Parting the crowd before them, the indian led the way to the middle of the village. They stopped in front of one of the earthen domes. An old man came out. He was dressed much like the others in that he was bare chested, and wore a breechcloth, with leggings and moccasins. He also wore a great bearskin robe over his shoulders, and wore a necklace of bear claws that hung halfway down his belly. Hugh assumed this was the chief.

The old man gave Hugh a strange look, almost as if he recognized him from somewhere. There *was* something. Hugh didn't know what it could be. There was no possible way that he and the old man could ever have met.

The old indian turned his attention on Clint, looking him over and nodding. Some words passed between him and the younger warrior that they both found amusing. Then the old man, with a broad grin at the two white men, made an expansive gesture and said something which, to Hugh, sounded like some sort of welcome. Immediately, the whole village crowded in on them, patting them on the back, smiling and chattering and ushering them into the nearest mound.

The mound had an entrance to it of about a dozen feet. The inside was quite large. Hugh guessed the diameter to be about forty feet. The center was held up by four poles, each about a foot thick, that formed a square in the middle of the room. A fire pit sat in the center of this. A large hole in the middle of the roof allowed smoke to escape.

The two white men were led to a spot just in front of the fire and, by gesture, were asked to sit. Food was brought to them. The entire tribe seemed to crowd in behind them to watch them eat. Bewildered, Hugh and Clint accepted the food, which consisted of a sort of stew, and both were surprised at how good it actually was.

The old chief seemed pleased. Hugh didn't know *what* to think. In an instant they had gone from being prisoners, bound hand and foot, to honored guests. Whatever it was that had turned the tide for them, he was thankful for it.

After they had finished eating, the chief called for one of the women to come forward. She was older than most of the women, about Hugh's age. Again, through gestures, the chief indicated that the two men should follow her. The woman led them to the edge of the village, to the river. As before, the entire village seemed to follow them.

When they reached the river, the woman immediately turned and began to remove Hugh's clothing.

"Whoa!" he said, stopping her and stepping back. "What's going on?"

The woman gave him a puzzled look, then reached once more for the buttons on his trousers. Again, he stopped her.

"Will you please stop?" he told her. The woman gave him an uncomprehending look.

Behind them, the indians who had followed seemed to find the whole thing amusing. Clint looked at them. When he turned back to Hugh and the woman, he was grinning.

"What's the matter, Hugh? Haven't you ever had a woman try to get your pants off before?"

"Very funny," Hugh said, not taking his eyes off the woman. "Go ahead and laugh. She'll be after yours next!"

Looking down at his own attire, Clint said, "She can *have* the bloody rags! They're about to fall off me as it is!"

Once more the woman started toward Hugh. When he backed away again she stopped. Giving him a perturbed look, she said something he couldn't understand. Immediately, fifteen or twenty women came down to them. Surrounding Hugh and Clint, the women forced the two men out into the river and began to pull at their clothes. Tattered as it was, their clothing tore easily. The women seemed to make a contest of seeing how much each one could get away with. In moments the two men were totally naked. The women withdrew to the shore, each with a prized patch of cloth which they had torn from the two men. Hugh and Clint sunk down into the water and waited.

"So, what now?" Clint asked.

"I think," Hugh said, "that they want us to bathe."

The two men stayed in the water for a short while, splashing around while the men, women, children, and dogs on the shore watched them. Finally, the woman who had led them to the river came forward again. She held up two blankets and motioned for the men in the river to come out.

"Well," Hugh said, "I guess we can't stay in here forever. So much for modesty."

Amid the open stares of the women, children, and men who were on the shore, the two men moved up and out of the water. They were at first wrapped in blankets, but the two men quickly understood that these were to be used to dry themselves. Then they were given buckskin leggings, breechcloths, and shirts, all new and decorated with beadwork. Hugh could not help but wonder why they were being treated so well. His only knowledge of indians was through what he had read and from seeing the Karankawas. None of that information supported this kind of hospitality.

Even though most of the men went bare-chested, the indians all seemed to be amazed at Clint's physique. As he was trying to get dressed, they crowded in around him, touching his arms and chest as if to see if he were real. Mostly, it was the women who did this, but some of the men did so as well. They were right to be awed, Hugh thought. He had never seen or known a more finely muscled man than his friend.

After they had dressed, the two men were taken once more back to the chief's lodge. They were seated by the fire, next to the chief. Another bowl of stewed meat was brought to the old man. Putting his hand into the bowl, the chief rolled the meat around for a moment, looking for the best morsel. Finding what he decided was a good piece, he then offered it to Hugh. Hugh, having already eaten his fill, started to decline, but when he saw the troubled look in the old man's eyes, he quickly accepted the meat. The chief then repeated the process, finding just the right piece to offer to Clint.

"Don't refuse," Hugh told him. "I think it might be an insult to them."

"We already ate, once." Clint said. "Are they trying to fatten us up? Maybe they really *are* Karankawas!"

"Let's hope not."

Behind them, a couple of the indians had begun to beat rhythmically on drums. A moment later they began to sing. Some of the others began to dance. Neither of the two white men understood the singing or the reason for the dance, if there was one, but they enjoyed it anyway. The old chief smiled and offered them some more meat.

Later, the two men were shown to a spot next to the wall, and were given mats to sleep on. Exhausted, both Hugh and Clint fell into a deep, dreamless sleep. The indians, meanwhile, continued to celebrate.

For the next two days, the indians treated the two white men like honored guests. Wherever they went in the village, the people smiled and spoke to them as though they were dignitaries. They were allowed to wander when and where they wanted, and no one tried to stop or molest them in any way. At breakfast, which consisted of the same fare they had been given the night before, Hugh tried to explain to the chief that they needed to get back to civilization, to St. Louis, but the old man didn't understand and merely offered Hugh more food.

Hugh found life in the village to be not too unlike most white towns. In many ways it was more practical. Everyone in the village contributed to the betterment of the whole. Each of the earthen mounds housed several families, and each of these had their own section along the inside wall of the mound. They shared the fire in the center of the room for all their individual cooking, and all the women seemed to take turns at keeping the fire going.

They were a curious people, and a curiosity to him. Almost all the men wore breechcloths, leggings, and moccasins, and went mostly bare chested. The leggings were fringed, and the fringes were often decorated with hair which, Hugh thought, must have been scalps. The women all wore dresses of what looked like deerskin, tied at the waist and decorated with beadwork. The women wore their hair long or braided. Hugh was surprised at how beautiful most of them were.

Among the men, most shaved their heads, leaving only a narrow strip of hair down the middle of their head or a small scalplock. This was usually decorated with feathers. The faces of the men, along with their heads and their chests, were often painted with red, yellow, or white. Even in repose, they were fearsome to behold.

Despite their frightening appearance, the indians seemed quite genial. Hugh saw evidence of kindness and affection between them. Children, especially, were treated with great tolerance and love. Hugh held all of this in contrast to the pirates, most all of whom were petty and vicious and mean.

Among the children, the young boys went completely naked, while the young girls wore only a short skirt. The boys, Hugh noticed, constructed bows and arrows that were not unlike the one Clint had made. No wonder that the men who had captured them found Clint's efforts so amusing. The bows that *they* carried were of much superior construction. That didn't negate the fact that Clint had used his bow successfully to help feed them.

The morning following their arrival, Hugh and Clint were taken to a lodge that, while similar in construction to the others they had seen, was several times larger. Once more, they were the center of attention. A huge celebration ensued, which involved everyone in the village. This went on throughout the day and into the night. It continued the next morning when they woke up and went on without letup through the second day as well. Hugh was puzzled at all the celebrating. Two days. And still going. For two white men. What could be the significance of that?

He was sitting by the fire, listening to the indians who were nearby, singing and thumping on their chests as they lay on their backs. He looked across to the entrance and saw a young woman walking toward him, carrying a basket. A surge of excitement went through him as he recognized her. Hugh had noticed her the morning before, when he had risen, the morning after their arrival. He had been walking down to the river and he passed her. When their eyes met, something in him stirred. He felt it again, now, as she walked toward him. There was something about her that was different from the other women in the village. Hugh couldn't place what it was, but it was there. She wore her hair the same as the other women, and dressed pretty much the same, but there was something that set her apart. She looked like she must be in her mid-twenties. She was certainly no better looking than the other women he had seen in the village, but when she looked at Hugh, he could feel it all the way down into the pit of his stomach. It had been a long time since any woman had that effect on Hugh Glass.

CHAPTER SIXTEEN

IT WAS late into the evening of the third day. Hugh wanted to rest, but the indians would not let him alone. Whenever he tried to rise and go to get some sleep, one of the young indian women—or one of the men—would intercept him and pull him back to dance by the fire, accompanied by the never-ending drumming that went on throughout the night. Hugh looked for the woman he had seen earlier, but she was nowhere to be found.

We must by nearing the end of the celebration, Hugh thought. *This is the only night they've kept us up this late.* He looked around for Clint and found him, droopy-eyed, sitting by the fire. An attractive young squaw came and sat down next to him, letting her hand rest on his thigh. Clint woke up.

A short while later, the drumming and dancing and singing seemed to increase in speed and intensity. Hugh noticed that nearly all of the indians had joined in. It got faster and faster, with the indians all dancing around, feverishly. Then, abruptly, it stopped. The few indians who were still sitting all rose. Hugh and Clint were ushered outside.

It was nearly dawn. The entire village seemed to have been assembled. There were more people here than Hugh had realized before. Hugh estimated that there were at least a thousand, possibly two thousand people here.

The indian that had led the party that captured the two white men suddenly appeared before them. Motioning for Hugh and Clint to follow him, he led the way through the village. The rest of the crowd of indians followed along behind. Together, they headed toward the eastern side of the encampment. Exiting through a large gateway, they continued on until they reached a large clearing. In the center of this, surrounded by twenty or thirty warriors, stood the old chief. Behind the chief, about twenty feet back, a sort of framework had been erected. This consisted of six poles, two of which were set into the ground, while the other four ran horizontally across the bottom, each about a foot apart, forming cross braces. The entire framework was about eight feet across, and about a dozen feet high.

The chief looked magnificent. He wore a long wolfskin robe that fell nearly to the ground and was almost as white as his hair. He wore no headdress, but about his neck was a collar of feathers which spread down over his chest. More than all of this was the man's presence. There was a vitality and power in his old eyes that Hugh had not seen before.

The two white men were led up to the edge of the clearing, the indians fanning out around and behind them.

Hugh looked over at Clint. The younger man gave him a very worried look.

"You know," Clint said, looking back at the chief, "I have had a really bad feeling ever since we left the ship…"

"Just relax." Hugh tried to sound more confident than he felt. "We've done all right up 'til now. Maybe they just want to honor us, somehow."

The old chief began to speak. For several minutes his voice droned on and on. Finally, he walked over and stood before the two men. He looked at Hugh, smiling and nodding. Then he looked at Clint. For a few moments he stood, regarding the two of them as if her were trying to make a decision. Suddenly, he pointed the end of his staff at Clint.

Instantly, six of the surrounding warriors stepped forward. Like the chief, these men all wore feathered collars about their necks. They made no move to lay hands on Clint, but motioned for him to step forward. Clint looked at Hugh.

"It's probably some sort of test of courage," Hugh told him. Even as he said the words, though, an uneasy feeling in the pit of his stomach told him it was more.

Nodding worriedly, Clint stepped forward. Hugh started to follow but one of the warriors stopped him.

They led Clint to the center of the clearing, stopping just before the framework of poles. Two of the warriors climbed up to the top cross-pole and waited, each bracing himself on one of the two upright poles at either side. The other four warriors, using hand signals, indicated that they wanted Clint to strip. Reluctantly, Clint did what they wanted. A moment later he stood naked before the entire village.

They now motioned for Clint to join the two warriors up on the pole framework. With leaden movements, Clint did so. Hugh could see the fear in his friend and it tore at him, adding to his own growing feelings of dread. Hugh had never known Clint to be afraid of anything.

When Clint was at the top, the two indians who were there tied his hands to the two upper corners of the framework. Again, Clint allowed them to do this. They then tied his feet to the two lower corners, pulling his legs wide apart in the process so that he half-stood, half-hung, spread eagle, from the framework. Watching from the edge of the crowd, Hugh felt a paralyzing numbness grow in the pit of his stomach. He tried reminding himself that, up until now, the indians had treated the two of them like honored guests; that this was probably some sort of test of courage. It didn't help. Something about this didn't feel right.

Without warning, several of the indians suddenly grabbed Hugh. He tried to fight back, but he had been caught off guard and from behind. There were way too many of them for him to fight effectively. Rough hands forced him face-down onto the ground, as his arms were pulled back and tied behind him.

"CLINT!" he yelled. "GET LOOSE! GET AWAY! WE HAVE TO FIGHT...!"

Something struck him hard on the back of the head. For a moment he blacked out. When he came to, he was being pulled onto his knees, so that he could watch the rest of the ordeal. Clint, meanwhile, was struggling with his bonds. His efforts were useless. The ropes held.

Several of the indians had begun to pile wood at the bottom of the framework. One man, carrying a torch, ran forward. Climbing up next to Clint, the indian thrust the torch up under Clint's left arm and held it there for several seconds, searing his underarm. Clint screamed in agony and tried once more to free himself.

Extending the torch, the indian then held the torch under Clint's right arm. Finally, he held it under Clint's groin, burning his genitals. When he was done with that, the indian climbed down and dropped the torch into the pile of wood that had been piled beneath the framework.

Clint seemed to swoon for a moment, from the pain. When he realized that the wood beneath him had begun to burn, he became frantic. He strained at the ropes that held him. As the fire grew below him, he began to rock, forward and back, in a desperate effort to loosen the two upright poles and topple the framework. Suddenly, the indian that had led the party that captured the two white men ran forward with a bow and arrow. Standing on Clint's left, the indian drew the bow and shot him. The arrow passed completely through Clint, so that the point stuck out one side and the feathered shaft stuck out the other. Immediately, Clint went limp.

As Clint's blood ran down into the fire, one of the indians ran forward and placed some sort of raw meat under it, so that the blood ran over the meat and then into the fire. A moment later, every man and boy from the village seemed to move into the clearing. One by one, they each shot an arrow into Clint's chest, until Clint resembled some huge, grotesque, pin cushion.

Hugh felt something deep within him shrivel and die. He continued to struggle at his bonds, but he was in a kind of shock. He was looking at the ground as he fought, no longer seeing what was before him. His best and only remaining friend was dead, killed in a useless, stupid manner. They had been together for years, suffering the hardships and dangers of the sea, the pirates, the swamps. Again and again they had saved each other. Not any more. Clint was dead.

The sun was just starting to rise. Two of the indians suddenly took hold of Hugh's arms, lifting him from behind. Expecting the same treatment that his friend had just suffered, Hugh fought back desperately. Instead of dragging him out into the clearing, however, they began half-dragging, half-carrying him back into the village. They took him back to the chief's lodge. Then, after tying his legs and checking to make sure that the ropes on his arms were still tight, they left him on his sleeping mat. For some time he laid there, shivering and in shock, teeth chattering, unable to close his eyes without seeing again and again the last moments of Clint's life, and his horrible, untimely death.

Sometime later, he became aware that someone was beside him. He was surprised when he realized it was the young woman, the one he'd been interested in before. She covered his shivering body with a buffalo robe, then leaned low and whispered into his ear:

"(N'avez pas peur.) Ne vous inquietez pas. Ils ne feront pas un autre (sacrifi) a l'etoile du matin jusqu' a la lune prochaine ~ ce que vous apellez un mois." "— *Do not fear. They will not make another sacrifice to Morning Star until the next moon—what you would call a month.*"

Then she was gone.

CHAPTER SEVENTEEN

A HUNDRED questions raged in Hugh's mind— Who was this woman? How did she come to know French? Why had these indians treated them so well if they intended to kill them anyway? If, as the woman had said, it as a sacrifice, why had they chosen Clint instead of him? Hugh had always heard that indians respected strength, honored it. Clint was stronger than almost any man. It would have made more sense to have sacrificed Hugh—he was ten years older and, while not exactly weak, was not in Clint's league when it came to raw power. Why hadn't they chosen him instead? He lay for hours, thinking about it.

Clint was gone. For the first time Hugh realized just how much he had depended on his young friend, and how much he had taken Clint's great strength for granted.

And now it was much too late for Hugh to thank him.

Hugh lay, no longer even bothering to strain at his bonds. He could smell the smoke from the fire and the scent of human beings resting in their lair. He could hear them snoring. Somewhere in the room, he could hear the sounds of a couple making love.

All of it meant nothing to him. He had lost his friend, and much, much more. He had lost hope. For the first time in his life he was truly alone.

Eventually, he dozed, but there was no rest for him. As soon as he began to drift off he found himself back aboard the *Gallant*. Tom Halpern was at the helm. Behind him stood Clint. Hugh was overjoyed to see his friend, alive and well again. Then Halpern looked over and realized he was there. When he saw Hugh his face became an almost insane mask of hatred and rage. Spittle formed at the corner of his mouth when he spoke—

"Life, you asked for, and life you have. But it is not, and never will be, an easy life. You will *NEVER* know peace—you will know hardship and suffering and pain of every sort. And when you die, you will die bloody!"

"Didn't I tell you?"

"Didn't I?"

"DIDN'T I?"

Hugh awoke, cramped and shivering under the buffalo robe. Nor did he sleep any more that day, but lay awake and staring until, hours later, the indians roused themselves and came around and untied him.

Once more, they treated him with the greatest courtesy. As though the events of the previous morning had never taken place, they went about their business. If anything, they seemed in even greater spirits than before.

But Hugh knew what they had done, and he knew what was in store for him if he stayed.

Hugh Glass had no intention of staying.

He walked through the village, unhampered, aware that, for all their friendly greetings and apparent good will, he was being watched.

It was hard for him to accept that Clint was gone. He found himself unconsciously looking for his friend wherever he went, half expecting to see Clint come walking around each earth-mound that he came upon. Clint would have a slight swagger to his walk, an easy smile on his genial face.

But Clint was forever gone.

Hugh moved through the village, observing the people in their daily routines. Looking at them, it was hard to believe they had taken part in the horror of the morning before. The children played; wives cajoled their husbands; the men, once they had gotten used to Hugh's presence, had dropped their grim, stern looks and were actually quite open and friendly. He saw none of the petty callousness and suspicion that had dominated Campeche. He saw nothing at all to indicate the eager disregard that they had shown in the way they dispatched Clint. None of it made sense to him.

For want of anything better to do, he began to count dogs. He counted about two dogs for every person he saw, which would figure out somewhere between two and four thousand dogs. That was a lot of dogs. they all looked half-starved, and indeed, he had never yet seen anyone feed any of them, but they were there.

He passed a group of squaws, but none among them was the one he sought. One *did* draw his attention, though. She was taller than the others, by head and shoulders. Her hair was gray and stringy. When she turned to look at him, he was shocked by how incredibly homely she was. She looked just like a man.

Hugh climbed up onto one of the earthen mounds and sat down. From here he was able to see the whole village. Hugh counted sixty-three earth domes, including the one upon which he sat.

Across from him, on another dome, four young men were beginning their daily preparations, which they appeared to take pretty seriously. Hugh watched them for awhile. First, they rubbed themselves down with grease until their skin glistened in the sunlight. After that, they meticulously began applying red, yellow and white paint to their faces and upper bodies. One of them had a small mirror, which they took turns using periodically to check their progress. Hugh watched them for near-ly an hour. When he finally climbed down off the earthen dome and went on his way, the four were nowhere near finished with their primpings, as far as he could tell.

It seemed to Hugh that all of the work was done by the women, including the little girls. The men lounged around or went hunting. Young boys chased each other around, or sat in small groups and gambled for arrows, or played a game that con-sisted of throwing a feathered lance through a four-inch hoop that one of the other boys would roll along the ground. No one appeared to be unhappy with this arrange-ment. It seemed to Hugh that everyone in the village was quite content.

Wherever he went, Hugh was met with friendly smiles and greetings that he didn't understand. Some of the older men would sometimes stop him and talk to him for several minutes at a time. Hugh would smile and nod, never comprehend-ing a word and never forgetting that these smiling, happy people had brutally mur-dered his friend.

It was almost a week before Hugh again caught up with the woman who had spoken French to him. He had been walking through the village, not really looking for her anymore and beginning to wonder if she had ever really been there at all, when suddenly, there she was.

She was older than he had first thought—probably about thirty. Once more he found something about her that was different from the other women, but he could not place what it was. There was a calmness about her, he thought, that made her almost seem plain. Certainly, she was by far not the most beautiful woman he had seen since entering the village.

Then she saw him and smiled.

Hugh immediately changed his mind. She was not only the most beautiful woman in the village, she was the most beautiful woman he had ever seen, any time, anywhere.

"What is your name," he immediately asked her in French.

"Not here," she said quickly. She looked around. "Over there, in the trees beyond the village. When the sun is high. I will come."

She moved away. Hugh watched her go, wondering why the intrigue. If she spoke a language that he understood, why not communicate? Why hide the fact from the rest of her tribe?

Hugh looked at the sun. It was early yet, probably three hours before the sun would be "high". He continued on, walking through the village. A stand of trees stood about three-hundred yards south of where the last earthen dome was built. In three hours Hugh would be there.

It was a hot day. The sweat ran down Hugh's back as he walked toward the woods. A flock of noisy, brightly colored birds filled the upper branches of the trees. Hugh had seen the birds before. He was pretty certain they were called parakeets.

She was already there, waiting for him when he arrived. Hugh didn't see her at first. He strolled casually into the woods. It was the first time he had wandered away from the village and he was a little nervous that he might be stopped. To his surprise, no one paid him any mind.

He walked a short way into the woods, stopped, and waited. A moment later he was startled to realize that she was beside him. Hugh hadn't heard a thing.

"What is your name?" he asked her again.

"Little Feather," she told him.

"Why do you not want your people to know that you speak the white man's tongue?"

"They are not my people. I am Sioux. They are Pawnee. If they knew that I speak your tongue, they might have thought I would warn you of the sacrifice."

"But you didn't…"

"It would have done no good. You could not escape. Telling you would have changed nothing. If I had warned you, it would have brought only worry to you and your friend. Would you have wanted his last days to be so filled?"

"No," Hugh said. "We might have escaped, though."

"You would not have escaped," she told him.

They were silent for a time. A dozen questions flashed through Hugh's mind at once. He wasn't sure where to start.

"So what happens now?" he asked.

"Now we must wait. There will be another sacrifice again when the moon returns. We must wait until then."

"And if I don't want to wait? What's to keep me from just walking away?"

She smiled at him.

"Your movements are awkward and clumsy, even for a white man. The Pawnees are good trackers. They will find you easily."

"What am I to do then? Sit and wait? Do nothing? Wait for them to decide to make a pin cushion of me? No thank you!"

"You must be patient," she told him. "There is a way."

CHAPTER EIGHTEEN

SO THESE WERE Pawnees. If Hugh had ever heard of them before, he didn't recall it. It would have had to have been when he was a child, before he left Pennsylvania. Hugh didn't think so, though. When he was a child, very little was known about any of the tribes that lived west of the Missouri. By the time Lewis and Clark had made their famous journey across the great American wilderness, he had already been at sea for eleven years.

Little Feather was Sioux. That was another tribe he'd never heard of. Apparently, the two tribes were bitter enemies. She had been taken in a raid, some time back, and had been adopted into the Pawnee tribe.

She had also told him that she was married to one of this tribes' principal warriors.

Hugh considered these things as he lay on his sleeping mat, watching the fire. Around him, others were involved in their nightly rituals. A couple of the women were pounding corn in what looked to Hugh to be wooden mortars. Others were already asleep. A few of the men lay on their backs, thumping their chests and singing a sad, mournful song.

They treated him, mostly, as they would a guest. He was allowed to come and go as he wished, unmolested. Sometimes, some of the older men would stop him as he moved through the village, recounting some tale of their deeds, or some bit of advice. Whatever it was that they said to him was lost on Hugh. He listened politely and nodded when it seemed appropriate, but not a word of what they said did he understand.

Actually, that wasn't completely true anymore. There was one word that he was just beginning to understand. Loo-ah, or rather, *Loo-ah!* The indians seemed to use it as a greeting, or when they were offering something to you. At night, when the evening meal was ready, the chief would offer some food to Hugh. Usually, the meal consisted of some kind of meat, boiled with corn and placed in a large bowl. The chief would take the bowl and roll the meat around with his hand until he found a large, choice piece. This he would take out and offer to Hugh, saying, *"Loo-ah!"*

Also, whenever someone would enter a lodge, they would do so with the greeting, *"Loo-ah!"*

A word for all occasions, Hugh thought. *Loo-ah!*

The next two weeks went by slowly for Hugh. He spent his days observing the Pawnees, trying to learn their ways and their language. Little Feather helped him with this. The chief, she told him, was called Old Knife. Under him there were four principal warriors, or sub-chiefs; Big Axe, Storm Dancer, Big Soldier, and the chief's son, Little Knife. Storm Dancer was Little Feather's husband. He was currently away on a raiding party, but would probably be back any day. Little Knife, she said, had fallen from favor two years earlier, when he had stolen the tribe's sacrifice away and set her free. At that time, it had been a young Comanche maiden who was to be offered. Little Knife had taken her at the last minute and had stolen her away on horseback. Everyone in the village expected him to be struck down by the gods. He wasn't, and managed to return the girl to within a short distance of her village before letting her go. When Little Knife returned, he was at once hailed for his daring and bravery, and chastised for breaking tradition. Now, whenever the sacrifice was made, he was watched to make sure he did nothing to spoil it. There had been some who thought that his actions would end the sacrifice forever, but it did not.

Hugh asked her about the game he had seen the indians playing, the one with the spear and the small ring. He'd noticed that not only the boys played the game, but the men as well.

"That is called Lance and Hoop," she told him. "Boys learn it at an early age. It helps them develop skill with the lance. The game is also used for gambling. The lance is set with feathers every few inches to prevent the hoop from slipping back in any way. The feathers are also used for measuring how far through the hoop the lance has passed."

"What do they gamble for?"

"That depends—if they are young boys, they might gamble for arrows. Older boys gamble for their bows. Men usually gamble for horses."

Hugh thought about that for a moment. He began to get an idea, but he filed it away. To think of beating an indian at a game he had played since childhood was folly.

Hugh was relieved to find that Big Axe was *not* the warrior that had struck him in the stomach at their first meeting, and whom Clint had knocked his feet. That, she told him, was Kicking Deer. Kicking Deer was one of the lesser warriors, and not someone Hugh should worry about.

Hugh looked out through the trees, toward the village. A group of women were walking out. Among them was the tall, homely squaw Hugh had noticed a couple of days earlier, the one who had reminded him so much of a man. Curious, he asked Little Feather who she was.

"That is Little Wolf," she told him. "He *is* a man. Little Wolf was once a great warrior. He counted many coup upon his enemies. One night, after returning from a successful hunt, Little Wolf went into his lodge. When he came out again, he had changed. The Great Spirit had visited him in a dream, and had told him that his days as a warrior were through.

Until that time, no one had been ahead of Little Wolf in battle. No man or woman doubted his bravery. Everyone knew Little Wolf to be a great war captain among the Pawnees. The Great Spirit told him that his warring days were over, and that he must put down the war club forever and, to gain knowledge, live the remainder of his days as a woman. He must give up all the ways of manhood and all the privileges of rank, and thereafter, do woman's work. Little Wolf was shaken, but he knew the Great Spirit did not lie. He gave away all of his horses and broke his weapons of war and, since that time, has lived as a squaw. His voice is no longer heard in council. Among the men, his name is spoken only with contempt."

Later, as he moved through the village, Hugh saw Little Wolf working with some of the women. He thought about what Little Feather had told him.

What an interesting people these were. They practiced human sacrifice with the complete belief that to not do so would mean an end to their tribe. They were fierce warriors and hunters, yet among themselves they were kind and obviously very religious. How hard it must have been for this man, one of their great warriors, to give up his rank and position and enter a life of toil—for it was the women, Hugh noticed, who did the work—all on the strength of a dream. That took a lot of faith. Hugh didn't know if he could have done it himself.

Then again, he thought, *your dreams have moved you to action, too!*

CHAPTER NINETEEN

THE MORE Hugh learned about these people, the more he found himself appreciating them—despite himself. They had a certain order to their lives; customs and beliefs that they had followed for generations. To their enemies, the Pawnees were savage and fearsome. Among themselves, it was a different story altogether.

He was walking by a group of men and boys who were playing the lance and hoop game. Hugh couldn't help but marvel at the participants. Some of the men were so skillful at it that they could throw the lance more than halfway through the four-inch hoop before the lance would knock the hoop over.

He watched for several minutes. When he was about to go on his way, the young indian who was to throw the lance suddenly brought it over to Hugh and offered it to him. Hesitating for only a moment, Hugh accepted it.

Hefting the lance to feel the balance, he looked around. The indians had made this look easy, but Hugh knew they had been playing at it and practicing their whole lives.

"Well Glass," he muttered to himself, "here's a chance to make a real fool of yourself."

He nodded to the young indian who was waiting to roll the small hoop, and said, *"Loo-ah!"*

The indians seemed amused at his usage of the word. The young brave nodded back and rolled the hoop. Hugh tried to judge the speed of the rolling hoop and then threw the lance. The lance struck the ground about a foot behind the hoop.

The indians laughed. Hugh shrugged good-naturedly. He started to turn away. The young indian who had offered the lance stopped him, offering it a second time.

Hugh hesitated. He looked around at the group of men and boys standing there. His eyes locked with those of one of the men standing opposite him. The man was shorter than some of the other indians, and darker skinned. Though slighter of build than Clint had been, his muscular frame was no less impressive to behold. Chiseled muscles, like burnished iron, stood out in stark relief beneath his skin. From this, and from his ferocious, indomitable presence, Hugh knew this must be Big Axe, one of the four principal warriors that Little Feather had told him about.

The indian gave him an almost imperceptible nod. Hugh nodded back and accepted the lance a second time.

There was a murmur of approval from among the crowd of men. Hugh noticed that many of the indians, including Big Axe, seemed to be making bets. He waited until they were done. When it was quiet once more, Hugh hefted the lance. Again, his eyes locked momentarily with those of Big Axe. The indian gave him a look of encouragement.

For some reason this game seemed a lot more important than it had a few moments earlier. Hugh nodded to the hoop-roller.

Waiting until the small hoop was almost directly across from him, Hugh threw the lance. The lance passed through the hoop, entering it by nearly a foot before the hoop fell.

The crowd of indians cheered. Hugh smiled and gave a slight bow, then moved away before they could ask him to do it again. He felt like a hero.

From what Little Feather had told him, that probably meant he'd make a better sacrifice.

Little Feather had seen nearly thirty summers. She had lived with her own people, the Sioux, until she was fifteen. At that time her father had given her in marriage to a French trapper named Louis DeLozier. At first she had been frightened by the white man. By indian standards, he was smelly and unclean. He did not pluck the hair from his face, from under his arms, or from between his legs, as her people did. He rarely bathed and did not rub himself down with grease, so at first she found it hard to be near him. Little by little, though, that would change.

They lived in a cabin, some distance away from her people. Slowly, as she began to learn his language, the strangeness of him went away. He treated her well, better than she had ever expected to be treated by the men of her tribe.

One summer night, after they had been together for some time, she decided that she could accept his smelliness no longer. Peeling off his clothes, she gave him and "indian" bath, using grease to clean him from head to foot. After that she no longer found his hairiness intolerable.

Louis was an insatiable lover, and he went to great lengths to ensure that their lovemaking was pleasurable for her. Little Feather gave him two sons, which Louis himself delivered. During the birth of their second child, there were complications. Little Feather nearly died. For weeks after, Louis nursed her back to health.

Some of the things Louis did for her would have been seen as weakness in an indian man. Little Feather knew he wasn't weak, but that he loved her. She loved him as well.

One afternoon, Louis was chopping wood. Little Feather and the boys busied themselves with stacking it for the coming winter. There was a sudden rifle shot. Louis collapsed on the ground.

Immediately, four Osage warriors on horseback swept down out of the woods. Little Feather tried to gather the boys to her and usher them to the house, but the men on horseback were quicker. Her oldest boy, called Edmund by his father, was shot down, while the younger boy was impaled on an Osage lance.

Louis, meanwhile, had managed to drag himself to his rifle. He aimed and fired, knocking one of the Osages off his horse but not killing him. The other three warriors immediately fell upon Louis and killed him.

Seizing her chance, Little Feather ran to where the injured Osage had fallen. His lance lay a few feet from him. Snatching it up, Little Feather finished killing him with it.

Little Feather turned. The other three Osages were off their horses and were moving toward her. Holding the lance before, she began to back away, toward the cabin.

The three warriors fanned out, moving slowly around her, approaching her from three sides at once.

Then, from out of the woods, a single Pawnee warrior was there. He came in like the wind, striking down one of the three Osages with his tomahawk before the man could react. The other two warriors turned to face the Pawnee. As they did, Little Feather ran forward with the lance and ran it completely through one of them. Unnerved, the remaining Osage turned to run. The Pawnee took two big steps and struck him down.

Little Feather and the Pawnee faced each other.

He was, without a doubt, the largest man she had ever seen. Little Feather regarded him for a moment. Then, turning, she knelt next to the Osage warrior nearest her. Pulling the knife from the dead man's belt, she quickly scalped him. Then she stood and extended the scalp to the Pawnee.

Before they left he had scalped everyone, including Louis and the two boys. After that the two of them loaded everything that was to be taken onto the horses, then rode out in the direction of the Pawnee village.

The name of the Pawnee warrior was Storm Dancer. Storm Dancer hated the Osages. He also hated the Sioux. He told Little Feather that he intended to fill her up with many Pawnee babies, but no babies ever came.

According to Pawnee custom, when Storm Dancer's nephew entered adolescence, it was Little Feather's duty to provide sex for him, up until the time of his marriage. This she submitted to, and even tried to instruct him in some of the ways of lovemaking that Louis had taught to her. The relationship ended some months earlier, when the boy was killed while participating in his third buffalo hunt.

Storm Dancer had been gone a long time. He had missed the sacrifice to Morning Star. Members of his family and other members of the tribe were worried that he might have been killed, and would never return.

But it was not Storm Dancer that Little Feather thought about when she lay on her sleeping mat at night, nor was it his nephew.

It was the white man that had come into the village. It was Hugh Glass.

The heat of Summer was already upon them. For three days it had been stifling hot, foretelling the season to come. The earthen domes offered protection from it during the day, but at night it became barely tolerable. Following the example of the Pawnees, Hugh dragged his sleeping mat outside and up onto the roof of the lodge, where an occasional breeze could cool him.

Finding a spot on the dome that suited him, he lay looking up at the sky. Above him, the stars were brilliant. Hugh had seen, painted on animal skins in some of the lodges, maps of this sky.

The Pawnees called themselves Chahiks-i-chahiks—men of men. They considered themselves civilized. They were astronomers and farmers, as well as hunters. They were skilled craftsmen and artists, and yet they were barbaric. Little Feather told him that the various indian tribes were always at war with someone, and the Pawnees seemed to be at war more than anybody. The only way for any tribe to keep from being completely eliminated was to be terrible and fearsome to their enemies. The Pawnees were fearsome. Little Feather told Hugh that among her own people, the Sioux, she had heard it said that it would one day be the downfall of the Pawnees that they had few friends, and many enemies.

Hugh lay on the roof of the lodge, drifting dreamily toward sleep. He could hear the voices of millions of insects in the plains around the village. Nearby, he could hear the murmuring of voices and, as always, the low, rhythmic singing of some of the men. Apparently, during the heat of summer, none of the indians slept inside. Every one of the sixty-three lodges was littered with people. Nearly two thousand people, maybe more, all lying outside and looking up at the stars. Strangely, it gave Hugh a sense of peace and safety that he had never quite experienced before.

But he never doubted for a moment that they still intended to kill him.

The time for the next sacrifice was drawing nearer every day, and Hugh was becoming anxious. He wanted to leave. After all, as he had told Little Feather, he wasn't watched. What was there to stop him from just walking away from the village and making his way down the river to safety?

"There are men here," Little Feather told him, "who could track you anywhere you would go. Besides that, your movements through the prairie and in the woods are clumsy and awkward. They would tell of your coming long before you arrived at any place. Other tribes would know of you. None would be your friend."

And so he waited, becoming more anxious as the days passed. At the same time, a strange thing was happening inside him; he was beginning to admire these people—the very ones who would, one day soon, kill him. Some of them he genuinely liked. They were different from him; had beliefs and customs that were different from his, but in their world, those customs made sense. If he had a choice between living with them and living among the so-called "civilized" pirates, Hugh would choose the Pawnees.

He was also certain that some of them had begun to like him. He didn't know if it would or could change what they intended to do with him, but he had made friends among these people.

None of this meant that he had forgotten Clint, or the fact that these were the people who had brought him to such an unsavory end, but Clint was gone. He had not been killed out of spite, pettiness, or out of meanness, as some of Lafitte's men might have done. Little Feather had told Hugh that the Pawnees were a deeply religious people. They believed in dreams and omens. Until Little Knife had stopped the sacrifice of the Comanche girl, it was believed that the Morning Star sacrifice *must* take place, or the tribe would perish. Even now many of them believed that Ti-ra-wa had been merciful. Ti-ra-wa, she explained, was the Pawnees' principal god. Ti-ra-wa was in and of everything, and had absolute power over everything in the universe.

Kind-of like the God of the Christians, Hugh thought. Well, perhaps Ti-ra-wa would intervene for him.

Hugh wasn't going to count on that.

CHAPTER TWENTY

THE TIME to try to escape had passed. The indians were watching him. Three days earlier they had begun, once again, to treat him like royalty. They fawned over him, gave him the finest morsels of food, and gave him new buckskin leggings, new moccasins, and a new buckskin shirt. The shirt was beautifully decorated with ornate beadwork that looked like stars. The brightest of these stars probably represented Venus, the Morning Star.

Now they were keeping him awake again, not allowing him to sleep, celebrating throughout the night. It didn't take a great deal of intelligence to figure out how this night was expected to end.

Little Feather had a plan that she thought might save him. It sounded plausible when she had told it to him. Now Hugh wasn't so sure. Earlier that day she had given him a large red rock, which Hugh recognized as vermilion. The rock was hidden in a leather pouch she had sewn, which Hugh wore under his breechcloth. He could feel it there now. It gave him only a small measure of relief.

The evening wore on. For awhile Hugh felt himself becoming morose and tired. Then, suddenly, his attitude lifted. If this was to be the last night of his life, then he was going to enjoy it to the hilt. He'd had a month to run away and escape, and he had not done it. It was too late to think about it now.

Beside, these people bore him no ill will. Not really. They had treated him pretty graciously, all in all.

He looked around at some of the faces of the men around him. Big Axe, Little Knife, Big Soldier, Old Knife—Chahiks-i-chahiks—Men of men. These were people who valued strength and courage above all else. They had their own set of values and they adhered to them. Little Feather had told him that they never lied, because the dishonor caused by the discovery of a lie would be worse to them than death.

So if it came to pass that he should die at the hands of these people when morning came, so be it. He would show them how a white man could face death.

Better to die in one of their religious ceremonies, no matter how painful it might be, than it would have been to die at the hands of the pirates of Campeche.

Hugh looked over at Big Axe. The warrior seemed to be dressed in his best and finest clothes. He wore a buckskin shirt and leggings, both fringed and decorated with fine beadwork. His face and head were painted completely red, and the thin patch of hair that ran down the center of his head was roached with feathers, making him look like some sort of fierce bird. Hugh counted a dozen scalps tied into the fringes of his shirt and leggings. Each was a trophy taken from an enemy in heated battle. Little Feather had told Hugh that, among the Pawnees, the exploits of Big Axe were legendary. *This,* Hugh thought, *was a man.*

Hugh stood suddenly. When he did all talk around the fire ceased and all eyes fell on him.

"Ta-rare-kak-scha!" Hugh said, loudly addressing Big Axe by his Pawnee name. The indians all looked from Hugh to Big Axe in shock, then back at Hugh. "Ta-rare-kak-scha! You are a great warrior! Ta-rare-kak-scha, if it passes that I must die tomorrow, then let your arrow be the first to pierce my heart! Let Ti-ra-wa make it so, Ta-rare-kak-scha!"

Hugh sat down again and resumed staring at the fire. From the corners of his eyes he could see the indians looking at each other in amazement. He hadn't spoken long, but in one breath he had used the name of their god and the name of one of their greatest warriors. He had also spoken Big Axe's name four times, as Little Feather told him to do.

It had begun.

The night passed slowly. The indians continued to celebrate, but it seemed more subdued than before, almost guarded. Hugh, by contrast, smiled at them all.

Finally, a general murmur seemed to pass throughout the village, followed by silence. It was time for the sacrifice.

Everyone stood up, including Hugh. It was important, from this point on, that the indians not lay hands on him. Without waiting for instruction, he walked proudly out of the lodge and headed toward the east side of the village, where he knew the framework of poles would be set up. Around him, on all sides and on the roofs of the surrounding earth-lodges, the indians made way to let him pass.

Hugh felt feverish, as he often had before going into battle. Instead of feeling dread, though, as had often been the case with the pirates, he felt strangely excited, eager to get on with it. He wasn't exactly afraid, but he had to fight to keep his body from trembling.

Old Knife was waiting, there in the clearing and looking magnificent, just as Hugh knew he would be. Hugh stopped just before he reached it. Looking at the anxious faces around him, he began to make a speech. It didn't matter that the indians didn't understand a word of what he said. Little Feather had told him that the words and his tone of voice had to be convincing.

"My Friends!" he began loudly. "For one month I have lived among you! I have eaten your food; sat at your fires; I have watched you laugh. I know the Pawnees to be a great and proud people! I know that your warriors are mighty! I have seen their skill with the lance, and with the bow and arrow. I have seen the scalps which hang from your lodge-poles!

Like you, I have fought many battles! For years, I had many enemies who tried to slay me, yet they are dead, while I have lived on! I came a long way to be here! If it is so that I must die now, I am proud that it is at the hands of my friends, the *Pawnees!*"

His speech over, Hugh took off the buckskin shirt. He folded it carefully, then handed it to the warrior nearest him. Then he took off the leggings, folded them, and handed them to another man. Turning, he quickly walked to the spot where the poles had been assembled for the sacrifice.

Hugh knew that he was supposed to be completely naked for the ceremony. When he reached the pole-structure he stopped and removed the breechcloth—carefully, so that he would not lose the rock that was hidden there. Leaning over, he folded the cloth. As he did he palmed the rock.

Turning, Hugh walked over to where the old chief stood. He could see, beyond Old Knife, all the warriors of the village, waiting, their bows ready. Long Hair, the man who had captured Hugh and Clint, and who had fired the first arrow into Clint when he was sacrificed, stood nearby. Behind him stood a man holding a torch, another who carried the carcass of an owl, and one other who carried some raw meat. Little Feather had told Hugh that the meat that they sacrificed was the heart and tongue of a buffalo. All the men, as far as Hugh could see, were wearing feathered collars, the ones they all wore when Clint was slain, and which Hugh had not seen either before or since.

Old Knife was regarding Hugh with something that looked like amusement. Looking him in the eye, Hugh brought his hand up. He held the hand palm down at first, then turned it over and presented the chief with the rock.

"A gift," Hugh said, "from Ti-ra-wa!"

The rock was a large, bright red piece of vermilion. Even in the dim torchlight there was no mistaking what it was. Old Knife regarded him for a moment. Then he accepted the gift. He looked at the rock for several seconds, thoughtfully. Turning, he held it up for everyone to see.

Old Knife began to speak to his people. Hugh had no idea what was being said, but by the astonished stares and murmurs of the indians, he knew it must be important.

Finally, turning, the old man took the wolf robe off his shoulders and place it around Hugh. Then, holding Hugh in front of him, his hands on Hugh's shoulders, Old Knife spoke to him. Again, Hugh had no idea what the chief said, but the words were strangely moving.

When the chief finished speaking, he leaned forward and gave Hugh a hug. Then he ushered Hugh through the crowd and away from the clearing.

The ceremony was over.

The feasting went on throughout the following day. Before it was over, Hugh had begun to wish they really *had* killed him. Immediately after leaving the clearing, Hugh was taken back to Old Knife's lodge, where they fed on buffalo meat and corn until Hugh was quite full. Hugh was tired from being up all night, but not really sleepy after his close brush with death. More than anything, he wanted to talk to Little Feather, to find out what it was the Old Knife had said.

After eating, they smoked from the sacred pipe. Old Knife then brought out three horses, which he presented to Hugh, making it obvious that they were gifts. More curious than ever, Hugh accepted the gifts.

No sooner had they finished, when a young boy came into the lodge. The chief indicated that Hugh should follow him.

The boy led Hugh over to the lodge of Big Axe. Big Axe had a feast of buffalo meat and corn waiting for him. Little Feather had explained to Hugh that one way to insult an indian was to refuse his hospitality, or to not fully indulge in it. Hugh wasn't hungry at all, but he ate again to be polite.

Big Axe welcomed him with open arms, but seemed, behind it all, to be a little guarded. That was understandable. Hugh had said some things earlier which Big Axe didn't understand. In asking that Big Axe's arrow be the first to strike him, he had used the indian's name four times—a number, Hugh had been told, that was significant to the indians. He had also used the name of their chief god, Ti-ra-wa, in that same speech. On top of all that, Hugh had done something special enough to save himself from being sacrificed. It was no wonder that Big Axe was a little reticent.

Still, Big Axe welcomed him as a friend and they feasted together. The warrior was a gracious host. He kept the conversation going, even though Hugh didn't understand a word of what was said. Hugh, playing the part of the good guest, managed to stuff himself, even though he had just done so already.

As before, when they finished, they smoked the pipe together. As they were finishing with that, another indian boy appeared. Big Axe indicated that Hugh should follow him.

The boy took Hugh to the lodge of Big Soldier. Like Big Axe, Big Soldier was one of the principal warriors of the tribe, or sub-chiefs. Younger than Big Axe, Big Soldier was taller than Hugh and thinner, even though he seemed to be all brawn and sinew. Hugh had seen men like this before, aboard ship. They could work all day, seemingly tireless, the extremes of weather having little effect on them.

Big Soldier had prepared a feast for Hugh of buffalo meat and corn, after which they smoked the pipe. Before they were done, another indian boy appeared to take him to the next lodge.

Before the day was over, Hugh would visit ten lodges altogether, and attend feasts in each of them. To refuse to partake in any of them would have been an insult to his host. Vomiting would have been an even greater one.

Hugh managed to not insult anyone in the village that day.

Barely.

It was two days before Hugh was able to meet with Little Feather again and find out what Old Knife had said. What he learned astounded him.

Little Feather had known that producing the vermilion and making a gift of it was something that would be considered a powerful sign, but even she didn't realize how far it would go. When she explained to Hugh, he was stunned.

"Many years ago," she told him, "long before many of the people in the village were even born, and certainly before Little Knife, Old Knife had another son. Before the first son had seen two summers, though, he was taken from Old Knife by a fever that swept through the village, killing many. Old Knife's wife, the boy's mother, died as well. Old Knife's grief over this was great. For a long time afterward he mourned and was poor in mind.

Time passed, and Old Knife recovered, but he never forgot his wife or his son, and he prayed to Ti-ra-wa to watch over them.

Last Winter, Old Knife began to have dreams about the son. At first this bothered him, and Old Knife worried that the boy might be coming back to haunt him, or that it meant that he, Old Knife, might die soon.

Over the past weeks, Old Knife has dreamt of his son again and again. Then, several nights ago, the son appeared to him again. In this dream, the son had grown into a proud, fine warrior. In the dream, as Old Knife watched, the son began to change. He became a white man. He became you. In the dream, the son said that Ti-ra-wa was returning him to Old Knife to give him wisdom about the white man, for the white man would one day come to the land in great numbers and the Pawnees would need this wisdom to know how to deal with them. Old Knife thought long about this dream. He prayed to Ti-ra-wa to give him a sign that this was a true vision and not just the dreams of an old man. When you gave him the sacred rock, he knew it was the sign he had waited for. You are his son. Old Knife has adopted you."

Hugh felt a strange mixture of emotions at what Little Feather told him. Most of it was shock, but there was some gratitude mixed in, along with disbelief. There was something else, too, that Hugh didn't quite understand. He felt oddly emotional at it.

He wanted to thank Little Feather for her help—for saving him. No words came to him, so he merely nodded.

CHAPTER TWENTY-ONE

IT WAS NOW well into summer. The corn the Pawnees had planted was getting tall. Every day the women of the village would go to tend it, sometimes walking miles to get to a spot that was planted in a favored patch of dirt. Sometimes, one or two of the women would not return and would never be seen alive again. The Pawnees had many enemies.

By his best estimation, Hugh had been among the Pawnees for nearly three months. Slowly, but steadily, he was learning to speak their language. He was learning their customs as well.

Storm Dancer, Little Feather's husband, had never returned from his warpath and was presumed dead. Hugh assumed she would be in mourning, but she explained to him that she was, in fact, a war trophy, and that their marriage was not based on love. In any event, he found her more and more beautiful every day, even though he was not at all sure if it was appropriate to think about her. He still had much to learn, he knew, about the ways of the Pawnees.

Sometimes Hugh thought about Sarah, his ex-wife, and about his two boys, Wes and Phillip. The boys would be into their teens now, probably tall and strong. He wondered if he would ever have the occasion to see them again. It wasn't likely, but the way his life had gone for the last couple of years, who could tell. Who could have known that he would have gone from sailor, to pirate, to being the adopted son of a Pawnee chief, all within two years. Certainly not Hugh Glass.

He wasn't sure if it was even wise to think about going back anymore. The authorities would have assumed that the *Gallant* had been lost to a storm or some other mishap, two years earlier. While Clint was alive, their plan had been to go back and set the record straight. Alone, without Clint to back his story, those same authorities might take issue with what he told them. Hugh, himself, might end up with his head in a noose.

So no, if he went back, he could never go back to sailing. What else would he do? The sea was all he knew. For the time being, he would stay with the Pawnees. He would learn their ways and, as Old Knife had said, would help to make them wise in the ways of the white man.

Hugh and Big Soldier were away from the village, near the clump of trees that grew by the river. Big Soldier had given Hugh a tomahawk as a present and was teaching him how to throw it. Hugh was amazed at the indian's skill and power. From twenty feet, Big Soldier could bury the tomahawk in a ten-inch circle drawn on the trunk of a tree. Hugh, by comparison, missed the tree trunk altogether, most of the time. When he *did* hit the tree, it was usually with the wrong end of the tomahawk.

"Practice much," Big Soldier told him. "These skills you must have to be Pawnee warrior. Also," he added with a hint of amusement, "to feed Little Feather, when time come."

Hugh looked at him.

"Everyone know," Big Soldier said. "You must wait for the proper time. Storm Dancer not come back, you go to Old Knife, make presents, ask Little Feather to marry. First, practice."

Big Axe had ridden up on a beautiful black mare as they spoke. He looked at the circle drawn on the tree. Without a word, he stepped down, took his tomahawk out and threw it, planting the blade squarely in the middle of the circle.

Hugh sighed.

"Practice much," he said.

The two indians laughed.

"You practice, you get good," Big Axe told him.

Big Soldier, meanwhile, had turned away and was looking back toward the village.

"Someone comes," he said.

Big Axe looked toward the village and nodded. Hugh looked but saw nothing that wasn't there before. He was beginning to wonder if the Pawnees had supernatural powers, when he saw a hint of movement out beyond the village. As he watched, the movement became six men on horseback.

In one, graceful move, Big Axe was back upon his horse.

"You like this horse?" he asked Hugh.

"Yes," Hugh answered. "She's very beautiful."

"I won her," Big Axe said, "when you threw the lance through the hoop."

He rode off. Big Soldier looked at Hugh.

"Maybe you not marry Little Feather after all," he said. "Maybe Storm Dancer come back."

They headed back toward the village.

It wasn't Storm Dancer, but a party of indians from another village. By their dress, Hugh thought they were Pawnees. Big Soldier corrected him.

"These men are Arikaras," he told Hugh. "Very close to Pawnee, like cousins. Come to trade."

One of the men, very tall and muscular, took an instant disliking to Hugh and glared at him whenever Hugh was nearby. Hugh tried to ignore him, not wishing to be impolite, but finally ended up returning the indian's malignant stare.

"Be careful that one," Big Axe told him. "He hates all white people. His name is, Kills-the-Whites."

Hugh thanked Big Axe for the information, taking note as he did, of the number of scalps hanging from the Arikara's belt, as well as from his saddle. Many of those scalps, Hugh observed, were too light in color to have belonged to indians.

From that point on, until the Arikaras left the village, Hugh was careful not to let his guard down.

Shortly after the Arikaras left the village, Hugh began to sense a change in the Pawnees. There was an air of excitement in the village, a sense of holiday. He wondered if they were getting ready for another sacrifice.

"No," Big Axe told him. "Sacrifice only in time of planting. Planting done now. Now it is time for the summer hunt. Soon we leave—whole village go, you go too. Kill many buffalo."

So that was it. Hugh tried to imagine the whole village packing up and leaving. There were almost two thousand people in the village. This would, indeed, be something to see.

The following day, Hugh was out among the trees again, alternately practicing his tomahawk throw and his skill with the bow and arrow. He was getting pretty good with the bow, but the tomahawk was something he just couldn't seem to get the hang of. Hugh kept at it, though. If he was going to be an indian, he would be a good one.

Walking back from the tree he was using for a target, he saw a figure ride out in his direction. As the figure drew close Hugh saw that it was Big Axe. He was riding the black mare. Hugh stopped practicing as he rode up.

"Lau, idad, tut-tu-ta-rik ti-rah-rek!" Big Axe hollered without getting off his horse. *"Come brother, they are going to dance!"* Then he turned, spurred his horse, and rode back to the village. Gathering up his things, Hugh followed him.

When he reached the village it seemed almost deserted. Hugh headed for the big medicine lodge. Before he reached it Hugh saw people crowding around the entrance and could hear the murmur of their voices.

Hugh made his way into the lodge. The people politely let him pass, so that he was able to get all the way to the front and see what was going on.

In the center of the lodge, on the floor, twelve buffalo skulls lay in a half-circle. Near these stood Old Knife, Big Axe, Big Soldier, Little Knife, and several others, all holding bows and arrows. Pipe Chief, Proud Eagle, and Yellow Fox were with them. These three men were the leading priests of the tribe. For days they had fasted and prayed, preparing for this sacred ceremony. Big Axe had told Hugh that, in this one hunt, enough meat must be secured to last the tribe for half the year, until the winter hunt. It was too important to them to leave *anything* to idle chance.

As the warriors all held their bows, so did the priests carry their own hallowed implements. Among these were the buffalo staves—slender poles made of spruce, each wrapped in red and blue cloth, and each decorated with elaborate beadwork. These were sacred tools and were used to help guide and lead the hunt. As the Pawnees felt that the very success of the hunt depended on them, they were guarded religiously at all times. Hugh had heard Big Axe speak of the staves, but this was the first that he had seen them.

When Hugh first arrived at the edge of the circle of men, women, and children who were looking on, most of the people were standing quietly with their heads bowed, as in prayer. Slowly, one of the priests began to murmur. One by one, the other priests joined him, followed by the warriors, their voices gradually becoming louder and more distinct.

"Father, you, who are the Great Ruler of all, take pity on us. We are your children and we are poor. Send us many buffalo, many fat cows. We are your children, Father, send us the meat on which to live and grow strong. Listen to our prayers, Father, for we are your children. Help us…"

As each man spoke, he passed his hands over and over the tools and weapons that he held. Each of them, from the youngest to the oldest, prayed ardently, with fire and intensity that Hugh had never seen in the prayers of white people. These men fairly shook with emotion. It was the most impressive display of religious faith that Hugh had ever seen.

With no cessation in their prayers, the men began to walk forward, each in turn. Each placed the implements he held on the floor of the lodge, all within the half-circle of buffalo skulls. When the last man had placed his tools within the half-circle of skulls, the prayers increased in volume and then faded away. Then a drum sounded, and sixteen young men leapt into the circle and began to dance.

The dancing continued without let up for three days. On the morning of the fourth day, when it stopped, every man, woman, and child left the village, and set out on the summer hunt.

CHAPTER TWENTY-TWO

THE LEADER of the raiding party that had captured Hugh and Clint was called Long Hair, because he didn't shave his head, as was the custom with the Pawnees. He wasn't the only one to let it grow, but he was the first in recent times, so he was the one who was named for it.

At the time that they captured Hugh, all among the raiding party were of the same countenance—all wore stern, sober faces. In Hugh's entire life, any time he had seen any indians, the expressions those indians wore was the same—serious and solemn. Like most whites, he assumed this to be the natural look of a race of people who lived hard, violent lives. Very grim.

Living among the Pawnees, Hugh learned the truth.

When they were around strangers, their expressions and manner became solemn, but when they were with their own, it was different. They laughed, they played, they joked, they were generous and unguarded and *guileless* in a way that Hugh never imagined adults could be. As time passed, he found it harder and harder to believe these were the same people who had visited such a cruel death upon his friend.

As the tribe set out upon the hunt, the amount of noise they created was tremendous. In addition to the indians themselves, which numbered nearly two thousand, there were several hundred head of horses being driven along, and at least as many dogs as people, all whinnying and barking and adding to the general din.

They had an interesting mode of travel. They attached poles (which were later to be used as lodge poles) on either side of a horse, so that one end was strapped to the horses' back and stuck out over it's head. The other end of the pole dragged on the ground. Between the two poles that trailed behind the horse, a buffalo skin was tied, creating a platform. Little Feather said this platform was called a *travois*. Upon this, they piled all their worldly goods. Children, or those who were too sick to walk, rode on top. The children, if they were young girls, usually had an armload of puppies to keep them company.

In this fashion, they headed southward, moving slowly. Hugh, still unaccustomed to sitting on the back of a horse, rode a spotted gray, which was one of the ponies that Old Knife had given him. Initially, his awkward attempts at riding brought the Pawnees great amusement. When he explained to them that he had lived his life on waters that were more vast than the prairie itself, their laughter turned to awe. Some of the older indians had heard of these great waters, but none among them had ever seen them. Hugh, meanwhile, resigned himself to the fact that he would never ride nearly as well as the Pawnees, who had lived on the backs of horses since the time they could walk. In time, though, Hugh would learn to handle his steeds well enough.

Hugh was riding next to a warrior named Lucky Hawk. He found this man to be extremely likable. He was amiable, as Clint had been. Lucky Hawk always had a smile for anyone he called friend, which seemed to be everyone. Lucky Hawk explained to Hugh that the hunt was governed by the Pawnee Soldiers, under the leadership of Big Soldier, who was the soldier chief. The soldiers commanded unquestionable authority in all matters regarding the hunt. No one was allowed to go off on their own, for if they startled the herd and drove it away before enough meat could be harvested, the entire village might be in jeopardy. Scouts were sent out far in advance, while the rest of the tribe followed behind. When a herd was discovered, word would be sent back. The tribe would try to camp as close as they could to the herd without startling them. The next morning, the killing would take place. They would surround the herd and drive it, first one way, then another, back and forth, until the buffalo were too tired to get away. Then the killing would begin.

As the day wore on, the Pawnees were joined by two other groups of indians, the Otoes and the Omahas. These were tribes, Lucky Hawk said, that the Pawnees had at one time conquered and were now friends with. Hugh estimated that by the end of the day, there were over thirty-five hundred indians spread out over the prairie. It would take an awful lot of buffalo, he thought, to provide meat for them all for six months. He wondered how they could do this without completely wiping out the herd.

"Ti-ra-wa send many buffalo," Lucky Hawk told him. "Plenty, plenty."

Late in the afternoon they made camp. Some of the women took the poles off the ponies and erected lodges, covering them with buffalo skins. Others went about collecting dried buffalo droppings—some well over a foot in diameter—and making fires with them. Hugh was surprised at how well they burned.

Hugh estimated that they traveled about eight or ten miles that day. Considering what a production it was to move the whole village, he thought it was good time.

The next day was much the same as the first. The same was true of the day after that and the day after that. By now, most of the excitement had worn away, leaving only the heat, the dust, and the noise. Often he would start out at the head of the column, slowly falling back to wherever Little Feather was, and would stay for a time near her. The sight of her never failed to lift his spirits, and she seemed to brighten whenever he was near. Little Feather traveled with Storm Dancer's sister, however, and after a while, Hugh would get the idea that it was time to move along.

One thing he noticed about some of the men who planned to participate in the hunt, was that they often walked their horses. Lucky Hawk explained to him that these were men who were generally too poor to own more than one horse. Rather than tire it out, these men walked, thereby saving the horse's strength for when they would need it most. Considering this, Hugh felt extremely fortunate. Old Knife had given him three horses as gifts.

He was learning more and more about the Pawnees every day. He noticed that those among the men who had rifles, almost to a man, put them away, in favor of bows and arrows. And for their arrows, they preferred the older, stone arrowheads over the steel ones they got from the whites. He asked Big Axe why this was.

"For buffalo," Big Axe answered, "bow and arrow almost as good as rifle. Make no noise. Stone arrowheads better than steel. With stone, even small wounds cause swelling and death. Stone better."

At least once a day, the procession would pass by a small wooded area or thicket. Whenever they did, all the young boys would get together, surround it, and drive out whatever was inside. Sometimes it was birds, like pheasant or wild turkeys. Sometimes it was rabbits or deer. Whatever it was, the boys would usually manage to bring it down, providing fresh meat for themselves and their families. Twice, small groups of buffalo were sighted. At those times it was the men who rode out, chasing them down and killing them, just as the boys had done with the smaller game.

This was the first time Hugh ad actually seen buffalo. He was fascinated by their size and magnificence. Some of the larger bulls had to be two or three times as big as the horse he rode. Like the indians, he rode out after them. He wasn't a match for any of the Pawnees, either in horsemanship or with a bow and arrow. Only one of his arrows struck a buffalo cow—for it was the cows and calves that they valued most—and his was not the arrow that killed it.

The sun grew hotter with each passing day. Hugh had almost lost track of time, but by his nearest estimation, he figured this to be early August.

He was getting pretty tired of sitting on the back of a horse. It had been over two weeks since they had left the village. As yet they had seen no sign of the great herd. The indians continued on, day after day, ever southward. They traveled slowly. At best, they had gone about one-hundred and fifty miles. The prairie continued to stretch on about them in ever direction, endlessly.

Hugh had never seen anything quite like this. In some places the grass rose all about them, growing to a height of ten or twelve feet. Moving through it gave Hugh an eerie, defenseless feeling. Men on horseback might be sitting ten feet from where the column of indians passed. The grass here was so thick and so high that the Pawnees might never have seen them.

Gradually, the tall grass gave way and grew shorter and shorter, until it was only about three feet tall, and they could see across the prairie for a distance of several miles. Hugh was relieved.

It was late in the day, nearly three weeks after the Pawnees had left their village, that the herd was sighted. The Pawnee scouts, far out in front of the column, had sent word back that the buffalo were about a day's ride away. In the morning, the men would ride out, leaving the others to catch up later. The men would camp near the herd the following night. The next morning they would make a "surround".

"Soon," Lucky Hawk told Hugh, "soon, you see many buffalo."

The following morning the men set out. Moving rapidly, unhampered by the bulk of their belongings and the slow-moving column, they moved within striking distance of the buffalo. At a sight selected by Big Soldier, they set up camp. Here they would wait until the following morning, when the killing would begin. This would give the rest of the tribe a chance to catch up. They would reach this spot tomorrow, in time to help with some of the butchering.

Hugh couldn't help getting caught up in the excitement. Here were nearly a thousand Pawnee warriors, along with four or five hundred Otoes and Omahas, all ready for their semi-annual hunt—an event upon which their survival, and the survival of their families, would depend. If Ti-ra-wa was good to them, they would get all they needed.

Big Soldier had chosen a spot far enough away from the buffalo to prevent the possibility of spooking them, and downwind so that the herd would not pick up their scent. The men, including Hugh, spent the evening smoking, dancing and singing, and getting their weapons ready. All in all, they got very little sleep.

The following morning they were up early and ready for the hunt. Big Soldier split the party of men into four groups. The herd was too big for a general surround, so a section of it would be cut out and attacked, leaving the rest of the herd to go free until the second day, when the Pawnees would repeat the procedure. If the rest of the herd stampeded, they would not go far and the indians would easily find them again.

As they rode out across the plain Hugh was puzzled. He could see for miles in all directions, yet he saw nothing looked remotely like a herd of buffalo. Three-quarters of an hour later this was still true. Then they passed over a low hillock and the buffalo were there, but it took Hugh Glass a few moments to realize it.

It would have been impossible to estimate the number of animals that lay before them. There could have been twenty-thousand—or ten million. At first sight, they did not even seem like animals at all, but like some great, undulating, brown sea, ever moving as though a great fire had swept through the plains, charring but not destroying or stiffening the grass, so that the slightest breeze still stirred and moved it.

The magnificence of the scene before Hugh thrilled him. Now that he could see the buffalo, they were all he *could* see. The herd stretched on and on, seemingly for miles, to the edges of his vision and beyond. In a way that the sea never had, it made him feel small.

The indians had split into their respective groups. Three of those groups, under Big Soldier's direction, had moved off to cut away a section of the herd and surround it on three sides. Hugh's group stayed where they were. It didn't take long before the other three groups had cut several hundred head away from the rest of the herd, and were driving them toward the small knoll where Hugh and the others sat waiting. It was a frightening sight—nearly a thousand head of buffalo, each one weighing two or three times as much as the horse Hugh sat upon, all charging down on them. Hugh felt a giddying impulse to turn his horse and run. None of the indians in his group had moved except to change horses. Hugh stood his ground with them.

"Plenty scary, eh?" Lucky Hawk said. Hugh knew they would be watching him, looking for signs of courage or cowardice. He merely smiled.

Starting far down on his left, the line of indians began to move, charging down in the direction of the stampeding buffalo. When the man next to him yelled and charged down with them, Hugh did likewise, followed a moment later by Lucky Hawk. Long before he reached them, however, the big animals veered off, moving in a counter-clockwise direction. The men on Hugh's right then charged down on them, keeping the buffalo moving, while Hugh's group fell back to their original position, to wait for the buffalo to come around once more. In this way, they kept the buffalo running in circles for nearly an hour, until the great beasts were exhausted and could run no more. Then, on a signal from Big Soldier, the indians all rushed down on them at once, killing them. Very few of the buffalo got away.

When the indians had finished, almost one-thousand dead or wounded buffalo lay before them. As the butchering began, Hugh looked around. The rest of the herd had moved a quarter of a mile away and were grazing, unconcerned about the fate of their brethren. The herd, to Hugh, looked every bit as huge as when he had first seen it, and seemed completely undiminished by the buffalo that had been killed.

Nor were the indians done with them. Before there were finished, the Pawnees would make three more surrounds, and would easily secure and dry enough buffalo meat to last them well into winter, until the winter hunt.

CHAPTER TWENTY-THREE

THE PAWNEES used the buffalo for nearly everything. Nothing was wasted. The skins they used for robes, blankets, and for covering their lodges when they were traveling. The hair of the buffalo was used for rope; the horns for ladles and spoons. The sinew was used for lariats, or for their bows—one piece being used for the bowstring and the other to back the bow, to give it added strength to keep it from breaking. The shoulder blade of a buffalo was used as a hoe. Most of the meat they dried. It would sustain them in the months to come. Hugh was amazed by it all.

One other thing he learned on the day of the buffalo hunt, that he hadn't known before, was about their arrows. It made sense that, as the various indian tribes were different, so would their implements and weapons be different. A Pawnee arrow would differ from the arrows made by the Otoes or the Sioux, or from any other tribe. What Hugh hadn't realized was just how far these differences went. Any arrow that a man made was uniquely different from the arrows made by any other man. Not *only* were the arrows from the various tribes different—the arrows a man made were as individualistic as his signature would be in the civilized world. Hugh had imagined that, since the tribe shared what was killed on the whole, that it did not matter who killed what. This wasn't exactly so. By looking at their arrows, everyone knew who had killed which buffalo. And they, of course, were entitled to that kill.

Not that he would have known himself by looking at the arrows, but the indians told him that he killed three buffaloes on that first day.

Not bad for a white man.

Of the four surrounds that were made, Hugh killed seven buffalo. Two of these he gave to Little Feather, two he kept for himself, and three he gave to the poor of the village. Neither the gift to the poor, nor the one to Little Feather, went unnoticed by the other members of the tribe. In return for the gift, Little Feather sewed moccasins and clothing for him. She helped him to dry the meat and store it, and showed him how to pound the meat in a bowl, adding berries and herbs to make pemmican. The two of them spent a great deal of time together—another fact that did not escape the notice of the Pawnees.

And although Little Feather was expected to wait a full year for Storm Dancer to come back before finding another mate, the village smiled on them.

After the hunt was finished and all the hides had been tanned, and the meat dried for later use, the Pawnees packed up their belongings and headed back to their village. Moving only a little slower because of the extra load, the trip took about three and a half weeks. When they arrived, it was almost time to harvest the beans, squash, and corn they had planted in the Spring.

As time went on, Hugh continually found himself comparing the similarities and differences between the Pawnees and the pirates at Campeche. Both groups stole, and both were capable of incredible acts of brutality and murder. The Pawnees called it going to war. For them, it was an ancient and accepted practice; appropriate in the world they lived in because all those around them did the same. To not to have practiced "war" upon their enemies would have meant weakness, and weakness would have meant the end of them as a people.

The pirates chose their way of life, mainly, through laziness and contempt for the rights and lives of others. Selfishness and greed had turned them from values that their society had believed in for centuries. There was a pettiness about them that Hugh hated.

The Pawnees had killed his only friend, true, but Hugh had never seen any signs of pettiness among them. In fact, on the whole, they were the most generous group of people he had ever known. To judge them fairly you had to judge them in the context of the world they lived in. In that world, they were no more guilty than lions or wolves.

Coincidentally, in indian sign language, the sign for Pawnee was the same sign that was used for "wolf".

Interestingly enough, the only pirate Hugh had ever been able to tolerate was Willie Brandt. Willie had been born a pirate, from parents who were pirates. Like the Pawnees, it was the only way of life he had ever known.

The Pawnees were on the move for six to eight months out of the year. Traveling with them, Hugh slowly learned their ways and developed the skills they found necessary for survival. In time, practice yielded results in skills such areas as the lance, knife, and tomahawk, as well as with the bow and arrow. He also learned what plants were good to eat and which ones held medicinal uses.

The one thing that seemed to elude Hugh, no matter how much he worked at it was tracking. Time and again he watched Big Axe or Lucky Hawk look at an area littered with leaves and pick out the tracks of a bobcat, deer, or a fox, when all Hugh could see was leaf litter.

"Eyes too hard," Big Axe told him. "Need soft eyes to see tracks in leaves." Patiently, they would follow the tracks with him, pointing them out as they went. Occasionally, Hugh would see indents that were supposed to be the tracks. Mostly, he saw leaves. Eventually, the animal they were following would step out of the leaves and into the soft earth, leaving a track that even Hugh could follow. This frustrated him all the more, knowing that the tracks really had been there all along and he had been unable to see them.

"Soften your eyes," Big Axe told him. "Eyes too hard. Practice much."

Eyes too hard. It would be months before Hugh figured out what Big Axe meant by that. In the meantime, he learned to identify the tracks of various animals whenever he came upon those obvious enough for him to see.

Hugh had been having nightmares again. They woke him up in the middle of the night. He would lay, shivering afterwards. Sometimes it would be hours before he could get to sleep again. Sometimes the dreams had Tom Halpern in them, usually with Clint standing somewhere behind him. Hugh figured those dreams were left over feelings of guilt, come back to haunt him for staying alive when the others had all died. It was the other dream, though, that really terrified him. Hugh didn't know what the significance of Sarah and the two boys was, but he was now pretty certain that the beast in the dream that kept tearing at him had to be a bear. He'd seen the necklaces of claws that some of the warriors wore. They were the same as the ones that tore at his flesh in the dream. Hugh had never seen a bear, but he knew those claws.

Once more they were back in their "permanent" village. It was nighttime. Unable to sleep, Hugh was standing at the outskirts of the village, out near the horses, letting his stomach settle and not really thinking much about anything.

He had learned quite a lot from the Pawnees, in the time he'd been with them. Despite having "hard eyes", as Big Axe called them, Hugh had learned to identify the tracks of quite a number of animals, as well as how to tell how old those tracks were. There was much more, however, that he still had yet to learn.

It amazed him to realize just how at home with these people he had become. They had accepted him as one of their own, even though he was different. He would never truly be *one* of them, but they made him feel comfortable with them, and they treated him as an equal.

A sudden noise off to his left startled him. As he looked to see what it was, he felt something fly past his head. Reacting instinctively, Hugh threw himself to the right. Rolling, he came back up onto his feet, pulling his knife from his belt as he did. A dark form rushed him out of the darkness, wielding a tomahawk. The indian struck two quick blows, back and forth across the front of him. The first one missed.

The second blow cut across the front of Hugh's deerskin shirt. Stepping in close, Hugh drove his knife into the indians' chest. Immediately, the man went limp and fell to the ground.

From somewhere in front of him, Hugh heard the distinct sound of a rifle being cocked. Again he threw himself sideways, this time sprawling face first in the dirt. Hugh heard the rifle bark loudly and saw the muzzle flash thirty feet away from him, but the shot missed.

Rolling back to the indian he had just killed, Hugh snapped up the dead man's tomahawk. The tomahawk had a thong on it, which the dead man had wrapped around his wrist. When Hugh tried to take the tomahawk, the thong caught. Hugh lost precious moments getting it free. Finally, pulling the tomahawk from the indians' wrist, Hugh jumped to his feet and ran toward the man with the rifle. The indian was reloading to take a second shot. The man seemed unhurried, as though he had all the time in the world.

Before he had covered half the distance to the indian, Hugh knew he wouldn't make it. The man was finished reloading. Hugh took two more steps, stopped, and let the tomahawk fly. The indian looked up from his rifle in time for the tomahawk to bury itself in his forehead. He wavered a moment, then fell forward over his rifle. Hugh reached him just as, with a yell, a third indian leapt onto one of the horses and began driving a number of other horses before him, out across the prairie.

Hesitating for only a second, Hugh reached down and rolled the body of the second indian off the rifle. Then, picking it up, he took aim. In the dim starlight, Hugh could make out only an outline of the man, hunched over the form of the galloping horse. Breathing, Hugh squeezed the trigger. In the darkness, the man seemed to give a little jump. Then he slipped off the horse and into the grass.

Almost instantly, the Pawnees were there, ready with their weapons, drawn by the two shots. Some of them had torches. When they saw that the excitement was over, they began checking out the devastation Hugh had wrought. Big Axe inspected the bodies of the two men who were killed near the compound. Grunting with satisfaction, he indicated the man Hugh had killed with the tomahawk.

"You practiced—you got good!" he said.

Big Soldier scalped the two dead men who were close by, while some of the others went after the third, who lay out on the prairie. Still others went after the horses that had gotten away. Big Soldier tried giving the scalps to Hugh.

"No, my friend," Hugh told him. "You take them. It is my gift for teaching me to throw the tomahawk."

Hefting the scalps, Big Soldier nodded with satisfaction at what was, to him, no small present. Then, lifting them into the air, he yelled, "Aye-Yi-Yi-Yi-Yi! My brother, He-Shoots-In-Darkness, has shown himself to be a great warrior! He has killed the Kansa's, our ancient enemies, who came to steal our horses! He is truly a worthy Pawnee warrior!"

The man Hugh had shot was not quite dead. Dragging him back by his hair, The Pawnees scalped and dismembered him. They also dismembered the other two and dragged the entrails of all three out into the prairie. Having become accustomed to their normally gentle, laughing ways, Hugh was shocked by this, and a little sickened. He accepted it though, and in time would learn to understand their reasons for doing some of the things they did. Had it been the other way around, the Kansa's would have done the Pawnees no differently.

The rifle, Hugh kept. It was different from those that the Pawnees had. Theirs were fusils—flintlocks that, while antiquated, could shoot a ball with considerable force and accuracy. The rifle Hugh took off the Kansa was a much newer design and better made, better even than the weapons he had seen and used while he had been with the pirates.

It would be some time before Hugh would come to know what he actually had, or how well known the name "HAWKEN" was becoming in circles where men knew firearms.

Later that night, after much celebrating and dancing, Hugh finally caught sight of Little Feather. Slipping away from the festivities, he followed her and caught up with her behind one of the earth lodges. Hugh was still strangely "keyed-up" from his experience earlier that evening. All of his senses seemed heightened, somehow. His skin tingled. He felt alive and powerful in a way he had not felt for quite some time.

As if she knew he was following, Little Feather stopped to face him. Hugh stopped only inches away, standing closer to her than he ever had before. The scent of her, drifting up to Hugh, was strangely intoxicating to him.

"I am glad you were not hurt," she said. Reaching up, she felt the spot where the tomahawk had cut across the front of his shirt. "I will sew this for you—"

Hugh reached for her and pulled her to him. To his surprise, Little Feather lifted her mouth toward him and kissed his as a white woman would.

Moments later, the two of them slipped away, disappearing into the tall grass just outside the village.

CHAPTER TWENTY-FOUR

ST. LOUIS—MARCH, 1820-
WEST OF THE Missouri, things were beginning to warm up.

That's what everyone said, anyway. Within the next ten years, settlements would sprout up in areas that were now nothing but wilderness and indian territory. Adventures would be had and fortunes would be made.

Young Jim Bridger wanted both.

Ever since the Louis and Clark expedition of 1804—the year Jim had been born—people had talked about the rich, fertile land the expedition had found. Up until now the government, *and* the indians, had kept any kind of expansion in check. The talk was that would change soon. Nine years earlier, in 1811, Major Andrew Henry had made his own expedition over the Rockies. Most of the expedition had been wiped out by Blackfeet indians, but those who returned in the spring of 1812 brought out tales of an unimaginable wealth in furs, waiting to be taken by whoever got there first and managed to survive. Since then, the cry had been growing louder every year: "Did the United States Government make the Louisiana Purchase just to leave the land to the indians?"

The talk around Baird's Blacksmith Shop, where Jim worked, was that they hadn't. Any day now, the government would open the land up for those who were bold enough to take it. Jim's greatest fear was that it would happen before he was old enough to join them.

Old enough legally, anyway. Emotionally and physically, he was as ready as anyone to take on the new world.

The past few years had been especially hard, both on Jim and on his younger sister. Four years earlier, their family had moved from their home in Richmond, Virginia, to a spot along the Missouri River called the American Bottoms, six miles from St. Louis. Jim's father was a surveyor by trade, and there was no lack of work in the St. Louis area, but the job took him away from home for long periods of time.

One year after they arrived at the American Bottoms, in the summer of 1816, tragedy struck. Jim's mother died. Then, as winter began to set in, his baby brother followed her. Jim's father was away on both occasions, leaving Jim to handle all of the details and funeral arrangements, and anything else that needed to be taken care of.

A year after the death of his brother, just before Christmas of 1817, Jim's father died, leaving a thirteen-year-old Jim Bridger to take care of himself and his younger sister.

Not waiting for starvation or for handouts, Jim immediately began to look for work. He managed to obtain a canoe and, with the help of Pierre Chouteau, at Chouteau's General Store, began to trap for muskrat and mink. In addition to this, he found occasional work as a deck hand aboard Antoine Dangen's ferry, which ran from the American Bottoms to Old Cahokio, or East St. Louis.

He learned right away to distrust and dislike the average riverman, as well as to keep his wits about him. He had more to think about than just himself. He had his sister to care for.

On March 17, 1818, while the Irish of St. Louis celebrated St. Patrick's Day, Jim turned fourteen. That same day, he signed a four-year apprenticeship at Baird's Blacksmith Shop. It was a big day for Jim. It meant that he would learn a trade—something he could take with him wherever he went. It also meant an end to the hand-to-mouth existence that he and his younger sister had been living over to past months. On top of this, a blacksmith named Phil Creamer had offered to let Jim and his sister stay with him and his family.

That had been two years ago. Jim had learned a lot since then. He'd grown tall and strong from blacksmithing—far stronger than most sixteen year old boys. His lack of schooling in other matters, though, led him to be painfully shy. He felt inferior to the other young men who lived in St. Louis, boys whose social position and advantages seemed to put them a step above him.

During the long, cold days of winter, the blacksmith shop was a good, warm place to be. When spring came, though, it brought the wanderlust to him. Jim missed the freedom of the river, the mystery of it. Every day men came into the shop and spoke of the wealth and adventure that lay to the west. Soon, things would begin to open up out there. Then a flood of men, all looking for the same things Jim wanted, would go surging out into the wilderness.

His apprenticeship would end on March 17, 1822, on Jim's eighteenth birthday. As yet, that was still two years away. If things broke loose too soon, all the wealth and adventure would be taken before Jim got a chance at it.

He prayed that the tide of events would be slow.

CHAPTER TWENTY-FIVE

THE CHIEF of the Arikaras had come into the village, along with several others. Among these were Kills-The-Whites, and two other principal warriors, Little Soldier and Elk's Tongue.

The chief's name was Gray Eyes. He treated Hugh with the utmost courtesy, but there was something in his eyes that belied it, a subtle hint of amusement and malice. Hugh's own response to this surprised him. He was as polite as the Arikaras were, but inside he was wary and tiredly angry. That the Arikaras carried a hatred for all white people was obvious.

As usual, they stayed but a short time and then moved on. And, as always, Hugh Glass was both happy and relieved to see them go.

Hugh was convinced that Big Axe had to be a magician. The indian could appear or disappear, seemingly at will.

At least, in the woods, anyway.

At home, in his lodge or around the village, he seemed almost as any other warrior. In the woods he was supreme. There was a silence within and about him, a stillness, that was *like* the forest. It allowed him to blend in and become a part of his surroundings almost without effort. Then, in an instant, the stillness would end explosively and Hugh would know exactly where Big Axe was.

At least Hugh was learning from the best.

That was, *if* he would just learn. They had come into the woods the day before. Big Axe was determined that they would stay until Hugh learned to "soften his eyes". They had spent the day doing exercises that Big Axe had designed to help

Hugh "see". Hugh thought he had the idea—Big Axe was trying to get him to focus on the outside edges of his vision in order to soften the focus in the middle, somehow. Hugh thought he had it once or twice, but whenever he tried to use it to see tracks that Big Axe said were in front of him, Hugh automatically focused on the area and, as a result, couldn't see a thing. Maybe it was something you had to learn when you were young.

Finally, at the end of the day, Big Axe had left him. It was nearly sundown. Big Axe walked to the edge of a small meadow near their camp.

"Look close at this spot that I leave from," he told Hugh. "Tomorrow, you start here. Come find me." Then he disappeared into the woods.

Now, having spent the night alone, Hugh was back at that same spot, looking for some trace of his friend.

Hugh knew this was where Big Axe had gone back into the woods. The area was glistening with dew. Any tracks recently made through the leaves should have been obvious. Hugh could make out nothing. Try as he might to soften his eyes, all he saw were leaves.

Some indian you are, he thought.

After trying for a good half hour without any luck, he decided to stop and give himself a break. He stood, staring, wondering how to proceed. He knew that he was in the right spot. The tracks had to be there, but he couldn't see them. Hugh also knew that if he didn't find them he would risk losing face with his friend. Big Axe had shown incredible patience with Hugh on this. Now it was time for Hugh to learn to see.

Unfortunately, he just couldn't.

He'd been standing there for some time, pondering and not really looking any longer, trying to decide what next to do, when he suddenly realized the tracks were there, before him, as clear and obvious as wagon tracks through a muddy field.

Hugh blinked and looked. The tracks disappeared.

But he had done it. *Finally,* he'd done it!

And, having done it, he would do it again.

It took only a few minutes for Hugh to "soften" his eyes a second time, so that he was able to begin following Big Axe's trail. At first it was tricky—his eyes kept wanting to focus—but Hugh kept at it with the enthusiasm of a child with a new toy. As he began to get the hang of it he realized that there was so much more, right there in the leaves, that he had never seen before. He likened it to someone who had never seen hues, but was now suddenly able to see all the different shadings of color. The difference was incredible.

Big Axe had intentionally left him an easy trail, although it would have been impossible for Hugh to have followed it the day before.

After awhile Hugh decided to rest a bit. This was a new thing to him, a new skill. He delighted in it, but the strain of keeping his eyes in soft focus was giving him a headache.

They were in the hills, a little farther north than Hugh had been before. It was lovely here, by far the most beautiful country he had ever seen. He had stopped in a stand of trees with white bark and small leaves that quivered constantly in the breeze. Big Axe had told him the indians called the tree "Woman's tongue, woman's tongue. Always shaking, never still."

One day, a white man would tell Hugh that the tree was called a "quaking asp". Hugh Glass would always prefer the indian name.

Finished with his rest, Hugh began to track again. This time, his eyes automatically went into soft focus when he wanted them to. What he saw disturbed him. He could see Big Axe's tracks ahead of him, moving through the leaves. Several feet ahead of Hugh, a second pair of tracks joined them. The second pair of tracks had come in after Big Axe had passed this way, for they obliterated some of the tracks the indian had left.

What bothered Hugh even more was that the second set of tracks were not made by human feet.

They were bear tracks. Hugh was certain of it. He had still never seen a bear, but he had seen the claws and the skins. Those claws—and an animal big enough to fill a bearskin—was the only thing he could think of that would make a track like this.

Hugh's eyes searched the trees around him. He had an eerie feeling that the bear might be here, hidden by the trees, watching him and ready to strike at any moment. Checking the load in his rifle, he continued forward.

Hugh felt a sense of urgency that he found hard to contain. Big Axe had left these tracks yesterday, the bear sometime after. Looking closely at the bear track, he noticed that the edges were still sharp and crisp. Some of the leaves in the tracks were turned over, so that the bottoms of those leave were wet, while the tops were dry. The wetness was from the dew. The tracks had definitely been made only a short time earlier. Dry mouthed, his heart pounding heavily in his chest, Hugh kept going.

Hugh suddenly realized that his palms were sweating. He kept remembering the dream, the one he'd had again and again since leaving the pirates, and from before he'd ever had any thought of being in bear country. It created in him a lethargy, a heaviness that he fought hard to control. The bear was following his friend. He had no time now, to let his fear stop him.

He passed the place where Big Axe had made his camp. The bear had been there, possibly only moments before. Hugh kept going.

He smelled the bear long before he saw it. It was a musky, unwashed dog sort of smell, only more stronger and more foul. Once he noticed it, the smell seemed to grow with each step he took. Suddenly the woods fell away and Hugh found himself in a clearing. Thirty feet in front of him and moving away, was the bear. Hugh gasped at the sight of it.

Instantly, the bear turned. When it saw Hugh it raised it's massive body up onto it's hind legs and began walking toward him.

Hugh stared at the bear, unable to move. It was enormous, terrifying, and at the same time, magnificent. It's long, shaggy brown hair was tipped with silver, giving it the appearance of being a ghostly white. Hugh judged it to be at least eight feet tall. As it drew closer he could see that it's teeth and claws were at least three inches long. Hugh knew those claws well, both from the necklaces that some of the warriors wore, and from his dreams.

Woodenly, he raised his rifle and fired. Almost simultaneously, a second shot rang out, from somewhere off to Hugh's left. The bear took two more steps and sprawled, face forward, in front of him, coming to rest only three feet from where Hugh stood.

Appearing next to him, Big Axe said, "Tu-ra-heh! —*It is good!* The white bear wanted you, but now he is yours!"

CHAPTER TWENTY-SIX

MARCH 20, 1822—

THREE DAYS after Jim's eighteenth birthday—three days after his apprenticeship was complete and he was free of obligation—and there, before him, was the notice he had been waiting to see. If there was such a thing as fate, it was working for him now.

> "To Enterprising Young Men: The subscriber
> wishes to engage one hundred young men to ascend
> the Missouri River to it's source, there to be
> employed one, two, or three years. For particulars
> inquire of Major Andrew Henry, near the lead mines,
> in the county of Washington, who will ascend with
> and command the party; or the subscriber, near
> St. Louis.
>
> —William H. Ashley"

The notice seemed personally written for Jim. After all, he was young, although taller and stronger than men he knew. He had a familiarity with traps and guns, and had just finished a four-year blacksmithing apprenticeship. If anyone was a natural for this trip, Jim was.

The notice didn't say what work there was to be done, or what the wages were, but anyone who had spent as much time as Jim had, listening to gossip in the blacksmith shop, knew that they would be trapping and building a fort. He really didn't care what the wages were. He just wanted to go. Getting rich would be a bonus.

James Baird had seen the notice, too. He knew Jim's mind. Jim had been a good apprentice in his shop, always eager to learn and to help. Baird would be sorry to see the boy go, but then, the boy wasn't really a boy any longer. Jim Bridger was a man now, and a damned good blacksmith.

"*You're* a blacksmith?" The skepticism in Major Andrew Henry's voice was obvious.

"That's right, sir. I finished my apprenticeship at Baird's Blacksmith Shop four days ago, on my eighteenth birthday."

"And you say you've hunted and trapped, too?"

"Yes, sir. After my Ma and Pa died there was just me and my sister. I had to fend for both of us. I got my supplies at Pierre Chouteau's. I sold my furs there, too. You can ask Mr. Chouteau about me, sir. He'll vouch for me."

Henry looked at the young man in front of him. He seemed *awfully* young. He was tall, though, and well-built. The boy had the arms of a blacksmith. If what he said was true, he would make a valuable addition to the expedition, more so than many of those who had already signed on.

Henry looked over at Jedidiah Smith, his chief hunter in the outfit. Smith was young, too, only twenty-four. He was highly educated, though, and had spent time in the woods. Smith was standing in on the interviews, but said little unless his opinion was requested.

Smith gave a slight nod. The Major turned back to the young man that stood before him.

"Well, Mr. Bridger," he said, "assuming that your references check out, you're in." He put out his hand. "Welcome aboard."

"Thank you, sir," Jim said, shaking hands. "Thank you. I won't let you down."

"I'm sure you won't, son. Just be at the St. Louis wharf at 4:00 AM on April 3rd. We'll be leaving at sunup."

"I'll be there, sir."

The boy left. When he was gone, Jedidiah Smith looked at Major Andrew Henry.

"Unless I miss my guess," Smith said, "he'll be one of the best that we take on this trip."

So, on April 3rd, Jim was back on the river again. It hadn't changed, the river hadn't, but Jim had. He was older now, a man, and able now to appreciate the things of men. As the boat was leaving the pier he could hardly contain the excitement within himself.

The keelboatmen were doing their work, pushing the boat upstream with their poles. Leading these men was a legend.

Mike Fink had been a famous riverman long before Jim Bridger was born, ranked in notoriety with Davy Crockett and Jim Bowie. Half-horse, half-alligator, according to legend, Fink had been barred from shooting matches from the age of seventeen, because no one could compete with him. He was a big man, a brawler, with heavy bones and hams for fists. Jim found him a little loud, but as rivermen went, he was said to be the best.

Only one of the two keelboats left St. Louis on that day, and this was commanded by Major Andrew Henry himself. The second boat would be brought upriver later by Jedidiah Smith, as soon as they received a shipment of rifles that they were waiting for.

The keelboats themselves were something to see. Sixty-five feet in length and fifteen feet wide, each would carry more than twenty tons of cargo. The two boats combined would carry more supplies than an entire train of wagons, put together.

As they were pulling away from the dock, some of the trappers were passing around a jug of corn whiskey. When it came to Jim he took a big swallow. The whiskey burned his throat, but he managed to not choke on it.

After the burning stopped, the whiskey seemed to add to the excitement he felt. Jim liked the feeling.

This was going to be a great trip.

The adventure of a lifetime.

After three days on the river, the excitement Jim had felt turned to monotony. There was nothing to do but sit on the deck with dozens of other men as, hour after hour, the rivermen slowly pushed them upstream. Nor did the scenery offer any relief. Aside from an occasional bluff or a stand of timber, the area they passed through was essentially the same—flat, unbroken prairie. To add to all this, it began to rain. The rain swelled the river, making it impossible to continue upstream. The keelboat was tied up, and the men were forced to remain on shore, huddled in their tents.

For all their planning, and for the great capacity of the keelboat for carrying supplies, the one thing they hadn't counted on was the rain. It was their plan to feed the company off the land, hunting for their food as they went.

When it rained, game became scarce. Henry was forced to resort to strict food rationing, which did nothing for his popularity with the men, and was forced to use food stores that were meant for much later on in the trip.

Three weeks after leaving St. Louis, the keelboat stopped for a short time at Fort Osage. The fort had been ordered closed years earlier. Some of the Osage indians were still there. The young women were definitely interested in the trappers, but Jim and the others would have nothing to do with them.

Jim felt there was something unclean about these people, something that went beyond their dirty clothes and unwashed hair.

"Try not to judge them too harshly, Jim," Major Andrew Henry told him. "Their way of life—all they knew and almost everything they believed, has been destroyed. Where we're going you'll see less and less of this." He nodded toward the West. "Out there," he said, "you'll see indians that will show you what these people were like, before they were contaminated by white people. Don't be surprised if you learn to respect them."

HughGlass

The monotony of the river grew even more tiresome as the days passed. Sitting on the deck of the keelboat day after day was hard for Jim. After four years in a blacksmith shop, his body was not accustomed to inactivity.

CHAPTER TWENTY-SEVEN

THE PAWNEES lived for war. Through war they attained honor and riches. When a young man wished to take a bride, he went to war to win the gifts he would give to her father. Nor did any of the tribes around the Pawnees think of this as murder, for it was a practice that was accepted by all.

Hugh Glass had seen enough killing to last a lifetime. Having finally learned to "soften his eyes", he became fascinated with tracking. Even without going to war, he did quite well among the Pawnees, just hunting and trapping. Not that he was better at it than they were, for he wasn't, but the indian men rarely applied themselves to anything that was not either religious or war related. You could win honor as a great hunter, but it was nowhere near as important as war, and not nearly as interesting to them.

Fortunately, after killing the three Kansas who had come to steal horses, no one doubted his bravery or his skill as a warrior. As time went on, he helped to defend the Pawnees from attacks by Sioux, Cheyenne, Kansa, and Osage war parties.

Besides all that, he was a white man. They accepted that his ways were different from theirs. Learning those ways was one of the reasons they wanted him among them.

It was almost planting time again. Once more the Pawnees were getting ready to move back to their permanent village of earthen domes. The snow was melting off the hills and was already gone from the flatlands. The streams and rivers were swollen, but not completely impassable.

And Hugh Glass was the happiest he had ever been.

He stood on the side of a hill, overlooking a lake. To his right, in an area next to the lake and sheltered by three mountains, the women were striking the teepees. Hugh hated to go. It was beautiful here, and it had been the most wonderful of all his winters, but where the tribe went, he would go.

There was still a bite in the air. Hugh felt it in the wind as he watched the scene below him. The wind carried something else, too, a strange feeling of anxiety and concern. Hugh shrugged it off. He would miss this place.

To look at him, he seemed as much a member of the tribe below as any of the Pawnees. His hair was long, and had feathers in it. He'd managed to trade for a razor, so his face was cleanly shaved. He did not, like the Pawnees, pluck the hair from his underarms and groin. Those differences, and the fact that he was light haired and light eyed, were almost the only things that set him apart from them. They were differences that Little Feather didn't seem to mind too much. She had been married to a white man once before. This would be his third spring with the Pawnees. Hugh was content living with the indians. Too long had he lived without a woman at his side, and the Pawnee way of life offered a freedom that restrictive "civilization" lacked. Warlike, they might be, but the Pawnees were honest almost to a fault, and were more deeply emersed in their own religion than nearly any white man Hugh had ever met. Overall, theirs was a good and happy life.

Tom Halpern had been wrong.

Actually, Hugh had Old Knife and a medicine man named Yellow Fox to thank for that. For nearly a year after coming to live with the Pawnees, Hugh continued to suffer from nightmares. One evening, just before supper, Old Knife and Yellow Fox came to him, asking Hugh to accompany them to Yellow Fox's medicine lodge. Hugh did as they asked.

Hugh stayed in the medicine lodge for three days. Before he left, he saw and experienced things that few white men would ever have believed. Yellow Fox told Hugh that two spirits followed him. One was the spirit of a man who had placed a curse upon Hugh at the moment of his death. The other spirit was the spirit of a bear that followed Hugh from another life. Although Hugh would doubt it all later, at the time it was happening Yellow Fox's words rang true to him.

In any event, when he left the medicine lodge, Hugh felt lighter of spirit than he had for a very long time, and he hadn't suffered from nightmares—either of Tom Halpern or of being attacked—since that time. Interestingly enough, after Hugh had tracked the bear, and he and Big Axe shot it, Big Axe gave him a new Pawnee name, "Ta'-Ka Kur'uks", which meant "White Bear", or grizzly.

This seemed to over ride the name that Big Soldier had already given him, "Shoots-In-Darkness", and became his permanent Pawnee name. Although Big Soldier was the Soldier Chief, Big Axe actually outranked him in the tribe and was second only to Old Knife.

Far down the hill from him, and onto the flat of the meadow, Hugh could see Little Feather pulling down their teepee. That was something that was considered to be woman's work. Hugh decided to go and help her with it anyway.

Little Feather was troubled by something, Hugh could see it as he came down the hill. The look on her face when she saw him was one of relief, more than gladness.

"Hello wife," he said to her. He began to help dismantle their portable lodge.

"Hello, my husband," she said absently, and kept working.

Hugh wondered what was wrong. In the three years he had known her, Little Feather had always been either joyful and happy, or calm and serene. There was a steadiness about her that Hugh admired. It was something he had seen in few men and fewer women. She reminded him of a ship, deep-drafted and stable, built to hold up under any kind of wind or sea.

Hugh watched her as the two of them began to roll and fold the hides that covered their lodge. Little Feather's face was shadowed with concern. Suddenly, Hugh turned and sat down on the hide as she tried to roll it up. Little Feather shot him an angry look and tried to roll the hide with him on it.

"What are you doing?" she demanded. "We have to make ready to leave! The others will leave without us!"

"Let them," he told her. "We'll catch up."

"But we need to make ready—!"

"Little Feather," Hugh said quietly, "what is wrong?"

She sat back on her knees and sighed, looking down at the hide in front of her.

"It is nothing," she told him without looking up, "a bad sign..."

"Tell me," he insisted.

She took a deep breath, then exhaled. "This morning, as you were leaving, I watched you go away, up the hill. When I turned back, there was an owl, over there in the tree, watching me. When our eyes met, he turned and flew away."

"That was it? An owl?"

"It was an omen," she told him. "A bad sign."

They were silent for a moment. Hugh wanted to say something, to tease her for being silly, but he could see that she was clearly troubled.

"There's more," she said suddenly.

"More?"

"Yes. I had a dream. You were in a great canoe, out on the big waters you have spoken of. There was another man there. This man hated you very much."

Hugh thought for a minute.

"What did this man look like?" he asked finally.

"He was a white man. He was tall, like you, but his hair was dark, except for here—" she touched her hairline, at the top of her forehead. "Here, his hair was white."

Hugh nodded. He knew he had often spoken to her about the sea. He *may* have told her about Tom Halpern, but he was certain he had never described him to her. This was eerie.

Abruptly, he reached down and picked up a stick. Using the stick, he drew four small crosses in the dirt. Then he drew a circle around them.

"There!" he said. "I have made a good sign, to counter the bad ones. Ti-war-Uks-ti! *Big Magic!*"

Little Feather smiled weakly and nodded. The two of them finished their preparations for the trip.

Later, as they were leaving, the travois that they made to carry their things brushed over Hugh's drawing in the dirt, destroying it, but neither Hugh nor Little Feather noticed.

Traveling as a whole, the Pawnees were rarely on the move for more than six hours a day, covering at best, fifteen miles.

It was late in the afternoon, nearing the time when the tribe would stop and make camp for the night. During the day, as they traveled, the sky had grown dark with clouds. It might only be a spring rain, or it could be a heavy storm that was headed for them. Wherever they stopped, the indians would have to be prepared to stay for several days. Although the tribe had been through this area many times in the past, Big Soldier had gone ahead to choose the best spot to camp. When he came back, it was already past the time when they would normally have stopped.

"River up ahead," Big Soldier told Hugh. "About half-mile. We cross, then make camp."

They continued onward. When they reached the river Hugh could see why Big Soldier wanted them to get across. The riverbed was a small gorge that ran about twenty feet deep. Directly in the middle of this, the river flowed at a depth of three feet. At this time of year it should have been deeper, and if the storm that threatened was as bad as it looked, it soon would be. Even after crossing, if it stormed, the movements of the tribe could be halted for several days.

Big Soldier had picked the best place for them to cross. Without hesitating, the column of indians began to move down into the river.

Hugh was riding a spirited, rust-colored mare—one of the original three that Old Knife had given him three years earlier—which he had affectionately named Annie. By his best estimate he was now forty-two years old, older than most men in the tribe ever expected to be. By any man's standards, he had led an interesting life. He had been a sailor, a pirate, and now he was an indian. He had expected to live and die on the open sea, and now he was as far away from that as he could ever hope to be, and happier than he had ever been. For all their warlike ways, the Pawnees were essentially a merry, light-hearted people, always ready for a joke, with a love for both the ridiculous and the absurd. Except for rare occasions, Hugh found it hard to be too serious around them.

The river hardly slowed the Pawnees down at all. Big Soldier had found a good spot to cross. The only difficult part of it was climbing the opposite bank, which rose several feet above the side that they approached from, which was a shallow, flat area that probably flooded whenever the river was high. Riding ahead of Little Feather, Hugh crossed the river, barely getting his feet wet. He rode up the opposite bank easily, turning when he reached the other side to wave at Little Feather.

Lucky Hawk was already there. He rode over to where Hugh was.

"Ta'Ka Kur'uks!" Lucky Hawk said, addressing Hugh. "Let us go and hunt! Big Soldier told me that there is a herd of antelope only a short distance from here, to the east. Let us go and get some fresh meat for tonight's meal!"

"That sounds good. Wait a few moment, though. I want to help Little Feather cross the river first—"

There was a rumble, which seemed to come from deep within the earth. Both men thought it was thunder, an advance notice from the approaching storm, but it continued on, growing louder until Hugh thought it must be an earthquake.

When he saw what was behind the noise, Hugh's heart shrank.

"Oh, sweet Jesus!" he said under his breath.

From around the bend in the river rushed a wall of water, easily ten feet high and crashing along at an unbelievable speed, pushing whole trees and brush and debris of all sorts along in its path. Hugh realized immediately that this was why the river had been so shallow. The trees and brush had formed a dam somewhere upstream, slowing the flow to a fraction of what it should have been. Now that dam had burst.

Hugh kicked his horse in the ribs and started back toward the river. Lucky Hawk cut him off, crashing his horse into Hugh's. Even as he did the wall of water went thundering by, washing the half-dozen or so Pawnees who were in the river away as if they had never been there.

"You cannot help her!" Lucky Hawk shouted. "You will only die! Little Feather may be all right! Look!"

In the shallow area where Little Feather and the others were, the water was as yet only knee-deep, but it was deepening quickly. Little Feather and the others had turned and were making their way back toward the opposite side of the river. Suddenly a second wall of water, four feet deep, came rushing around from that side, trapping them and washing them into the center of the raging stream.

Spurring their horses, Hugh and Lucky Hawk raced along the river's edge, trying their best to keep sight of Little Feather and the others who had been caught in the flood. The horses were unable to match the speed of the rushing water, and the amount of debris was so great that it was impossible to keep sight of those who had been washed away in the deluge.

At length, the two men were forced to stop and let their horses rest. Before they started up again, rain began to fall in heavy, pelting drops.

Hugh and Lucky Hawk searched along the river, through the storm, for five days. Then the rain stopped. The two men continued looking for six more days. Finally, they turned back, hoping for some sign that they had missed before.

Others, on both sides of the river, joined them in the search. Despite their efforts, no trace of Little Feather, or of eleven others, was ever found.

CHAPTER TWENTY-EIGHT

IT WAS LATE August before the Ashley-Henry trappers finally stopped traveling and built what the men were calling "The New Fort Henry". The "Old" Fort Henry had been built and abandoned eleven years earlier, in 1811, on the other side of the Rocky Mountains. Andrew Henry had gone that way to escape a disastrous encounter with the Blackfeet. Unfortunately, *that* fort had been built in the middle of Shoshone territory. The Shoshones were no happier to see the white men that the Blackfeet had been.

When the spring of 1811 arrived, only Henry and a few of his men were left alive. They managed to make it back to civilization, barely. Now, eleven years later, Andrew Henry was trying again. This time, he was hoping for better luck.

If nothing else, they were at least better outfitted for the second expedition. In partnership with Henry was Missouri's first Lieutenant Governor, William Henry Ashley. Ashley was known as a man of wealth and authority. If anyone could get the west opened up, it was he.

The second Fort Henry was located a little over four-hundred yards past the mouth of the Yellowstone River. By their best estimation, the trappers were now about eighteen-hundred miles from St. Louis.

For Jim Bridger, that wasn't nearly far enough.

Jim wanted to be in the mountains. He'd seen enough prairie to last him the rest of his life. And while there were trees along the river, everything beyond was an unchanging as it had been for the last one-thousand miles, which had been nothing but open plains.

The trip had not been entirely uneventful. A month earlier they had met, for the first time, the Arikaras. The Arikaras had a reputation for hating whites, but when the trappers stopped at their village, the indians received them warmly. Jim was surprised at how beautiful some of the women were. Henry traded with the Arikaras for forty horses, and the company continued on its way.

From that time on, the company split into two contingents—one on land and one on the water. Tired of sitting in a boat, Jim Bridger was more than happy to be traveling with those who drove the horses.

A week after leaving the Arikara village, they encountered a group of Assiniboines. These indians made a great show of friendship. At the first opportunity they disappeared, taking with them thirty-five of the horses the trappers had purchased from the Arikaras.

There had also been a good many missed meals on the trip. Quite the opposite of what everyone had thought, a lot of the country they traveled through had been amazingly sparse. When you added to that the fact that at least fifteen days had been lost to heavy rains, it meant that a lot of rations had to be consumed that were never meant to be touched before winter.

In early June, the troop had stopped at Cedar Fort. Nine men, under the leadership of a man named Daniel T. Potts, had deserted there, blaming the shortage of food.

Now at least, things were different. They were able to find enough game along the river to feed themselves, and the building of the fort was going well.

But Jim Bridger still yearned to see those shining, Rocky Mountains.

The second Fort Henry consisted of four small, log houses that were built in a square and connected by a palisade. It would provide shelter for the men and protection against potential attacks by indians, but there were some who thought it was *way* too small.

Mike Fink was a big man. He was raw-bone and powerfully built. At seventeen, his skill with a rifle was so great that literally no one would compete against him. He had been a riverman his whole life. *Legend* had it that Mike was half-horse, half-alligator. He'd been in innumerable scrapes, some of them quite well known. One story had it that he and Davy Crockett had fought for three days, neither getting the better of the other. According to Mike, he had never been bested.

That was about to change.

Now in his fifties, Mike's legend had begun to decline. Like many men who had done much but amassed little, Mike Fink took it upon himself to keep his legend alive. Not content with having the reputation of being the best keelboatman on the Missouri, Mike talked about himself constantly. Loud by nature, he was gregarious, but not above bullying those around him if he felt the need for it. One man that he bullied once too often was his adopted son, Carpenter.

Mike Fink and Carpenter had been together for years, since Carpenter was a boy. Mike had taught Carpenter to shoot, and for quite a few years the two of them entertained crowds in shooting exhibitions, their favorite trick being to shoot tin cups off of each other's head. Dangerous, but it was a real crowd pleaser. As far as

Mike was concerned, Carpenter was his *boy*.

But the boy had grown into a man. Carpenter was every inch as big as Mike was, and had become an expert riverman in his own right. He chafed at being ordered about by Mike, and by Mike's treatment of him in general.

This was old business between these two, but it was made new again by the unending days of close confinement. One afternoon, Mike pushed Carpenter a little too far, and Carpenter rebelled.

Right or wrong, Mike Fink was not a man to back down from anybody. A bitter fight ensued. When it was over, Mike lay on the ground, with Carpenter standing over him.

Another man might have let it go and realized that he had made a mistake in pushing Carpenter too far. All Mike saw was that he had taken his first real beating, and from a man he considered to be his lesser, a man who, as far as Mike Fink was concerned, owed him everything.

He was not *about* to forget it.

The days passed quickly while the fort was being built. Henry's men watched the river eagerly, expecting the second keelboat to arrive any day, under the command of Jedidiah Smith. The second keelboat would bring them fresh supplies and men, as well as news of anything that might have happened in St. Louis after the first boat had left.

Although he was the youngest man in the company, Jim Bridger was stronger than a good many of the others. Four years as a blacksmith's apprentice had given him strength that would have been, otherwise, almost impossible to earn.

Jim enjoyed the building of the fort. He was able to learn some things about construction that he hadn't known before. It was good to use his muscles again after months of sitting on the keelboat.

He was down next to the river with some of the others, cutting timbers, when he saw the boat. A quick thrill of excitement ran through him. This turned to curiosity when he realized that the boat wasn't theirs.

This boat was smaller than the two that Ashley-Henry owned, and it carried about one third of the men that the trappers were expecting. Jim was surprised to see another group of men this far west. His surprise turned to concern when he realized who they were and why they were there.

Like the Ashley-Henry group, these men were trappers. They worked for a man named Joshua Pilcher, of the Missouri Fur Company. The two men in charge were Micheal E. Immel and Robert Jones. Their plans were simple—get ahead of the Ashley-Henry party and stake out the best trapping areas for themselves. The way they planned to do that was almost an insult.

In 1807, a man named Manuel Lisa had gone up the Missouri with a crew of forty men. Ahead of his time, Lisa built a fort at the mouth of the Bighorn River. He returned a year later with a rich load of furs.

In 1810, Andrew Henry had stopped at Fort Manuel before going on to what turned out to be a disastrous encounter with the Blackfeet at Three Forks Basin, in which thirty of his party were slain, and resulted in his going over the Rockies to establish the first Fort Henry.

Immel and Jones were planning to repeat that move. They were heading upriver, past the Ashley-Henry party, and on up to Fort Manuel, at the mouth of the Bighorn. They would spend the winter there, spreading westward toward Three Forks with the spring thaw. This would put them way ahead of the Ashley-Henry men, and would give them the rights to the rich load of furs that waited there.

Immel and Jones didn't stay long, nor were they made to feel particularly welcome.

The second keelboat arrived at Fort Henry on October first. To everyone's surprise, it was commanded by General Ashley himself, with Jedidiah Smith second in command, and was not the same boat that Henry and the others had left behind in St. Louis at all. The first boat had been sunk shortly after it's departure from St. Louis, on May 8. An overhanging limb had caught on the mast, turning the boat sideways—broadside to the current—capsizing it and losing its $10,000.00 cargo. Undaunted, Ashley had replaced the entire shipment of supplies in three weeks time and, commanding the boat himself, headed upriver again.

Along the way, Ashley managed to re-recruit some of the men who had deserted at Cedar Fort, including Daniel T. Potts.

No sooner did Ashley arrive and unload his supply of goods, than he turned and headed back to St. Louis, taking with him the furs that the company had collected up until then.

One of the boxes that Ashley unloaded was full of blacksmith tools. Jim was delighted. He may have been the youngest, and in many ways the least experienced, but there was no man working for Ashley and Henry's Rocky Mountain Fur Company that knew blacksmithing like Jim Bridger did. It was his chance to shine.

PART TWO

Large of bone,
Deep-chested, that his
Great heart might have
Play
—It seemed
That he had
Never been young…

—John G. Neihardt
"The Song of Hugh Glass"

CHAPTER TWENTY-NINE

IT SEEMED that each time grief reached for Hugh Glass, it touched him in a different way. For three months he alternately searched and waited for some sign of Little Feather, but no sign was forthcoming. More than any time before in his life, he was now a man fully lost. Surrounded by friends, he was alone once more. Toward the end of summer, when word came requesting a delegation of Pawnees to go to St. Louis and meet with the representatives of "The Great White Father", Hugh decided to go with them. There was little doubt of his intentions. Ta'-Ka Kur'uks was returning to live once more among the whites.

"My people believe," Big Axe told him, "that the moon, who is female, gave us the bow, and that the Sun, who is male, gave us the arrow. One without the other does little good. Perhaps it is good for you to go back to your people at this time. In my heart, though, I am sad at your going."

"You have taught me much that I will never forget," Hugh told him. "You have been my true friend. Wherever I go, I will hold your memory strong here, in my heart." Hugh touched his chest as he spoke.

"Tu-ra-heh!" Big Axe declared. *"It is good!"*

The delegation left in late August. By October, Hugh Glass was a white man once more.

He had lost most of his worldly possessions in the river. That meant little to Hugh. Losing Little Feather made everything else unimportant. She had been the one thing in his life that had brought him only joy. When he left, the Pawnees gave him many gifts. When he said good-bye to Old Knife in St. Louis, Hugh had half a pack of furs and four horses. He sold the furs and two of the horses, all of which brought him nearly four-hundred dollars. That would last him quite a while, if he was careful. At least it would give him time to figure out his next move.

What Hugh hadn't realized before about white people was that most of them smelled bad. Living among the indians, he had developed the habit of bathing regularly, or else cleaning his body with oil or grease. White people, he remembered suddenly, rarely bathed more than once a week, whether they were male or female.

Hugh bought himself some clothes and checked into a moderately expensive hotel. His first night there he had a hot bath in a fancy tub, ate a fine meal, and bought a bottle of expensive whiskey. He took the bottle back to his hotel room, where he proceeded to get mildly drunk. When the tears began to fall, he tried to stop them and couldn't. Months of stored grief began to pour out of him in wave after wave. Away from the Pawnees, Hugh was forced to recognize and accept the fact that Little Feather was gone, and that he would never see her again. The weight of that realization was almost too much for him too bear.

After awhile there was a gentle knock at his door, and a feminine voice meekly asked if he was all right. He managed to choke back that he was. For the remainder of the night, until he finally fell asleep, Hugh bit down on his pillow to keep from sobbing too loudly.

Hugh Glass was finally back with his own people. He was a free man and he had money. Without Little Feather, none of that meant anything to him.

Hugh was slow to adapt back into civilized life. He didn't seem to fit in anymore, didn't feel as if he belonged. He roamed the streets of St. Louis, looking for the most part like everyone else, but inside he was an empty man. He drank too much and spent too much money. A couple of times he bought prostitutes. Nothing seemed to help. When his money began to run low, he moved out of the hotel and took a room in a boarding house.

Thanksgiving came and went, then Christmas. One week later, Hugh celebrated the arrival of 1823 along with the rest of St. Louis. His thoughts, though, were over a thousand miles away.

It would soon be time for the winter hunt. The buffalo would have their winter coats now, the ones that made the best and warmest robes. Hugh thought about Big Axe and Lucky Hawk, Old Knife, Big Soldier and all the others. He would never go back to them—Little Feather was gone and, without her, it would never be the same. He thought about them a lot, though. Wherever they were, out in the plains or nestled in the hills, he hoped they were fat and happy.

He wished them well.

On January 16, 1823 Hugh was sitting in a restaurant, waiting for his breakfast and reading the *Missouri Republican*. Outside, it was shaping up to be a miserable day, cold, dark, and snowy, but in the restaurant it was warm. Hugh sipped coffee from a china cup and read the newspaper.

In a little over two and a half months, he had gone through a good portion of what most people would have considered a good years' salary. Hugh didn't regret it, but now he was beginning to feel the pinch. He needed to find something to do, and soon.

About halfway down the page, Hugh saw the ad.

FOR THE ROCKY MOUNTAINS
    The subscribers wish to engage One Hundred
MEN, to ascend the Missouri to the Rocky Mountains,
    There to be employed as hunters. As a compen-
sation to each man fit for such business,
$200.00 Per Annum,
will be given for his services, as aforesaid. For
particulars, apply to J.V. Garmier, or W. Ashley,
at St. Louis. The expedition will set out for this
            place on or before March next.

ASHLEY AND HENRY

Hugh felt a surge of excitement when he read the ad. The thought of going back into the wilderness intrigued him. He was already beginning to grow tired of the city. He had no other prospects, and his supply of funds was seriously deplet-ed. If he was careful, though, he could make what was left last until March.

He had no trouble getting Ashley to hire him. He was an expert tracker and hunter; he knew how to survive out on the open plains or in the hills. He was famil-iar with many of the indian tribes and their ways. In all probability, Hugh would be more at home in the wilderness than any man Ashley had. In addition to all this, Glass was educated. Not that it made much of a difference where they were going, but only about five men out of the hundred that Ashley would hire would be able to read and write. Ashley knew that one could never tell when that might come in handy.

"I ascended the Masuri and arrived at the mouth of the Mussel Shell, on the latter end of November where I wintered with thirteen others here was a remarkable escape of my scalp as two large parteys of indians wintered within twenty miles of us and our better enimys the black feet....."

—Daniel T. Potts

CHAPTER THIRTY

THE EXPEDITION left St. Louis on Monday, March 7, 1823. Hardly had they gotten under way when a mishap took place that took the life of one man. *The Missouri Republican* reported it this way:

> Two keel boats belonging to General Ashley left
> this place Monday for the Yellow Stone, for the
> purpose of hunting and trapping... We understand
> a man fell overboard from one of the boats on
> Monday and was drowned.

One week later, the two boats stopped at St. Charles, to take on more supplies. Another accident happened. The *Republic* carried that story:

> AFFECTING OCCASION
> On Thursday last, three men belonging to General Ashley's
> expedition to the Yellow Stone were conveying a quantity of
> powder in a cart to the boats at St. Charles, when fire was
> communicated to the powder by means of a pipe... The men
> were blown into the air to the height of several hundred feet,

and the cart shivered to pieces, and the horses much injured. One of them survived a few minutes after his descent to the ground; the others were entirely lifeless and burnt in the most shocking manner.

To Hugh Glass, who had seen more than his share of bad luck, these were not good signs...

For the first of the Ashley-Henry trappers, things were faring no better. In an effort to stay ahead of the Immel-Jones party, Henry took 13 men and moved upstream, to the mouth of the Milk River. They wintered in a spot known as The Musselshell. It had been a frigid winter, with ice running to four feet thick. The trappers were snug in their camp, though. A small herd of buffalo remained close by for most of the winter, so for once, they had plenty to eat.

After months of strained tolerance, the trappers managed to repair the damage that had been done between Carpenter and Mike Fink. At least they *thought* they had. Carpenter was willing—he'd felt bad about giving his adopted father a beating, even though Mike had it coming. Fink had been stubborn. He nursed his anger through the winter. As far as Mike was concerned, his pride and his manhood had been injured. He felt he'd been betrayed, and by someone he had given everything to.

Finally, though, the trappers got him to relent, and the two men became friends once more. After all, Mike had been King of the River for most of his life. Who better to take away his crown than his *boy*, Carpenter.

As a show of friendship, they decided on their old game of shooting cups of whiskey off each other's head. As always, Carpenter's aim was true. Then it was Mike's turn. Mike missed the cup, shooting Carpenter between the eyes.

Mike tried declaring his innocence, but there was at least one man in the group who refused to believe it. Insisting that the killing was intentional, a man named Talbot, who was Carpenter's best friend, shot Mike Fink dead on the spot.

Three days later, while crossing a river, Talbot drowned. Some of the trappers said it was the ghost of Mike Fink, King of the River, taking his revenge.

So far, the year 1823 wasn't starting off too well.

By April, the spring thaw had softened things enough for Henry's men to continue upriver. The party had gone only a short distance before yet another mishap occurred. As one of the trappers was loading his rifle, it discharged and drove the ramrod through both knees of one of the other men—Daniel T. Potts. Two men were selected to take Potts back to Ft. Henry. Eleven others continued upriver.

On May 4th, the party was moving past the Great Falls, near the mouth of another, as yet unnamed river. It was a warm, lovely spring day. The men had taken the canoes out of the water to move them past the falls. The area they were passing through was breathtaking. This, Jim Bridger told himself, was what he had come to see.

They were at a spot just beyond the falls, near the shore and getting ready to put the canoes back into the water. The air about the trappers buzzed and twittered with the sounds of insects and birds. Over this could be heard the muffled sound of the falls. Jim was just putting one of the canoes back into the water, when he noticed the buzzing had stopped.

He stood up to listen. When he did an arrow struck the canoe he had been pushing into the water.

In a moment the clearing was ablaze with gunfire and arrows. Jim dove for his rifle. A second arrow narrowly missed him as he rolled into the bushes.

He resisted the urge to fire blindly back in the direction the arrow had come from, aware that, under these conditions, the indians could reload their bows much faster than he could his rifle. He force himself to wait for a target.

No target appeared. The attack broke off as quickly as it began, leaving the woods silent except for the sound of rushing water. They waited.

After fifteen minutes Major Henry called out, "I think they're gone!"

Jim and two others moved carefully forward, scanning the bushes and looking for signs. The indians were nowhere to be found.

The arrows the indians left behind showed them to be Blackfeet—a tribe that Major Andrew Henry had become very familiar with twelve years earlier. In their wake, the indians left behind four dead and two wounded among the whites.

Carefully, the men turned their canoes back down river and headed back to Fort Henry.

CHAPTER THIRTY-ONE

MAY 31, 1823—

THE TWO KEELBOATS had stopped at a place that, at this moment, Hugh Glass did not want to be. They were at the Arikara village. General Ashley had gone ashore with a man by the name of Ed Rose. Rose had lived with the Arikara's for a number of years and knew Gray Eyes well. Ashley and Rose were going to barter with Gray Eyes for horses.

Ashley really didn't like Rose, and only half-trusted him. It was easy to see why this was. Rose was one-half Negro. He was big and dark and surly, with a manner that did little to invite friendliness. Ashley was Lieutenant Governor and General of the Missouri militia. He preferred his men of color to be a little more servile and a lot less independent than Ed Rose would ever be.

Personally, Hugh thought Rose was all right. Like Hugh, he had spent a lot of time with the indians. It showed when he was in the woods.

Ashley and Rose came back after being in the village for only a short while. The Arikaras were going to barter with them. The dealing would take place the following day, on the beach between the village and the river. This was Ashley's idea—to conduct their business on neutral ground—and it was a good one. Hugh knew Gray Eyes well enough to know that the Arikara chief's hatred of whites should not be underestimated.

As for Hugh, he planned to stay out of sight as much as possible. For three years now Gray Eyes had looked upon him with the same amity and good will that a fox watches a rabbit with. It would have been very bad manners for Gray Eyes to have killed Hugh while Hugh was living among the Pawnees. It would also be con-

121

sidered bad manners now, for Hugh not to pay a visit to his "friends", the Arikaras.

He planned to be bad mannered, and alive. Old Knife couldn't protect him here.

He didn't care much for the way the negotiations went. Ashley had gotten the horses he wanted all right, but in doing so he gave the Arikaras something they wanted very badly, and that was gunpowder.

To make matters worse, a storm had moved in during the negotiating, which made it impossible for the trappers to continue on their way. In a show of good will and hospitality, Gray Eyes invited the trappers to come into the village to trade for other things they might need, like moccasins—or women.

Arikara women, Hugh knew, were seductively beautiful. Far too many of the trappers went into the village for him to be comfortable.

Hugh stayed in his tent by the beach and listened to the storm. He kept his rifle close to him.

Lt. Governor William H. Ashley was not a man who was used to having his sleep disturbed, especially by a man he had no particular trust or liking for, like Ed Rose.

"All right!" he grumbled. "All right, give me a minute to get my pants on! This better be important! What the devil time is it, anyway?"

"It's about——" Lightning flashed very close to them. Thunder drowned Rose's words.

"It's about three A.M. sir," Rose repeated.

Ashley came out of the tent, pulling his suspenders up over his shoulders.

"This damn well better be important!" he growled.

"It is, sir," Rose said. "Mr. Stephens has been killed."

"Aaron Stephens? How?"

"The Arikaras, they killed him. There were about a dozen of us there, at the village. The others left a few hours ago. Mr. Stephens and I stayed on. Then, a little while ago, a fight broke out over a squaw that Mr. Stephens had been spendin' time with. Three of the Arikaras got him down and gutted him"

"Damn!" Ashley swore. "Are you sure of this? Did you see it yourself?"

"Sure as I'm standin' here, sir. He's dead all right. And there's more. I'm pretty sure they're gettin' ready to attack."

Lightning flashed again. Ashley looked at Ed Rose.

"No," he said after a moment. "They won't attack in the rain."

"Beggin' your pardon General, but—"

"No!" Ashley cut him off. "Listen to me! They won't attack in the rain! There was some excitement. A man was killed and it's unfortunate, but by tomorrow things will have calmed down some. We can't do anything about it tonight. We'll deal with it tomorrow."

"General, I don't think…"

"Damnit Rose, listen to me! I am Lieutenant Governor and General of the militia for the state of Missouri! I didn't get there by flying off half-cocked every time some fool gets himself killed! Now, do as I tell you! Go to bed and get some sleep. We'll straighten this thing out tomorrow!"

Rose straightened, suddenly losing his self-effacing manner. He gave Ashley a look that caused the General to take a step backward. Then he turned and strode off in the direction of his tent.

Ashley watched him go. He didn't like Rose. The man was much too arrogant for a darky—even if he *was* free and lived with the indians. If anything, that fact made Rose even less trustworthy in the General's eyes.

Hugh was dozing. He had stayed in his tent since the day before, rising only to eat or to relieve himself. He knew, as Rose had, that the Arikaras would probably attack if they saw a chance for it and the trappers stayed there long enough. The indians outnumbered the trappers ten to one. Ashley had given them gunpowder. Now they had only to kill the whites—which was what they all wanted to do anyhow—and they would have more. A lot more.

Hugh didn't know about Aaron Stephens. None of the trappers knew. Angered by Ashley's stupidity and by his attitude, Ed Rose had gone straight to his tent, readied his rifle, and went to bed.

An hour later he was up again, moving from tent to tent and warning the trappers that they'd best get ready to defend themselves.

Just before sunup, the Arikaras attacked. Slipping up under the cover of the rain, they fired a sudden, massive burst into the tents on the beach. This was followed by a volley of gunfire and arrows, which seemed to go on for several minutes. The trappers, as ready as they could be under the circumstances, fired back, keeping the Arikaras at bay.

Even though they had known of the impending attack, there was almost no cover to be had on the beach. A number of the trappers were killed in the first barrage.

The trappers were fanned out in a semi-circle, the keelboats and the river behind them. Hugh Glass was on the right flank. Arrows and rifle-balls struck the ground near him. Flattened on the rain-soaked grass, he kept his rifle in position and waited, thankful that none of the missiles had struck him.

After a little while, the firing died down. Now the Arikaras would be moving in closer, saving their ammunition and looking for definite targets to fire at. If they rushed down all at once, the weight of their numbers would be enough to crush the trappers and end the battle in moments. Hugh knew the Arikaras well enough to be certain they wouldn't do that. The art of indian warfare lay in inflicting the greatest amount of injury to your enemy, while incurring the least amount of risk to yourself. The Arikaras would creep down slowly upon them, picking the trappers off as they came.

An arrow suddenly struck the ground next to Hugh's arm, missing him by inches. Hugh rolled to the right, over and over on the grass, before coming once more back into position. A moment later a dark form raised up, twenty yards in front of him. Hugh squeezed the trigger on his Hawken and the form crumpled out of sight.

He reloaded quickly, careful to keep his gunpowder from getting wet. The trappers were in a bad spot. The Arikaras had them pinned down on the beach and were able to pelt them with bullets and arrows from three sides. Hugh knew there were at least eight or ten Arikara warriors for every white man. There was no way the whites could win. Their only chance was to board the boats and escape down river.

He began to edge slowly backward through the wet grass, toward the water's edge, wishing for cover where none existed. Lightning flashed, illuminating bodies of the men around him, both alive and dead. Hugh recognized the faces of two of the men, James Clyman and John Gardener. Like Hugh, they were moving backward toward the water, firing whenever a target appeared and reloading as they went.

Hugh knew well the indians methods of attack. They seemed to be everywhere—and nowhere. They appeared like ghosts, then disappeared. The trappers rarely knew if they had hit one of the Arikaras or not.

Amazed that he was still unscathed, Hugh continued moving back. Suddenly Four Arikara warriors rose, not more than thirty feet away. Wielding tomahawks and lances, the indians rushed the three white men. There was a quick volley of rifle shots. Three of the indians fell. The fourth came on, swinging his tomahawk at John Gardener's head. Gardener rolled to one side and the blow missed.

The Arikara struck again. This time Gardener managed to block the tomahawk with his rifle stock. Then the indian was on top of him.

The two men fought, rolling together on the grass for several feet before the indian emerged on top again. The Arikara drew back to strike, then stiffened suddenly. The tomahawk slipped from his grasp. Then he slumped, lifeless, over John Gardener. Gardener pushed the indian away. There was a tomahawk buried between the Arikara's shoulder blades, thrown from twenty feet away by Hugh Glass.

Gardener kicked the indian away from him, then quickly retrieved and reloaded his rifle. When he was done he pulled the tomahawk from the dead indian and crawled to where Glass lay waiting and watching for another target to appear.

"Thanks!" Gardener told him over the storm.

Keeping his eyes ahead of him, Hugh said, "You're welcome." Then, looking around at the two men near him, he said, "Listen, we can't stay here! There are too many of them to fight. Our only chance is to get to the boats!" He looked around as he spoke, toward where the keelboats were tied.

The boats were gone.

General William Henry Ashley was not a man accustomed to having his commands ignored.

"What do you mean....*NO!*" he boomed over the storm. "You men get on your poles and move us back upstream! *I mean NOW!*"

The keelboatmen fidgeted, but made no effort to move the boat.

"As Lieutenant Governor of the State of Missouri and General of the Missouri militia, I'm *ordering* you men to get us back there—!"

"We ain't in Missouri, General," one of the men said, cutting Ashley off.

"I don't care *where* we are! Those men on the beach are trapped! They're depending on us!" Ashley pulled his pistol from his belt, cocked it, and aimed it at the lead boatman.

"You!" he shouted. "Get your men in line *NOW* and get us moving back upstream or, by God, I'll shoot you dead on the spot! So help me, I will!"

The man looked upstream, then back at Ashley.

"Well General," he said calmly, "I reckon I'd just as soon be killed by you as by the Arikaras." He looked around at the other men. "I reckon we all would."

Ashley was beside himself. His arm shook, not from the cold or from the weight of the pistol, but from frustration and anger. He *should* shoot the man.

"General, listen," the leadman said. "It's no good. If we go pushin' this boat back upstream now we'll be the easiest targets the Arikaras could ask for. You cain't push a boat pole with one hand an' shoot with the other, and you cain't do it any other way than standin' up. We won't do those men any good if we go an' git ourselves kilt!"

Ashley continued to point the pistol at the man for several seconds. Finally, he let the pistol drop to his side. He looked down at the deck of the keelboat. Water ran off his hat and onto the deck. He looked like a beaten man.

Why didn't I listen to Rose, he thought. *Why?*

After a moment, he straightened.

"All right," he said. "You win. But this is how it's going to be! We will hold this spot on the river! We're pretty much out of range here, and it will be light soon. The men on the beach will see us and swim for it. We *will* catch them as they go past! And I swear to you—any man who fails to do this because of cowardice will be left here for the indians to butcher!"

"Fair enough, General," the lead man said.

Dawn was only moments away. Neither Hugh Glass, nor any of the other men who were pinned down on the beach wanted to be there when it got light. The river, on the other hand, had risen considerably after two days of rain. Any man who was not a strong swimmer would almost certainly be lost if he tried to swim for it.

Then Glass saw the boats.

They were about three hundred yards downstream, out of the Arikara's line of sight, waiting. They had anchored. Some of the river men had their poles buried in the river bottom at steep angles to help keep the boats steady in the raging current. They were waiting for the men on the beach.

"Pass the word!" he yelled to the others. "The boats are waiting for us on the river! We have to swim for it!"

One by one, the trappers turned to see that what Hugh said was true. Several of them immediately began moving toward the water's edge.

"Come on boys!" Hugh said to Clyman and John Gardener. "It's time we were movin' out!"

He began edging toward the water, Clyman ahead of him. Gardener brought up the rear. Around them bullets whistled. Arrows struck the earth. The arrows were actually more frightening to Hugh than the rifle shots, for even a small wound from an arrow could cause infection, which would almost certainly lead to death.

When they were only a few yards from the water, John Gardener suddenly cried out.

"I'm hit! Oh Lordy, please! Somebody help me! I've been shot!"

Glass looked at Clyman. The two men nodded at each other and began moving slowly back up the beach toward the injured man. Hugh was the first to reach him.

"Mr. Glass!" Gardener said, teeth chattering as shock began to set in, "Oh, thank you for coming back for me!"

"It's all right, Johnnie." Hugh tried to soothe him. "We're going to get you out of here. Just relax." Gardener had been hit in the side. It was hard to tell how bad the wound was, but it didn't look good.

"You're going to have to hold that closed with your hand, Johnnie," Hugh said, indicating the wound. "We don't have anything to put on it. James and I will get you out of here."

Taking Gardener by the collar, Hugh began dragging him toward the water. Clyman, pulling Gardener by the arm, helped him.

"TA'-KA KUR'-UKS!" *WHITE BEAR!*

Hugh's head came up sharply at the sound of his Pawnee name. Kills-The-Whites and Little Soldier were standing, less than one hundred feet away. They were taking aim, even as he looked at them. Hugh and James Clyman brought their rifles up. Four rifles seemed to explode at once. Kills-The-Whites crumpled as two balls hit him at once. Little Soldier dove aside and disappeared. Hugh felt something strike his leg hard. He felt, as well as heard, another ball strike John Gardener. Clyman was unscathed.

Hugh looked at John Gardener. The young man's eyes were wide with fear.

"Mr. Glass!" Gardener gasped. "I'm hit again! I-I think they've done for me this time..."

"Just hold on, Johnnie," Hugh told him. "We'll get you out of here." Once more they began pulling the young man toward the water.

Some of the rivermen, shamed by Ashley's words, managed to bring a skiff up from one of the keelboats, and were collecting wounded men to take back to the boats. The two men managed to drag Gardener over to it and get him inside.

"Mr. Glass—don't leave me, please!" There was panic and desperation in Gardener's voice. He clutched at Hugh's jacket. "Don't go."

"You been shot in the leg, Mister," the boatman broke in. "We got room for one more. Whyn't you climb on in?"

Putting his rifle in ahead of him, Hugh did as the man said. Turning back, Clyman took refuge behind a log and began firing at the indians. The skiff left the shore. Halfway to the keelboats, Gardener spoke again.

"They say..." his voice had grown weak. "They say that you can read an' write, Mr. Glass. Is it true?"

"Yes, Johnnie," Hugh told him. "I can read and write."

Gardener fumbled in his heavy coat, removing a small, waterproof packet. He gave it to Hugh.

"In here…my Papa's address." Each word seemed to take more effort than the last. "Write to him…promise me…you'll tell my Daddy…"

"I promise, Johnnie," Hugh told him. Gardener nodded once and passed out. A moment later, the skiff struck the waiting keelboat with a heavy thud. Hugh grunted in pain when it did. The initial shock of his bullet wound had worn off and agony had set in. He felt the impact of the two boats coming together all the way up his leg and into the middle of his back.

As they were being loaded up onto the deck of the keelboat, the last of the trappers finally left the beach, tumbling into the water under a hailstone of arrows and gunshots. Among these was James Clyman. Clyman swam out far enough to let the current take him, realizing too late how fast the river was actually running. Keeping his feet out in front of him, he hit the end of the keelboat hard, then bounced around the side. Desperately, he tried grabbing one boat pole after another as he rode past, missing every time. The boatmen, likewise, were unable to catch hold of him. Then, just as he reached the stern of the boat and was about to be swept away in the current, a man named Reed Gibson caught a handful of Clyman's hair and pulled him up on board.

No sooner was Clyman safely on board than a shot came from the riverbank. Reed Gibson fell to the deck of the keelboat, shot through the heart.

As soon as the last of the trappers was aboard, the boatmen lifted their poles and allowed the current to take them downstream, moving at an alarming rate. They traveled for more than an hour before getting into shore again and making camp— a good twenty-five miles from the Arikara village.

Halfway there, Glass checked on young John Gardener. The boy had died.

HENRY and ASHLEY'S

June 7, 1823

Dear Sir:

My painfull duty is to tell you of the deth
of yr son wh befell at the hands of the indians 2nd
June in the early morning. He lived a little while
after he was shot and asked me to inform you of his
sad fate. We brought him to the ship where he soon
died. Mr. Smith a young man of our company made a
powerful prayer wh moved us all greatly and I am
persuaded John died in peace. His body we buried
with others near this camp and marked the grave
with a log. His things we will send to you. The
savages are greatly treacherous. We traded with
them as friends but after a great storm of rain and
thunder they came at us before light and many
were hurt. I myself was hit in the leg. Master Ashley
is bound to stay in these parts till the traitors are
rightly punished.

Yr. Obdt. Svt.

Hugh Glass

Author's Note: This letter to John S. Gardener's Father, discovered by John G. Neihardt, is the only item from Hugh Glass that has survived to the present day.

CHAPTER THIRTY-TWO

WITH SOME help from herbs that Yellow Fox had taught him to use when he was with the Pawnees, and a good deal of rest, Hugh's leg was mending quickly. He still winced sometimes when he put weight on it, but it seemed to be getting better every day. Fortunately, it had been a clean shot, through the meaty portion of his leg. No bones or major blood vessels had been hit by it.

After the Arikara attack, most of those who had hired on as trappers quit and headed back to St. Louis. Only thirty out of the original one-hundred stayed on. They were camped twenty-five miles south of the Arikara village. It was here that John Gardener had been laid to rest, and Jedidiah Smith had prayed powerfully over him. Afterward, Ashley had sent Smith overland to Fort Henry, asking for every available man to be sent back to help finish out the trip. He also sent a report to Major Benjamin O'Fallon, the U.S. Indian Agent at Fort Atkinson. Ashley wanted help from the Army, and he was a man who knew how to get what he wanted.

In the meantime, there was nothing to be done, except to wait.

Colonel Henry Leavenworth sat in his office at Fort Atkinson, reviewing the reports that lay before him, reports that were all bad:

—The Immel and Jones party, of the Missouri Fur Company, attacked by
Blackfeet.
Seven men dead, including Micheal E. Immel and Robert Jones.
—Major Andrew Henry, of the Rocky Mountain Fur Company, also attacked

by Blackfeet. Four men dead.

—General William H. Ashley, also of the Rocky Mountain Fur Company, attacked by the Arikaras. Fifteen men dead, and a dozen more wounded.

Things were getting out of hand. Leavenworth could see that. He could also see something else—an opportunity. He was an ambitious man, Leavenworth was. He had risen through the ranks quickly, building a name for himself. During the war of 1812, he had developed a reputation for recklessness, daring, and quick, decisive action in the face of the enemy. He had risen to the rank of Colonel...

But the war of 1812 had ended several years earlier, and little had happened for Leavenworth since. It galled him that he was still only a Colonel. He should have made General by now. And he should be in Washington, not stuck here in the middle of nowhere.

He looked at the reports again.

Here was opportunity. It was more than that, though. The indians needed to be taught a lesson, to make it safe for the whites once more. General William H. Ashley was a powerful man, well-connected. If Leavenworth acted quickly on this, it would go a long way toward getting his name back into the limelight again. Opportunities like this didn't come along any too often. Not in a peacetime Army.

With Leavenworth's superior, General Atkinson, out of reach in Louisville, Leavenworth decided to go it alone. On June 18, 1823 he gave orders for six companies of his regiment to ready themselves for a trip upriver, to teach the Arikaras that they couldn't attack whites and go unpunished. The Colonel himself would lead the expedition. He would strike quickly and hard, and would show them once and for all that whites were not to be trifled with.

The expedition began on June 22nd. It consisted of six companies of men, which added up to two-hundred forty soldiers. These were joined by one-hundred men from the Missouri Fur Company, led by Joshua Pilcher. General Ashley and his men waited for them upriver. Before they left, Joshua Pilcher sent word to his friends, the Sioux. The party was joined by four-hundred Sioux warriors. The Sioux were ancient enemies of the Arikaras. If the Arikaras were to be obliterated by the awesome power of the whites, the Sioux nation would be there to witness it.

They headed upriver in several keelboats, with the indians and some of the trappers following along on horseback at the river's edge. It would be a long, slow trip, ultimately marred by mishap.

Hugh Glass had begun to spend more and more time away from the other men, on his own. During the day, while they waited for the Army to join them, he scouted and hunted, bringing back to the camp whatever game he killed. He took his evening meals with the others, then went off to make his own camp some distance away. He did this for a number of reasons. His years at sea had taught him that the old adage was true—familiarity really could breed contempt. He also felt safer in a camp of his own choosing. At night the trappers drank whiskey and became loud.

Glass had no objection to the drinking, only to the effect it had on some of those who drank.

The trappers thought him odd and stand-offish. Hugh didn't care about that. Men were entitled to their opinions. If a fight developed and they needed him, he would be there.

They had lost all the horses back to the Arikaras. Whenever Hugh shot anything, he was forced to construct a litter and drag it back to the camp, which limited him to smaller game. The first time he did this, he was almost too far from camp. With his injured leg slowing him down, he barely made it back before nightfall. Thereafter, he kept a shorter radius on his daily trips, then worked in a circle to keep from straying too far. As wood was relatively scarce here, he also carried his litter with him whenever he went out.

One afternoon, after managing to kill two small antelope, he returned to camp and noticed that the ranks of the trappers had swelled considerably. When he spotted Jedidiah Smith he knew the men had arrived from Fort Henry. Before too many days had passed, the Army would be there as well.

He gave the meat to the camp cook and headed off to wash himself and rest his leg, which had begun to throb an hour earlier. It had been nearly a month since he had been shot. He was certain that using the leg was the best thing for it, but still it bothered him.

He was moving toward the river when two men intercepted him.

"You must be Hugh Glass." The man who addressed him was the older of the two. He was about Hugh's age, tall and slim, with clear, blue eyes and an air of sureness about himself that spoke of authority. The other man was much younger. He was taller than Hugh was, with a strong build and bright red hair. But for his height and mature frame, he could have been sixteen.

"I am," Hugh told the man.

"I'm Major Andrew Henry," the man said, putting out his hand. "And this young fella is James Bridger."

Hugh shook hands with both men. There was a solidness about the two of them that he immediately liked—Bridger, especially. There was a maturity in the young man's eyes that was at odds with his youthful appearance. Hugh took note not to underestimate him because of his years.

"Pleased to meet you, Major," Hugh said, then added, "...Mr. Bridger."

"The cook tells me you brought us some antelope," Major Henry said.

Hugh nodded.

"Well, we appreciate it. They also tell me you used to live with the indians."

"That's correct."

"What tribe?"

"Pawnees," Hugh told him.

"How long were you with them?"

"Almost four years."

"And before that?"

Hugh looked at the ground.

"I was a mariner," he said.

"What ship—"

"Excuse me Major," Hugh interrupted him, "but can we continue this interrogation over by the river? I was shot in the leg last month when the Arikaras attacked. I've been *on* that leg all day today, and it hurts like hell. I'd like to sit down."

"Yes, of course," Henry said, suddenly embarrassed. "Please forgive my manners."

Hugh turned and started away.

"Just one more thing," Henry stopped him.

"Yes?" Hugh breathed with disgust.

"James Clyman says that, during the attack, a couple of the Arikaras seemed to recognize you?"

"They recognized me, Major." Hugh told him. Then he turned again and walked away, trying not to limp.

Henry watched him go, saying nothing more. A single thought leapt into his mind about Hugh Glass.

What's he hiding?

A short while later, Hugh was sitting by the water, massaging his injured leg and thinking about his conversation with Major Henry.

That was almost too close, he thought. Henry had been on the verge of asking him what ship he had served on. If Hugh told him it had been the *Gallant* and the Major checked on it, questions would be raised. *The Gallant* had gone down six years ago, with all hands, and that was the way Hugh Glass wanted it to remain.

Even if he had given Henry the name of a different ship, trouble could follow. He had been fairly well known, six years ago, and had enjoyed a good reputation in the shipping trade. There might still be those in the industry that would remember that Hugh Glass had served on a ship that never returned to port.

Henry wasn't through with his questions, Hugh was certain of that. Hugh had cut him short, but the man would be back. Hugh had to decide, before that time, just what he would say.

He thought about the Major and what kind of man he was—things Hugh had heard and his own impressions of the man—and immediately made his decision.

If and when Major Andrew Henry again asked him about his past, Hugh would tell him the truth.

The Arikaras, almost more than any other tribe, were known by a variety of names, all given to them by the whites. Walking through the camp, Hugh Glass was surprised by the number of ways the men referred to them: Picareens, Rikaras, Picarees, Rikarees, or just Rees—they all meant Arikara. As the days and weeks passed and word came back that the U.S. Army was on their way, enthusiasm was high. The Arikaras were going to be taught a real lesson, and word of that lesson would travel to all the tribes, making it safe for white men to travel in the wilderness once more.

On August sixth, Leavenworth finally arrived. With him were two-hundred-forty U.S. Regulars, eighty men from Joshua Pilcher's Missouri Fur Company, and the Sioux, whose numbers had swelled to around one-thousand.

The expedition almost didn't make it. Shortly after leaving Fort Atkinson one of the boat commanders, Lt William Wickliffe, unhappy with the slow progress they were making, went looking for more wind. He found it, and promptly crashed into a sunken tree. The keelboat split in two and sank. About fifty rifles and seven men were lost. Concluding his report on the matter, Leavenworth wrote that, "most of the flour and all of the whiskey was saved."

Less than a week later a second craft, the *Yellowstone Packet*, also capsized. Again, a considerable amount of ordinance was lost, but most of the flour and all of the whiskey were retrieved.

At least the Army knew their priorities.

What was vitally important about the second mishap were two things: First, the hull of the *Yellowstone Packet* remained sound, so the craft could be righted and continue upriver. Second—and more important—was the fact that one barrel of gunpowder had also been retrieved. Without this, their cannons would have been useless. Leavenworth would have turned the expedition around and gone back to Fort Atkinson.

With so many Sioux warriors around, Hugh was careful to keep anything that would have linked him with the Pawnees out of sight, knowing that those two tribes had been bitter enemies even longer than the Sioux had been at war with the Arikaras.

On August ninth the expedition, now joined by the Rocky Mountain Fur trappers, arrived at the Arikara village, led by Colonel Leavenworth and his Regulars. Morale was high among both the whites and the Sioux. Both groups looked forward to a quick and absolute victory, possibly followed by the complete obliteration of the Arikara village. Such an action would send a message to all the tribes and let them know what they could expect if they decided to move against the whites.

Not one among them could have predicted what would really happen.

CHAPTER THIRTY-THREE

COLONEL HENRY LEAVENWORTH had never spent time around indians before. He had seen them, even worked with them to a limited degree during the War of 1812, but those were indians whose long contact with the whites had tamed them. They were nothing like the proud, fierce warriors that rode alongside him now. Warriors whose numbers outweighed his own troops by four to one.

Those numbers worked on Leavenworth, worried him. After all, he was responsible for this expedition, as well as for the men who made it up. What would happen, he wondered, if their supposed allies, the Sioux, decided to turn on the white men? Even with the addition of the two companies of trappers, the Sioux had them outnumbered more than two to one. Not good odds.

As they grew closer to the Arikara village, another possibility occurred to him—one that anyone truly acquainted with these two tribes would have laughed at. What if the Sioux and the Arikaras decided to join forces against them? The whites wouldn't stand a chance. The two tribes were said to be ancient, bitter enemies, but who could say for sure with indians. As military commander, Leavenworth had to be aware of every possibility. The closer they got to the Arikaras, the more this possibility occurred to him.

Leavenworth was also aware that he had taken action without waiting for authorization. It had been a bold move, the kind of thing that gained him a reputation in the War of 1812. In those days, his decisions had been followed by quick action that had always worked out well for him, and he never had much time to think about consequences.

134

This time it was different. He'd had a month of hard travel—and plenty of time to look for holes in his scheme. What had started out as a grand, bold plan began to seem foolhardy to him. If the indians turned on them, the whites would all be destroyed. Even if he, miraculously, escaped unharmed, his career would be ruined, for he had acted without orders.

He would have to be careful here. Very careful.

When they arrived at the Arikara village, the Sioux were in the lead. Seeing them, the Arikaras immediately rushed out of their town to do battle. The Sioux were more than anxious to engage them. A fight ensued, which went on until the U.S. Army appeared on the horizon. Seeing this, the Arikaras beat a hasty retreat back to the shelter of their town, leaving thirteen of their own dead upon the plain. Only two Sioux warriors had been slain.

Instantly, the Sioux began dismembering their dead enemies, cutting off the arms and legs of the Arikaras, dragging the entrails over the plains. They tied thongs about the various body parts. These they also dragged around, cat-calling to the enraged Arikaras, who watched from their village walls. One Sioux warrior, donning a bear robe, crawled from corpse to corpse, growling and tearing chunks from each one with his teeth.

Far from allaying Leavenworth's fears, this spectacle heightened them. Watching the Sioux, he felt sickened by what he saw. After all, if they would do this to their own kind, what would they do to the whites?

Hugh Glass knew that the indians west of the Missouri had seen very little of the American military, but they had heard a great deal. He, himself, had perpetuated stories of the Great White Father's might, while he was among the Pawnees. This exaggerated myth was what kept many tribes on friendly terms...and kept many a white man alive.

Having finished mutilating the bodies of the slain Arikaras, the Sioux now pulled back and waited for the U.S. Army to show their power. From all they had heard, they expected nothing less than total destruction to descend upon the Arikaras. Thunder and lightning, earthquake or tornado—none of this would have surprised them.

The Arikaras actually had two separate villages. Both were walled, as Pawnee villages were, and consisted of earth-dome lodges. The villages were bordered on one side by the river—where the attack on Ashley's party had taken place. Leavenworth had the Sixth Army stretch out in a thin line, which began on one side at the river and nearly surrounded the villages. The line was completed by Ashley and his men, who stretched the line around to the river on the opposite side of the village. Joshua Pilcher's men, along with the one-thousand Sioux warriors, waited in the rear. The Army set their cannons up on the low, rolling hills that faced the villages, and everyone waited.

Nothing happened.

Finally, one of the cannons barked, but instead of blasting away the palisade that surrounded the village, the artillerist merely lobbed a ball over the top, where it struck one of the earthen dome lodges and did some minor damage, certainly nothing that would impress any of the indians.

After the first cannon shot, a second gun spoke. They then began a general firing which continued for a short while but was, for the most part, ineffective. The Arikaras withdrew into their earthen homes, which the missiles had little effect on. Not once were the cannons directed at the palisade, which would have opened the village and allowed the whites and their allies, the Sioux, to attack.

The remainder of the day was spent in what Leavenworth, in his report, would refer to as "brisk marches, clever shifts in position," and, "daring advances down the throat of opposition".

The great, decisive battle that they had all come to take part in never occurred. The following morning a delegation of Arikaras, led by Little Soldier, came out to talk. Little Soldier told them the surprising news that, of the few deaths that had actually been caused by the shelling, one had been their chief, Gray Eyes. Apparently, Gray Eyes had stuck his head up over the palisade at the wrong time, and had lost it to a cannonball.

After describing this to the whites, Little Soldier then told them that the Arikaras wanted an armistice. This was fine with Leavenworth, who had mysteriously lost his taste for battle. Leavenworth conducted the negotiations himself, even though he legally had no authority to do so. Major Andrew Henry and Joshua Pilcher, both agents for the Bureau of Indian Affairs, refused to take part.

Even this Leavenworth botched. Sensing fear on the part of his adversary, Little Soldier began to dictate the terms of the treaty.

The peace talks, which took place on August eleventh and twelfth, were not without incident. Of all the whites, only Leavenworth seemed unaware of the mess he was creating. Joshua Pilcher was furious with him. Pilcher had spent enough time in that part of the country to understand the way that the various tribes thought and felt. The *only* thing that had made it safe for white men to travel in that area, up until now, was the total awe with which the indians held the white man's army. Leavenworth, in one blundering move, was destroying that awe, turning it into something laughable.

Indians, Pilcher knew, loved a good joke. *Especially* if they could turn it around.

At one point in the proceedings, Pilcher alerted the Army Surgeon, Major John Gale, to the very real possibility that the Arikaras might attempt to capture Leavenworth and hold him for ransom. After the capsizing of the *Yellowstone Packet*, Major Gale had been responsible for retrieving the one barrel of gunpowder, which had allowed the expedition to continue upriver. The Major responded to Pilcher's warning by firing his pistol into the group of Arikaras. Pilcher and one other man joined him, also firing toward them. The Arikaras responded by firing back. Pilcher was wounded, although only slightly. It was enough to put an end to the peace talks for that day.

In the end, for the murders of fifteen whites, the Arikaras agreed to pay General Ashley three rifles, one horse, and sixteen buffalo robes. Disgusted, the Sioux left without a word, stealing seven of Ashley's horses and a half-dozen Army mules.

Aware that there was still some unsettled wrath on the part of the whites, but not aware that the Sioux had left, the Arikaras left their villages in the middle of the night. On the morning of August 13, the whites awoke to find the villages abandoned.

Hugh Glass was awed and amazed at this. How, he wondered, could several thousand men, women, children, dogs, and horses sneak away from an armed siege, without being detected? It raised his appreciation of the Arikaras considerably.

The following day, Leavenworth sent his interpreter, Toussaint Charbonnau, with a message for the Arikaras, telling them all was well and asking them to come back. Twenty years earlier, Charbonnau and his Shoshoni wife, Sacajawea, had led Louis and Clark on their famous journey across America. He knew the land and he knew the indians, and they knew him.

Charbonnau was no fool. He chased the Arikaras but never caught them.

On the morning of August 15, Leavenworth declared the Arikara siege ended. The Army packed up their things, and headed back toward Fort Atkinson, leaving the late chief Gray Eyes' aged mother, who had been left behind by the Arikaras, in charge of the village.

Before the Army was out of sight, two of Joshua Pilcher's men, Angus McDonald and William Gordon, burned the villages.

CHAPTER THIRTY-FOUR

WITH THE Army gone and the near-comical siege at an end, it was time for the trappers to get back to their work. Joshua Pilcher and the men of the Missouri Fur Company went their way, as did the Rocky Mountain Fur Traders. The Ashley-Henry group traveled enmasse as far as the Grand River. Then Ashley took the bulk of the men and headed south. Moving west along the Grand, Henry headed overland toward Fort Henry, at the mouth of the Yellowstone. Since the mishandling of the Arikaras, the upper Missouri would not be safe to travel.

With Henry were Hugh Glass, Jim Bridger, and eleven others. Henry would have preferred to have more men with him. Most of those who traveled south with Ashley did so because they had decided to find easier and safer ways of making a living.

Due to the shortage of mounts, Henry's party were forced to use their horses as pack animals. This made going slow. The men were lucky to manage twenty miles a day. At night they made their camp close to the river. As was his habit, Hugh made his own camp, some distance away from the others.

Andrew Henry tried to persuade Hugh to stay with the other members of the group, but Hugh flatly refused. Following the directions of others had brought him nothing but grief. He would work with the others and be there when they needed him. Other than that, he would keep his own counsel and make his own camp, and would accept whatever consequences that brought to him.

And he always kept the Hawken loaded, and close at hand.

Jim Bridger came awake suddenly. He did not move, but lay fully alert, listening to the darkness. Something wasn't right.

Slowly, he eased his hand out from under the blanket, to where his rifle lay. With painstaking slowness, he pulled the hammer back until it cocked. Someone, or some *thing* was moving around in the darkness just outside the camp.

Probably coyotes, he thought. Whatever it was, it was causing Jim's inner alarm to sound, sending him into a near-paralyzing panic.

Moments passed. Jim lay, listening to the night, not moving, eyes wide open and searching the area in front of him. He wanted nothing more than to raise himself up and look around, but he knew that if someone *were* out there, that might be a deadly mistake.

He never saw them appear, but he was suddenly aware of six silhouettes standing silently at the edge of the camp—human silhouettes.

Without thinking, and without rising, he brought the rifle up in one hand and fired.

Hugh Glass awoke to the sound of gunshots. Rolling out from under his blanket, he set out at a run in the direction of Henry's camp, carrying the Hawken and ready to fire at any enemy that rose out of the darkness before him.

No enemy appeared, and by the time Hugh reached the camp the excitement was over. Two men—James Anderson and Augie Neill—were dead. Two others were wounded. Indians had attacked in the dead of night. They had struck quickly, then fled at the first resistance from the whites.

Henry's men had fired only two shots, but it left one dead indian.

"Damn Leavenworth!" Henry swore. "*Damn him!* This is a direct result of his monumental incompetence! He let the Arikaras go, and now two more men are dead! Damn him to Hell!"

The rising of the sun showed the situation to be even worse than Major Andrew Henry had thought. The dead indian was not Arikara after all, but Mandan. Of all the tribes, the Mandans were the friendliest toward the whites. In fact, there was no record of the Mandans *ever* attacking white men.

Until now.

If the Mandans were attacking the whites, it could mean only one thing—that word of Leavenworth's incredibly inept handling of the Arikara siege had gotten around to all the tribes. As far as every indian west of the Missouri River would be concerned, it was open season on white men.

As the small group of men moved out, no one spoke. Each of them knew how grave the situation had become. Each man kept his weapons loaded and ready.

For the next two days the party moved silently along the river, winding their way northward in an effort to get back to Fort Henry without further incident. The men, for the most part, were nervous to the point of being edgy. After all, if a peace-loving tribe like the Mandans were attacking, what might the more warlike tribes—the Cheyenne, the Sioux, the Pawnees, or the Arikaras—do if they were encountered? Those tribes were ready to fight under the best of circumstances, and any of them were likely to cross paths with the trappers at any time.

Only two men seemed to be immune to the hysteria that was brewing in the other men. One was a man called Black Harris. The other was Hugh Glass.

Hugh didn't feel that this was bravery on his part. There had been too many instances in his life when he had known he was about to die—and hadn't. Although he knew that one day it actually would happen, he found it hard to take his own death too seriously.

On the third morning after the attack by the Mandans, Hugh woke up feeling uncomfortable and out of sorts. He had slept wrong, and he'd had some unsettling dreams about Little Feather. He couldn't remember the dreams, only that she had been in them. It left him in a somber mood.

He reached the camp in time for coffee and a biscuit. While he was eating, young Jim Bridger approached him. Hugh liked Bridger. The young man talked very little, but he handled himself better than most men who were ten years older. What Hugh really wanted right now, though, was to be left alone.

"Mr. Glass...?" Bridger said tentatively.

"Mornin' Jim," Hugh said. "What can I do for you?"

Bridger looked around awkwardly. He wanted something from Hugh, but he hated to ask.

"Mr. Glass, is it true you know how to read sign, the way the indians do?"

"Yes," Hugh told him. "I can read sign."

"Well...I was wonderin'... Could you, maybe, teach me? I-I can pay. I'll pay you. I don't expect nothin' for free."

Hugh immediately thought of Big Axe. His mood softened somewhat. He smiled.

"You don't have to pay me," he said. "I'll be happy to teach you, as soon as we get to Fort Henry."

"Is there some...some secret to it? I mean, I can tell what tracks are, when I can see 'em. Trouble is, they always disappear."

Hugh scratched the back of his neck. Looking up at Bridger, he said, "Yeah, there is a secret. You have to learn to soften your eyes."

Bridger looked puzzled. It made him look even younger than he was. It made Hugh think of his own sons, whom he had not seen in more than six years and who, he knew, he would almost certainly never see again.

Hugh threw the dregs of his coffee into the fire.

"Come on," he told the younger man. "We have a few minutes. I can show you enough to get you started."

He led Bridger over to a spot just past the edge of the camp, to a stand of cotton-woods. Casting about for only a moment, Hugh pointed at a pile of leaves.

"What do you see there?" he asked Jim.

"Leaves," Jim said. "Just leaves."

Getting down on one knee, Hugh looked at the pile.

"I see three different sets of tracks," he told Jim. "Over here—" He pointed to a spot just to his left. "—you can see where a fox followed a rabbit, probably yesterday. He wasn't chasing the rabbit yet, just following. Then, over here on the right, you can see where a prairie chicken walked through, scratching around, lookin' for *his* dinner."

"But how…?"

"You have to teach yourself to focus on the outside edges of your vision—it's called peripheral vision, like seeing something out of the corner of your eye. When you do that the vision in the middle, which you normally use to look at things, softens. That allows you to see the things that aren't obvious. Takes practice. Indians learn to do it when they're young, which is why they're so good at it."

Jim Bridger, Hugh could tell, wasn't sure whether to believe him or not.

"Just practice it whenever you get the chance and it'll happen. When it does, it'll seem so obvious you'll wonder how you never saw the tracks before."

"That," he added, "I can promise."

As he had tried to do in the past, Henry insisted that Hugh remain with the others in the party.

"Especially now," Henry told him, "with the danger of attack from every known tribe imminent, we have to stay together." He wanted a tight, compact group, with no strays or stragglers.

"I'm sorry, Major," Hugh told him. "Can't do it. Don't worry—I'll stay within earshot. If anything happens, I'll come running."

"And what if something happens to you?" Major Henry shot back.

"I'll take my chances."

Disgusted, Henry moved off.

Hugh was not about to change his mind. Too many times in the past, he had trusted his welfare to others. Too many times, that had almost proved to be his undoing. After spending nearly four years with the Pawnees, he found the movements of the whites to be clumsy and loud. Their lack of harmony in the wilderness spread out from them in all directions, like the ripples that were created when you threw a stone into a pond. The unnatural movements of birds and animals would telegraph the coming of the white men for anyone with eyes to see, just as the movements of the grass told of the coming of the wind. If anyone was in danger of detection here, it was they, and not Hugh Glass.

Besides that, he needed to be by himself today. His dreams had gotten him thinking about Little Feather again, and he wanted to be alone with her in his thoughts.

And that's exactly where he was when the grizzly attacked.

It was late in the day. Hugh was about two hundred yards to the left of the group, between them and the river. Several times during the day, he had walked over to within sight of them, although they were never aware that he was there. Almost automatically, he stayed parallel to their position. In his mind, though, he was a thousand miles away, thinking of Little Feather. She had been the one bright spot in the last six, miserable years. Being with her had been the only time in his life that he could remember being really, truly happy. Now she was gone.

He spotted a large clump of berry bushes and decided to pick some. It would make a nice change from the constant diet of fresh meat, and bringing some back to the others might go a long way in softening Henry's attitude toward him.

The wind was against him. Hugh's first indication that he wasn't alone was an all-too-familiar cough. And when she stood up, the grizzly was only ten feet away.

It wasn't the largest grizzly he had ever seen—only about seven feet tall—but it was a female. She-grizzlies were far worse to encounter than the males, especially if they had cubs. This one had cubs.

Raising the Hawken, Hugh fired at her at point-blank range. The bullet seemed to have no effect. In a moment she was upon him.

Hugh knew that a grizzly was capable of breaking the neck of a small horse with one good swipe of its paw. At first he tried to get in close so that she couldn't use those paws. He managed to get his knife out and began stabbing at her, desperately hoping that the bullet and knife wounds would take effect. He could feel the weight of the bear as it raked his back again and again with three-inch claws, tearing away his shirt and destroying the flesh underneath. He felt it's hot breath as it's teeth bit deep into his skull. Screaming in pain, he raised his left arm to try to protect himself, while continuing to stab at it with the knife in his right. The bear seemed not to notice, but began biting at Hugh's left arm while it continued to rend his back with it's claws.

Pulling away in agony, Hugh tried to run for a nearby tree. He was nearly blind from his own blood running into his eyes. He made it to the tree, but found that his left arm was now nearly useless to him. Dropping the knife, he attempted to pull himself up, using only his right hand.

Too slow. The bear, taking Hugh by the right leg, pulled him out of the tree. With Hugh's leg still in it's mouth, the bear began to shake it's head angrily from side to side. Hugh heard and felt the leg snap. An intolerable wave of agony roared through him.

That was all he knew.....

CHAPTER THIRTY-FIVE

IT SEEMED he was back with the Pawnees again . He was being pulled along on a travois. Something had happened...he was in incredible pain. Every part of him cried out in agony.

The trappers were there too...where was Little Feather?

The pain...oh God, it hurt! Why didn't they do something to stop it? Why didn't they just shoot him? What had happened?

He remembered. The bear... Had he died? Was this what it was like to be in Hell?

He tried to move, but couldn't. It was as though he had a body, but it only existed in order to bring him unendurable agony.

Mercifully, he passed out again.

Through lapses in consciousness, he was aware of the passage of time. Pain followed him everywhere, even into his dreams. Awake or asleep, his awareness only lasted for a short while. The blackness would take over and the pain would go away for awhile...only to return again later.

After awhile, the movement stopped, but the pain continued. It was daytime, but they weren't moving.

Two men were there. Once in a while one of them would check on him. He couldn't remember their names.

Hastings...one of them was Clint Hastings. Clint!

No. Not Clint, Bridger. Jim Bridger. Young Fella. Capable. It made Hugh glad to know he was there. Bridger would take care of him.

God, it hurt!

The name of the other man finally came to him. Fitzgerald. John Fitzgerald. Hugh didn't really know him. This didn't make any sense. He *knew* why Bridger was there—Hugh had promised to teach him to track. Why was Fitzgerald here? Where were the others?

He felt as though he were on fire. It hurt to breathe. *Everything* hurt. He tried calling to Clint, tried to warn him. He tried to apologize to Clint for letting the Pawnees kill him.

"I tried," he cried out. "I really tried!"

It hurt to talk. Anyway, he was wrong. It wasn't Clint. It was Bridger.

Sometimes he would wake up and lay there, listening, waiting for the blackness to come and take him back to where it didn't hurt.

Bridger didn't talk much. Fitzgerald did. Fitzgerald was worried about the indians coming. Christ, let them come! They would kill him and put an end to this agony!

How long it continued like this, he had no idea. Time could not be measured by hours or minutes, not even in light or dark. Half the time he was out of his head. The rest of the time he was unconcious.

Later, much later, he would remember snatches of conversations:

"What's taking so long—why doesn't he die?"

"He can't last much longer…"

"The indians, they're gettin' closer…"

"I tell you, kid, I keep seein' signs…"

"Why doesn't he die?"

"I tell you…we're not gonna do him any good if we *all* get killed—"

"We *can't* leave him!"

"What's taking so long?"

"Damnit! He's gonna get us killed, too!"

"We promised to stay and bury him…"

"Damnit! Why doesn't he die?"

"We promised…"

"Damnit!"

"Promised…"

"Kid, they're just on the other side of that ridge. If we're gonna get out alive, it's got to be now!"

"…Now!"

"Now!"

"Promised…"

God, it hurt!

It was quiet. No movement from the two men. No smoke or crackling of the fire, only the hot wind blowing over him.

Bridger and Fitzgerald must have gone off to hunt. Maybe they were asleep. No.

They had left him.

It took awhile for it to sink in—he'd been abandoned. When the realization finally took hold, it alarmed and frightened him. The two men who had been charged with his care were gone. No one was going to feed him. No one would bring him water.

They expected him to die.

It was a sobering thought. They *expected* him to die. When he hadn't done it quick enough, they up and left him. Let the bastard bury himself. Better yet, let the wolves have him.

Not quite yet.

He had too much pain and too little strength to be very angry about it. That would come later—if he lived.

He had to find out exactly how bad off he was. He was nearly paralyzed. His left arm and right leg were useless. Trying to move or use either of them sent shock-waves of pain through him.

He passed out again.

He awoke with an incredible thirst, this time fully aware of the situation he was in. Using his right hand, he began to probe, gingerely, checking his wounds. He remembered little about the actual attack. He remembered seeing the bear rise up on its hind legs and rush toward him, remembered getting off one shot at it with his rifle…

His rifle—where was that?

He tried to turn his head to look around, causing splinters of pain to shoot through his neck and scalp.

When that pain subsided, Hugh felt those areas to assess the damage. What he felt were stitches. Someone had gone to a lot of trouble to sew him back togeth-er. The stitches stretched along half his neck and most of his scalp. What had the beast done? Ripped his head off?

That still didn't answer the question about his rifle. Through enormous effort, he managed to roll over, nearly passing out once more in agony. There seemed to be no part of him that the bear had left untouched.

When the pain subsided enough he opened his eyes. What he saw startled him. It was a grave, open and waiting for him. Hugh Shivered. Then he gave a small, mirthless laugh.

All you got to do, he thought, *is crawl in and cover yourself up. Simple as pie.*

He looked for his rifle, but could find no indication that it had been left behind. Nor could he find his tomahawk or his knife. Not only had Bridger and Fitzgerald abandoned him, they had robbed his grave before he was even in it. A man, even a healthy man with two good arms and two good legs, needed those tools to survive in this country. Chances of surviving without them were slim, indeed.

His next immediate concern was water. God only knew how long he had been lying there before he realized that those two had left him. His mouth and throat were dry, both from summer heat and from fever. He *had* to have water, and soon.

Rolling onto his stomach seemed a monumental task, which seemed to take all of his will and his strength. After he had done it, Hugh lay for several minutes, eyes closed, waiting for the roar of pain to subside. Then he listened. From his low vantage point he could see very little, but with his eyes closed he could tell that the rushing water sound was coming from his right. Moving in that direction, he began to crawl.

He didn't get very far. His left arm and right leg were useless to him. Before he had gotten ten feet, Hugh passed out.

He wasn't out for very long. Almost as soon as he was out he was awake again. By late that afternoon—after hours of struggling—Hugh made it to the river.

He had no illusions about his predicament. He knew that he could not long remain where he was. He needed food, and he needed tools if he was to survive. There would be no honor in his death for any indians that discovered him, but on the other hand, a scalp was a scalp. If the scalp of a woman or a child were worth taking—and they *were*—then Hugh's would be worth taking as well.

I'll just have to not let them find me, he thought. But that would be easier said than done.

Major Henry and the others were somewhere off to the northwest. Their trail would be cold long before Hugh was in any shape to pick it up. Behind him, east and then south, the nearest white settlement was Fort Kiowa. Lying in the dark, Hugh calculated the distance at about three hundred miles.

He would go there.

The following morning he set out, using his right arm and left leg to push himself along. As it had been the previous day, the pain of movement and exertion was too much for him. He traveled only a short distance before unconciousness again overtook him.

Whenever he awoke, he would continue onward, staying close to the water, sometimes crawling *into* the water, to relieve himself and let the river wash some of the stink and decay away from him.

By the end of the first day he make it to the top of a small rise, where he decided to stop for the night. Looking back, he could still see the camp, where he had awoke the day before, along with the grave that the two men had dug for him.

It wasn't that far behind him.

CHAPTER THIRTY-SIX

THERE ARE times in a man's life when he has to follow his instincts, no matter how much logic, or other people, might tell him otherwise. If he doesn't, he will have regrets. Those regrets may be small, or they may be enormous. They may even follow him for the rest of his days.

Jim Bridger knew he'd made a mistake. He knew it the moment he gave in to Fitzgerald and agreed to leave. But once he made that agreement, he felt bound to follow through. Strangely, he felt almost as obligated to follow Mr. Fitzgerald now, having said that he would, as he had originally felt toward the promise that Fitzgerald had persuaded him to break. It was confusing.

Leaving Hugh Glass was wrong. There was nothing confusing about that.

Jim took a sharp, deep breath at the thought. Unconsciously, he looked back at the trail behind them.

They had taken his weapons.

Everything about what they were doing was wrong. Everything.

And yet, there was no denying that Fitzgerald's arguments had been valid. No one expected them to stay as long as they had. Even Major Henry expected Mr. Glass to die that day, or at least the following day. *No one* expected Hugh Glass to still be breathing five days later, which was when they had left.

"We won't do him or *anyone* any good if we hang around and get ourselves killed!" Fitzgerald had said. "Who'll bury him then?"

It was an argument that Jim didn't have an answer for. The reason Major Henry had asked for volunteers to stay with Mr. Glass in the first place was because Glass was slowing the party down. With the probability that every indian tribe in the area

147

having declared war on the whites, the men needed to get to Fort Henry fast. Discovery might mean death to them all.

So, Henry had asked for two volunteers, to stay with Hugh Glass and bury him when he died, while the others got away. He offered a reward—eighty dollars for the men who stayed—and James Bridger and John Fitzgerald had volunteered. Now they were running away, their duty unfulfilled. They'd left him.

It had taken Fitzgerald five days to get Jim to leave. In the end, it seemed to happen so fast, the danger seemed so imminent, that Jim had just panicked. For five days they'd waited for one of two things to happen—either Hugh Glass would die, or they would all be discovered and, most likely, killed. It had been a nerve-racking wait, with nothing to do the entire time except to look over his shoulder and listen to John Fitzgerald speak of their coming doom. In the end, Fitzgerald's words had gotten to him.

So, that had been the truth of it. He panicked. Fitzgerald had come running into camp, out of breath and white-faced, and said they had to leave, right now, or it would be too late—the Arikaras were right over the hill.

And Jim had gone for it. Now, he wasn't so sure. Had the indians really been there, or was it a trick, to get Jim to leave? For two days now he'd been watching. He saw no sign that they were being followed.

Stopping once more, Jim checked their back trail again. Hugh Glass was back there, his body probably stiff and cold and, most likely, being worked over by wolves or vultures. Certainly, he was dead by now.

What if he wasn't?

And if he was, was he at peace? What about his ghost?

Major Andrew Henry and his small group of trappers arrived at Fort Henry late in the afternoon. Upon arriving, they immediately opened a jug of whiskey and passed it around to celebrate their arrival. Breathing a deep sigh of relief, Andrew Henry joined them. Only now did he realize the terrific strain he had been under—that they had *all* been under. Since the attack by the Mandans, there had been a growing certainty among them that they would be attacked again at any moment. Every dip, every hollow that they walked through, had been an ambush which, fortunately, never came.

Finally, having reached the relative safety of the palisade, they were able to breathe easy again.

Henry's alleviation from strain was short lived. Daniel T. Potts gave him the news.

"It was the Blackfeet again, Major. They hit us while you were gone. They managed to make off with 22 of our best horses."

"Damn it!" Henry swore. "And damn Leavenworth! This is his fault! If he had done what he set out to do—what he *said* he was going to do, none of this would be happening! Word would have spread among the tribes that the whites aren't to be trifled with. Even the Blackfeet would have hesitated to bother us! Instead, look what we have. Through his own weakness he's left things in a state *ten times* worse than they were! Damn him for the imbecile he is!"

Potts simply raised his eyebrows and said, "It's a problem..."

Looking out through the open gate, Henry thought for a long minute about where they were and all that had happened. So far, their losses had been almost immeasurable, while their gains had been small. Was all this really worth it?

He shrugged that thought away quickly. He had more immediate concerns. He had to think ahead to winter, and about the problem of the Blackfeet. Altogether, Henry had less than fifty men at his disposal, including two who might or might not make it back to the fort.

The fort itself was built well enough for what it was. Against a medium-sized war party, it was defendable. Against a large force, however, it would fall. Considering recent developments, it was not inconceivable that the Blackfeet might try that. It would be great coup for them.

He thought again about the two men he had left behind—and about the man they had stayed behind to care for. Both Fitzgerald and Bridger were good men. Hell, Bridger, if he lived, might well turn out to be Henry's best. In every emergency, he had kept his head and reacted coolly. The boy was only nineteen, not even a man. Yet, when the Mandans struck, he had been the first to react, catching the indians off guard. In Henry's mind, Bridger's good instincts had probably saved them all.

Now Bridger might well die because he stayed to care for a man who, by refusing to obey orders and stay with the others, had gotten himself mauled. It had been Glass' own fault, but his foolishness might well cost the Rocky Mountain Fur Company three men instead of one.

Damn Hugh Glass, and damn Henry Leavenworth.

The Major continued to stare out through the open gate, thinking.

No, he thought, *it was my fault, too.* He had been too lax, too easy. He should have insisted that Glass stay with them and obey orders or go back to St. Louis. Then none of this would have happened. At least Bridger and Fitzgerald would be here.

Well, hopefully, Hugh Glass was dead and buried, and the other two men were no more than a day behind. And safe.

Potts was still standing there, leaning on his crutches. Henry looked at him.

"Have someone close that gate," the Major ordered. "Tell them to keep a sharp lookout. And spread the word for everyone to start packing. As soon as Bridger and Fitzgerald get back, we're moving upriver."

Henry walked away, heading for his cabin. Before he reached it he heard someone say:

"Hey, that's a nice bearskin! Who killed the griz?"

"Hugh Glass," another answered, "but it killed him right back."

CHAPTER THIRTY-SEVEN

HE DREAMED he was with the Pawnees again. Yellow Fox was working over him, chanting, performing one of his magic rituals to keep the bad dreams away.

"It isn't a dream!" Hugh yelled, half awake and dilirious. "The bear...!"

Yellow Fox kept working. Little Feather was there too, somehow. Not really *there*, exactly. It was more as though she were nearby, just out of sight, waiting.

Yellow Fox kept chanting.

He awoke late in the day, soaked with sweat and parched from lying in the late summer sun, and from fever. He had the feeling that Yellow Fox and some of the others had just been there, but now they were gone.

The previous evening, when he had stopped, he'd made it a point to position himself close to the river. Reaching out, he managed to scoop a handful of water and threw it into his face, missing his mouth altogether. It alarmed him just how much effort that took. The fever had drained him. He needed to get a lot of water into himself, and he needed food. If he didn't meet both of those needs soon, he would be too weak to continue, and he would die.

It took everything he had just to get enough water into himself. When he was done he fell back, exhausted.

As he drifted off to sleep he thought he could hear someone laughing.

It was late into the second night. The two men were sitting by the fire, not talking. Jim was staring at the flame, not really seeing it. He was thinking about Mike Fink.

Fink had been a big man, a powerful man, known far and wide as the King of the River. He had been a legend before Jim Bridger was ever thought of. Talbot had killed him. Three days later Talbot drowned in the river.

To Jim, that was no coincidence

Like most of the trappers, Jim was not formally educated. He had grown up on the river and in a blacksmith shop. One thing he *had* learned was that there were things not of this world—not of the flesh—that were just as real as hammer and anvil. Jim was certain, as many of the trappers were, that it had been the ghost of Mike Fink that had caused Talbot to drown. The King of the River had taken his revenge on the man who had killed him. It was as simple as that.

Jim had a real strange feeling that Mr. Glass would rest no easier than big Mike Fink had.

Looking across the camp, his eyes fell on Glass' rifle. It was a beautiful piece, one of the earlier Hawken's and definitely one of the finest Jim had seen. Fitzgerald had taken possession of it and intended to keep it as his own. That was fine with Jim. He wanted no part of it.

He looked back at the fire, trying to shake his feelings of dread. Fitzgeralds voice startled him.

"Boy, you better stop lookin' at that fire. Anythin' happens and you gonna be blind *and* useless!"

Self conciously, Jim looked away. Fitzgerald was right. Looking at the fire destroyed his ability to see into the darkness around them. Hell, they shouldn't even *have* a fire.

But Jim wanted one

When Hugh awoke again the sun was up. He was lying on his stomach, with one hand in the water. He could hear as well as feel flies buzzing around on his lacerated back. Weakly, he tried to shoo them away. In doing so he caught a whiff of something rotten, and he knew it was him.

The flies were back before his arm had completed to pass.

"What the hell," he said. "I need a bath!"

The sound of his voice startled him. It was deep and gutteral—not his own voice at all. The throat wound.

Pulling himself forward, Hugh entered the river, letting the cool water wash over him. This felt better than anything he could remember for a good, long time. Where the pain had numbed his mind to little more than survival, the water made him feel more alert. The bouyancy helped relieve his weight, which in turn helped to relieve some of the pain. Although the pain itself was undeniable, he felt alive again.

Staying in the shalows, Hugh began to move downstream, with the current. This worked well, much better than crawling on land, but he had to be careful. If the current got hold of him, he would drown. There was no way Hugh could swim this river in the condition he was in.

He noticed that something kept catching on his right side whenever he would turn a certain way, sending tremors of pain down into his right leg. Reaching back carefully, Hugh made two discoveries. The first one delighted him.

It was his side pack. It had been there all along and he had been too dull-brained from pain to realize it. The pack contained a small tin cup and a razor—two items that would come in very handy.

The second discovery wasn't so pleasant. During the attack, the grizzly had bitten away half of his right buttocks.

Hugh managed to stay in the water for the better part of an hour, nearly losing conciousness twice when his injured leg banged against rocks hidden below the surface of the water. He had no way to guage the distance he traveled, but he was certain that it was greater than the previous two days. He was nearly at the limits of his strength when he spied a patch of buffalo berries growing alongside the bank. With great effort he pulled himself up out of the river, and passed out.

Later, when he awakened, he would drag himself up to the berry bushes and eat.

Hugh stayed by the berry bushes throughout that day, eating and sleeping. Twice he made trips to the river to drink.

He was starting to feel a little better about his chances for survival, although he still harbored no illusions about the danger he was in. As far as he knew, every indian tribe in the area would consider him their enemy. If that weren't bad enough, there were a hundred ways a man could die out here alone, even a healthy man. Another bear might find him, or a pack of wolves, or a sudden storm might create a flash flood, drowning Hugh before he could crawl to higher ground. Anything could happen.

Living with the Pawnees, Hugh had learned their methods of traveling through the countryside undetected. He had also learned which plants and herbs were beneficial. The buffalo berries relieved the hunger and provided some nutrition for him, but Hugh knew that to recover from his wounds and get back his strength, he would need protein and that would mean meat. That would be a problem.

One thing at a time…

Once again he awoke with the knowledge that something was wrong. He waited, not moving, listening and trying to detect whatever it was that had alerted him. His eyes searched through the early morning darkness. He was lying on his right side, his broken, right leg stretched out straight, his mangled left arm lying along his side. He had the berry bushes at his back, and had a clear view of the river.

Nothing moved in front of him. Gradually, Hugh began to relax. He shifted slightly. Realization came suddenly. As he had done with the flies on his back, Hugh both heard and felt the rattle beating against his leg. A wave of panic washed over him.

It was a prairie rattler, about three feet long. In the cool of the night it had crawled up next to him for warmth. Hugh lay as still as he could, praying that the snake would crawl away again.

After awhile the sun came up. Moving slowly and with great effort, Hugh managed to turn his head slightly and peer down at the rattlesnake. What he saw made him want to laugh, both from nervousness and relief.

There was no way this snake would leave him today, or tomorrow, for that matter. A huge lump in its belly showed that it had recently eaten. As such it would be in a state of torpor, which meant that, unbelievably, it was even more helpless than Hugh was.

Here was meat.

His pace was impossibly slow. Each slight obstacle that lay in his path had to be skirted around, easily taking him an hour or more out of his way. For Hugh, the daylight hours seemed an ongoing, relentless wave of pain. The sun scorched him. Insects feasted undisturbed on his already weakened frame, or else ran away from him at speeds which eclipsed his own sloth-like efforts. Day or night, his body seemed either to be racked with fever or shaken by shivering chills. His efforts seemed wasted and useless and hopelessly weak. Only one thought kept him moving.

If you die, he told himself, *they win.*

Bridger and Fitzgerald expected him to die. They had even planned for it by digging a grave for him. They had made a mistake, though, by not putting him in that grave. They should have finished the bear's work. Slitting his throat or putting a bullet in his brain would have been far more humane than just leaving him, but they hadn't even had the decency for that.

So, he continued to push himself, hour after hour, passing out often from pain and from exertion. Rocks and sticks tore at his flesh, adding to his agony and wearing his right elbow and left knee raw and bloody. There was nothing to be done for it. Each new and old needle of pain gave him another reason to live long enough to kill the two men who had deserted him.

CHAPTER THIRTY-EIGHT

BRIDGER AND FITZGERALD arrived at Fort Henry in the early afternoon. The fort was in an uproar. The Blackfeet had been there once again, during the night. Seven more horses had been stolen. Major Henry was furious. His anger was softened by relief when he saw Bridger and Fitzgerald.

When the two men entered his office, the Major was packing. He stopped long enough to welcome them back.

"So, Glass finally passed on, eh?" Henry asked them.

"Yessir, Major," Fitzgerald told him. "Dead an' buried. Got his fixins right here, so's the injuns couldn't pack 'em off. Figured I'd keep the rifle—if it's all the same to you. A momento, sort of."

Henry nodded. He was looking at Jim Bridger. The young man seemed pretty upset. He kept staring at the floor of the office.

"Did you see any indians?" Henry asked them.

"Nossir." Fitzgerald spoke up. "Not a one. We were lucky."

"Yes. You were. We've lost twenty-nine horses to the Blackfeet in the last two weeks. They're definitely on the prowl."

"Twenty-nine! That's a lot!"

"Too many. Well, you men get some rest, then get yourselves ready. Tomorrow morning we're moving the fort, lock, stock, and barrel. We're getting out of range of the Blackfeet, altogether."

"Whew!" Fitzgerald exhaled. "Alrighty Major." The two men turned to go.

"Oh, and Jim..." Henry suddenly added.

Bridger froze. After a moment, he looked up.

"Yes?"

"Welcome back," the Major told him. Jim simply nodded, then went out.

Major Andrew Henry watched him go, wondering. He'd never seen Jim bothered this way before, about anything. The young man must have really taken a liking to Hugh Glass.

Well, he would get over the man's death, eventually. In the meantime, there was a hell of a lot of work to be done.

After five days, Hugh realized he was healing. Or rather, that he was *starting* to heal. It was still going to be a long, slow process, but within his pain-ridden brain, he saw the beginning signs, and it gave him hope.

Fortunately for Hugh, there were a lot of berry bushes along this part of the river, so he wouldn't starve. He also ate grubs and insects, worms—anything that came within his reach. Sometimes he gagged when he would eat them, but eat them he did. All the while he was aware that, if he were *really* going to heal and get his strength back, he needed to get some meat. Berries might keep him alive, but they also gave him diahrea, which left him feeling weak. Hugh needed protein.

In the beginning, he had been able to crawl only short distances before passing out from pain or exhaustion. This continued to be the case, but each day the time and distance he traveled between rests grew longer. He was still aware that his chances of making it to Fort Kiowa were slim at best. But he kept his mind focused on one thought at all times, and that kept him going. Hugh wanted revenge. He would endure any form of Hell that stood in his way and find a way to overcome it, just to confront the two men who had abandoned him. He wanted to see the fear and shame in their eyes. He wanted to watch them die, suffering as *he* was suffering. Somehow, some way, he would do this.

By God, he would.

At mid-morning on the sixth day, Hugh made what was, to him, a great find. He was crawling up over a low rise, starving, looking for anything that might come within his reach that he could use to feed himself. The berry bushes along this section of the river had grown sparse. He reached the top of the rise and stared down into the gulley beyond. Before him was a sight that most men would have avoided, but which held great appeal for him.. It was the stripped-bare carcass of a buffalo. There was no meat on the bones, but the smell of putrefaction was still strong and the bones were green with mold. Hugh crawled toward it.

By the time he reached the carcass, Hugh was gagging from the smell and was no longer sure he could do what he needed to do. With great effort, he managed to break off one of the rib bones, fighting off flies and a horde of angry ants as he did. Then, crawling some distance away and into the wind, he found two large rocks. Placing the rib bone on one of the rocks, he used the other rock to strike the bone. After several tries, he managed to crack the bone open. Then, scraping the marrow out, he placed it in his cup.

He repeated this process several times, until he had what amounted to several spoonfuls of marrow in the cup. Then he crawled back a ways, to a berry bush he had spotted earlier. He picked some of the berries and put them in the cup, mixing them with the marrow. After he had mashed them together, he began to eat.

It wasn't the most delightful meal he'd ever endured, but it was food. Hugh spent the afternoon repeating the unsavory process, finally crawling away at dusk to find a place to sleep.

He awoke with a strange, morose heaviness that he found disturbing. He didn't feel *physically* heavy, exactly. He was emotionally weighted, and in a way he was unnacustomed to. He felt depressed.

He'd had some bad dreams, but he really couldn't remember them. His father had been in one of them, but Hugh couldn't recall any more than that. Hugh's father had been a hard man, a Pensylvania coal miner who had a tendency toward meanness whenever he drank. He was the main reason Hugh had run away to sea at such an early age and had never looked back. Hugh had not thought of him in years. Nor had he wanted to.

He tried to shake off the depression, but it clung to him. What had he been thinking? Did he really believe he could crawl all the way to Fort Kiowa? He tried to guage how far he had come in the past week. It was a mile or two at best. Hugh still had three hundred miles to go. At this rate, Winter would be on him before he was even a third of the way. It was hopeless.

Hugh made a weak start at trying to crawl again, but gave up before he had gotten six feet. He tried to bolster himself, speaking out loud. His unfamiliar voice, though gutteral, was flat and without enthusiasm:

"C'mon, Glass, pull it together. You can do this..."

After a few moments, he added, "No...I guess you can't."

He lay there, face down, eyes open but not seeing the grass and dirt before him, until he fell asleep again.

Once more he dreamed of his father. This time, though, the images were confusing. *Sometimes* they were his father. At other times the image of his father was intermingled with the image of another man from Hugh's past. Tom Halpern.

The final dream had four men in it—Hugh's father, Tom Halpern, Jim Bridger, and John Fitzgerald. They seemed to be having a party, were drinking and laughing. Something was hilarious to them. Hugh realized it was him.

"Go to Hell!" he yelled. "All of you! Go straight to Hell!"

His own voice woke him up. Hugh blinked several times, slowly realizing that he was once more awake.

"That's right," he growled. "You can all go to Hell."

A moment later he added:

"Better yet, I'll send you."

He began to crawl again.

CHAPTER THIRTY-NINE

THEY HAD REACHED an impasse with the river. Waterfalls blocked their progress. The keelboats could not continue upstream. Camping near the base of the falls, the trappers pondered their next move.

It was a beautiful spot, but Jim Bridger was reminded of another time, when they had stopped at a waterfall, and the Blackfeet had been waiting.

Others remembered too. Nervously, they watched the trees and the surrounding countryside, each man trying to keep some cover near him as they worked to make camp.

Without any particular pushing from Andrew Henry, the small group of men had become more cohesive, in the way that men in constant danger sometimes will. No one balked at his orders. No one argued. They were a small group, but they were well-armed, alert, and ready.

Henry was still puzzled about Jim Bridger's behavior. Since returning with Fitzgerald, he had continued to act nervous, edgy, and —if the Major didn't know better—somewhat guilty. Fitzgerald, on the other hand, acted as if everything were right as rain.

Like Bridger, Andrew Henry also remembered the incident at Great Falls. He knew that the falls themselves were a diversion that would work against the trappers in case of attack, creating noise and confusion that could allow a hostile party of indians to close in unobserved. With every tribe in the area a potential enemy, the sooner they found a way past this obstacle, the better.

Not for the first time since they had returned from the Arikara siege, he felt a sudden longing to be back in St. Louis, among his books and playing his violin.

157

Hugh Glass

This is crazy, he thought. *Why am I here? What are we gaining?* In less than a year's time, more than twenty men had been killed, mostly by indians. Could they ever hope to make up for that? Not to mention the staggering financial losses. True, Ashley was a man of credit, but how far could that credit go, and for how long?

As it turned out, the thing the trappers feared the most became their salvation. While waiting at the falls, a party of indians materialized. These turned out to be Crows. Signalling peaceful intentions, Henry followed them to their village, where he traded successfully with them. When he returned to the camp, he brought with him forty-seven horses.

The party continued upriver.

Hugh Glass did not so much as breathe. He lay, hidden by a thick growth of scrub brush, not moving, not even blinking. Thirty feet away from him, six Cheyenne warriors were watering their horses.

If they spotted him they would kill him. Hugh had no doubt about that. Nor would it be an easy death. The Cheyenne, like all the tribes in the area, liked to take their time when they captured an enemy. Hugh had been fortunate, both in his timing and in the direction they had come from. The indians had come up from the south—the direction Hugh was heading toward, so they hadn't crossed the hopelessly obvious trail that a crawling, injured man would leave. If they had arrived five minutes later than they had, Hugh would have been caught out in the open, for he had been about to exit the protection of the brush and crawl to where they now stood watering their horses. Instead of crawling out, he froze where he was and tried to blend in with his surroundings.

Reading the party, Hugh decided that they had probably been out for some time and that, by the look of them, they hadn't done too well for their trouble. Often, when a raiding party went out, they would go on foot, the intention being that they would ride back on the horses they would steal. That clearly wasn't the case here. These ponies all wore Cheyenne saddles and markings. The men looked gaunt and tired. They had traveled far and had little to show for it. Hugh didn't want to be the one to change their luck.

The wait began to grow painful for him. One of the irritating things about Hugh's injuries was that they made it difficult for him to be comfortable in any one position for any length of time. Even in his sleep he was shifting every few minutes. He was lying on his stomach, resting on his arms. Both his lacerated left arm and his broken leg began to throb.. Hugh forced himself to remain still.

One of the warriors suddenly looked directly at him. At the same moment, sweat ran into Hugh's eyes, forcing him to blink.

Miraculously, the Cheyenne didn't see him. He'd seem *something*, though. He continued to stare at the spot where Hugh lay, searching the area with his eyes. Abruptly, the leader of the group barked an order. Almost instantly, all six men were again on horseback. Moving single file, they turned their horses into the river. The last one in was the indian who had looked at Hugh. As his horse entered the water, he turned back once more to let his eyes search the area where Hugh lay. Seeing nothing, he turned his attention back to what was before him.

The six men crossed the river, floating back but still holding onto their mounts as they entered the deeper water, so that their weight wouldn't push the horses under, then settling in again as they reached the shallows on the opposite side. The Cheyennes rode up and over the opposite bank and quickly disappeared from view. Only then did Hugh resume normal breathing.

He waited a full ten minutes without moving from where he lay, just in case they decided to come back. Then, as quickly as he was able, he crawled down to the river. Entering at exactly the same spot that the Cheyennes had, he swam out a short way and allowed the current to carry him downstream.

This time he stayed in the water for quite a while, allowing the current to put as much distance as possible between him and the raiding party.

Finally, exhausted again, he made his way back to the bank and crawled out of the water. For a few brief moments he allowed himself to rest. Then he crawled up into the brush, hid himself, and slept.

It was an unrestful sleep. He dreamt that the Cheyennes had returned. Finding the spot where he had entered the river, they followed him downstream. Aware that they were growing close, he laid where he was, not moving, his eyes closed. By their voices, he could tell that they had found where he had left the river. He could hear them moving closer.

One of them had found him. Now Hugh lay in a sort of dream-paralysis, *unable* to move. Roughly, the man rolled him over.

It wasn't a man at all. It was an enormous bear, twice larger than any bear Hugh had ever heard of. It loomed over him, snarling, snarling…

Hugh woke up. He lay for several moments, chest heaving, his breath coming in great gulps. Slowly, he realized that once again, he had been having a nightmare.

Then he had a second realization.

The snarling was real.

It was a wolf pack. With great relief Hugh realized that it was not him they were snarling at. They had separated a buffalo calf from the rest of the herd, which must be somewhere nearby. It was a large calf, about six months old, and it was doing its best to keep them at bay, but its moments were running short. Hugh could tell from its heaving sides that the wolves had run the calf as far as it would go. In a few short minutes it would take its last breath, probably not more than a few paces from where it now stood.

One of the wolves made a run at it, growling. The calf took a step toward the wolf, swinging its big head defensively to protect itself. The wolf leapt away. Even as it did, a second wolf came in from the other side. Unseen until it was too late, the second wolf succeeded in clamping its teeth firmly on the throat of the buffalo. Bawling in pain, the calf managed to move forward a little, stepping on the wolf but not dislodging it. Another wolf grabbed the calf by the tail and started pulling it back. At first this had no effect. Then the calf once more stepped on the wolf that held its throat.

This time the wolf let go. The wolf that held the calf's tail held firm, pulling with all its might. Suddenly free of the weight of the first wolf, the calf was now off-balance. It sat down hard on its rump. Without waiting for it to recover, two more wolves struck the calf at once, knocking the young buffalo onto its side.

The calf would never rise to its feet again. The wolf that had been stepped on once more found purchase on the buffalo's throat and held it down. Avoiding the calf's flailing hooves, the rest of the pack rushed in. Not bothering to wait for death to arrive, the wolves tore open the belly of the calf and began to devour it.

The fight was over.

Having killed many buffalo himself, Hugh was yet not unmoved by the scene before him. The calf had died in fear and in pain. Hugh's sympathy, however, was tempered by the fact that he was starving.

As the wolves commenced their feast, Hugh eased himself backwards, slowly moving out of sight.

An hour later he was back, dragging two heavy poles with him. Crawling back to the spot he had left earlier, Hugh looked down upon the scene. Having sated their hunger, the wolves lolled about their kill. Hugh watched them for signs of aggression. He saw none.

It's now, he decided, *or not at all.*

Moving as quietly as he could, Hugh managed to raise himself up onto his knees. Then, using one of the poles as a crutch, he pulled himself up to his feet for the first time since being attacked by the grizzly. His broken leg was tender, but it accepted the weight, with the help of the crutch.

One of the wolves looked up and saw him. In an instant all of them—five wolves in all—were on their feet, staring at Hugh, growling at him. Not hesitating, Hugh rushed down at them, using the makeshift crutch under one arm and wielding a club with the other, yelling at the top of his voice as he went. Only one of the wolves approached him. Hugh struck it hard in the side of the head with his club. Yelping, the wolf leapt away.

If he had attempted this earlier, before all the wolves had eaten their fill, they would have pulled him down and killed him as they had the calf. Instead, with their stomachs full, they retreated into the dusk.

The kill was his.

Hugh stayed at the kill for four days, eating his fill again and again and resting. He had no means of making a fire, but for a man who was starving, the raw meat was heaven. Considering the amount of blood he had lost and strength he needed to regain, the bloody meat was probably the best thing for him.

During the time he spent by the buffalo calf, Hugh pre-occupied himself by cutting the meat into strips, pounding it and mixing it with berries, and allowing it to dry in the sun. He also practiced walking with the makeshift crutch. He was awkward at first, and the leg was pretty tender, but after four days of practice and rest he found he could move pretty well. On the morning of the fifth day he moved on. When he left, he did so walking upright, as a man, and he had with him more pemmican than he could comfortably carry.

For the first time since meeting with the grizzly, Hugh Glass felt like a man again.

CHAPTER FORTY

IT WAS NOW the middle of September. Hugh was making good time—not as good as he wanted, not as good as an *un*injured man—but good time just the same. He estimated that he was making between five and ten miles a day. He still had far to go.

At night he slept little. His right leg throbbed with pain from walking over the uneven terrain. Hugh knew that would pass. He was more concerned with the wounds on his back. They weren't healing properly. They were open and festering. Hugh could feel insects crawling over them. His back gave off a bad smell. Hugh was aware that he was fighting a fever.

There was nothing to be done about any of this. Hugh couldn't reach the wounds, couldn't clean them or dress them, or even shoo the insects away. All he could do was keep moving.

A week after leaving the buffalo calf, his supply of pemmican gave out. Hugh continued along, making the best time he could, eating buffalo berries or whatever came within his grasp. He was beginning to recognize the area he was traveling through, having passed through more than once while traveling with the Pawnees. He developed a plan.

As near as Hugh could figure, he was now within a couple of days walking from the Arikara village. The village had been burned and abandoned, but that was precisely why Hugh was headed there. Like the Pawnees, the Arikaras would have one or more food caches hidden somewhere in the village. Hugh doubted that they'd had the time to clean them all out before they fled into the night. If he could make it to the village and find one of the caches, he would feast like a king. Besides that, the village was along his path back to Fort Kiowa.

He reached the village four days after his supply of pemmican ran out. By then he was nearly starving again.

Instead of going directly in, he watched the village. Despite his hunger, he spent hours circling the village, making sure there was no sign of habitation. Only when he was certain did he venture in.

The village was laid out almost exactly like the Pawnee villages. The Arikaras used the same type of earth lodges as the Pawnees, only these had been burned. Many of the lodges had fallen in. Those that hadn't were unsafe to enter. None of that mattered to Hugh. If the Arikaras built their caches the way the Pawnees did, then they would not be inside one of the lodges, but outside, somewhere within the compound.

Knowing *what* to look for was a big advantage. After entering the village, it took Hugh less than two hours to find the food.

He ate his fill of the raw corn. Suddenly exhausted, he then lay back on one of the earth lodges that were still intact There he slept. During the night he awoke to find a strange pair of eyes looking at him. Startled, Hugh relaxed when he realized that it was an indian dog, somehow left behind by the Arikaras. The dog kept a respectful distance, and was still there when Hugh drifted off again.

When he woke up the dog was gone. After eating some more of the corn, Hugh washed himself in the river. Then he sat back once more on the earth dome, to try to plan the next leg of his journey. His best bet was to try to salvage enough lumber from the burned out village to construct a raft. That would be no easy chore, but if he could manage it, the rest of the journey would go much easier for him. A raft would also enable him to carry enough corn to last him until he reached Fort Kiowa.

The disadvantages of this plan were all too obvious to him. Any indians that happened to be in the area as Hugh floated by would be bound to see him. This time of year, the river ran slowly enough that a man on foot, or swimming with the current, could catch him easily. This would be even more true for men on horseback. With every tribe in the area potentially on the warpath, the this would be asking for trouble. Hugh still had no means of defending himself.

It was a knotty problem. Hugh didn't get to ponder it for very long. Suddenly aware that he was being watched, Hugh looked to his left. On a hill just outside the village, a dozen mounted Sioux braves sat regarding him. Calmly, they began to walk their mounts toward the village. Cursing his clumsiness, Hugh waited for them. It would have been a wasted attempt to try running or hiding from them. They had seen him long before he became aware that they were there.

One thing you could never show to the Sioux, or to *any* of the tribes, was fear. The indians respected bravery, but to display fear was to court their contempt— and a slow, painful death.

Hugh Glass waited. He was determined that, whatever happened, he could not let them take him prisoner. If they tried, he would have to make them kill him quickly. No one knew better than he did what kind of creative tortures they were capable of. Better to force them to kill him quickly, if it came to that.

Hugh hoped it wouldn't. He had things he still needed to do. Specifically, he had two men to kill.

The Sioux entered the village, taking their time. Like Hugh, they would have watched the village for some time before making their presence known. They knew he was alone.

Standing on the slope of the earth lodge, Hugh tried not to look too dependent on the crutch. The Sioux warriors rode up to him, fanning out in a semi-circle. There were thirteen in all. Behind them ran a string of six extra ponies. Thinking they were going to surround him, Hugh took an awkward step back and prepared to fight. The indians stopped.

For a moment nothing happened. Hugh stood, waiting as the indians regarded him. Then one of the warriors spoke—not to Hugh, but to another member of the war party. Without a word, that indian got off his horse. Carrying his lance, the brave walked up to Hugh. Not knowing the indian's intention, Glass balanced on his left leg and held up the crutch to protect himself. The indian held up his hand in an un-threatening way. Warily, Hugh lowered the crutch.

The indian seemed to be examining Hugh's wounds. Hugh knew that he looked a mess, but aside from an occasional dip in the river, there was nothing to be done about it. He could only imagine what his face looked like. The wounds on his neck and scalp were nearly healed, but Hugh had been unable to remove the thread that Henry and the others had sewn him up with. To the indians, he must have looked like a patchwork quilt.

The indian on the ground spoke to the man who ordered him to examine Hugh, then moved around to look at Hugh's back. Watching from the corner of his eye, Hugh Glass allowed him to do so.

Wrinkling his nose at the smell, the indian peered closely at Hugh's back and began talking excitedly to the others. As he spoke, he made a clawing motion in the air. Those who were on horseback gave murmurs of astonishment. The man who had spoken first—who seemed to be in command of the group—was wearing a bearclaw necklace. Holding it up, he addressed Hugh in a questioning way. Hugh didn't speak their language. He could only guess at what he was being asked. He nodded.

The indian then noticed the bundle of corn that Hugh had taken from the cache. Pointing at it, he once more asked what seemed to be a question.

So that's why they're here, he thought. *They're after the corn. Just like me.*

"Over there," he told them in English, "in a small clearing, three lodges over."

The indian with the bear necklace spoke quickly to two of the others. Without hesitation they rode over to the place Hugh had described. Hugh smiled.

"You speak english," he said to the indian.

"Little," the man answered. Then, indicating the man who was on the ground, he added, "He say, you back, full worms."

Hugh exhaled.

"Well," he said, "I knew something was going on back there."

The indians found the corn. Immediately, they began to scavenge poles from the burned out village, and started constructing travois', which they fastened to the extra ponies they had brought. It was clear that they intended to take all the corn they could possibly carry.

The indian who had spoken to him said nothing more as the others worked, but he stayed next to Hugh. Finally, he spoke again.

"Where-you-gun?" the Sioux warrior asked.

"Gone." Hugh told him. "Two white men stole it—long way back." He pointed back in the direction he had come from. "They thought I would die. I'm going to Fort Kiowa to get a new gun, so that I can find those men and kill them."

The indian accepted this as perfectly logical. Nothing more was said between them.

After awhile the others came back, having loaded all the corn that was in the cache. Without a word they mounted their ponies and began to exit the village. Just before they reached the gate, the indian who spoke English said something to the man that had examined Hugh. Abruptly, that man turned and rode back to where Hugh was. Turning his horse sideways in front of Hugh, the indian put out his hand. Hugh accepted. None too gracefully, he managed to climb up behind the indian and onto the horse. In moments, they had left the burned village behind and were riding toward the village of the Sioux.

CHAPTER FORTY-ONE

IT WAS ANYTHING but an easy ride. Hugh's wounds were not yet healed. The fact that a large chunk of his right buttock had been bitten away made it awkward for him to sit in the saddle, as well as painful.

Hugh wasn't sure what to expect from the Sioux. He didn't think they intended to kill him. If that was what they wanted he would already be dead, or would be undergoing a slow, painful torture. Since that hadn't happened, and since he'd helped them find the corn they were looking for, it was likely that they intended to help him. Indians respected bravery. The fact that he had survived the attack by the grizzly and was intent on killing two white men would be big medicine to them.

It's probably because I'm going to kill two white men, he thought humorously. Two less white men would be a plus to them.

They traveled until late in the afternoon, heading west, finally stopping to make their camp next to a stream. For Hugh Glass, it was none too soon. The last hours of the trip had been spent in agony. Knowing the Sioux would be watching for signs of weakness, he kept his face impassive and didn't wince. The exertion of this feat caused the sweat to roll down his body. By the time they stopped he was soaked from head to foot.

Tomorrow, he knew, would be no better.

Out of respect for his hosts, Hugh limped downstream a short distance, then walked out into the water and washed himself. Perhaps later the Sioux would kill him, but for now they were treating him kindly enough. It seemed to him that the least he could do was to try not to smell bad.

165

When he came back he found a familiar scene. A fire had been constructed. A few of the men were around it, lying on their backs, thumping their chests and humming. Hugh felt a sudden homesickness for the Pawnees. He missed Big Axe, Big Soldier, Lucky Hawk, and the others. He made up his mind that, when this was over, he would go and pay them a visit.

That was, if he lived through it.

Almost as soon as Hugh returned from his bath, one of the indians came up to him carrying a small bowl. At first Hugh thought it was food, then he realized that the bowl contained a liquid that had healing herbs in it. Turning, he allowed the man to clean his back wounds.

The effect was almost immediate. Instantly, the itching ceased. The liquid caused the wounds to dry up, where before they had been open and runny. By the following morning the wounds would be scabbed over and would finally be starting to heal. When the indian was done, he showed Hugh the "worms" that had infested his back. They were actually maggots. That made Hugh feel only slightly better about having them there. He remembered a ship's doctor telling him once about deliberately putting maggots on a wound. The maggots ate the dead flesh, which helped to prevent putrification from setting in. Disgusting as it was, these little "worms" might well have played a major part in saving his life.

For supper, they ate pemmican and corn. Hugh ate only a little. Then exhaustion overtook him and he crawled off to sleep.

The trip back to the Sioux village took three days. Each of those days was the same for Hugh Glass—agonizing and exhausting. He nearly fell from the back of the horse several times. On the second day, his buttock wound broke open. By the end of the day his right leg was soaked with blood. The indians seemed to find some humor in this. Working together, they managed to produce a piece of cloth, which they folded and, after some difficulty, tied into place, giving him a new "butt". This improved his balance and made it easier to stay on the horse. Sitting on the cloth, though painful, kept the wound from bleeding.

Hugh greeted the sight of the village with mixed emotions. It was a relief to know that the long hours of painful jostling on the back of a horse would soon end, but Hugh was apprehensive. What he knew of the Sioux came mostly from when he lived with the Pawnees. The Pawnees and the Sioux were mortal enemies and would kill each other on sight. Living as a Pawnee, Hugh had fought them, but he knew little about their customs of hospitality. So far they were helping him, but you could never know when that might change.

They entered the village amidst a chorus of greets and yells, and a lot of curious stares. Hugh knew the indians in the village would have been hopefully expecting the loads of corn, but the sight of a busted up white man riding along was a surprise to them.

The village itself was much like the portable villages of the Pawnees, and consisted of teepees made of buffalo skins. Hugh didn't know if the Sioux kept permanent lodges or not. The Pawnees did, but they were on the move for about eight months out of the year.

Like the Pawnees, the Sioux men were clean-faced and probably considered facial hair unclean. This made Hugh a little uncomfortable. Since being mauled he had not even *attempted* to use his razor for anything other than survival. His neck wound alone made it almost impossible to shave. Hugh knew he must look a real sight to them.

They rode into the center of the village and stopped. Immediately, the women began attacking the bundles of corn, pulling them off the travois' and piling corn into baskets. With help from the man he was riding with, Hugh gingerly let himself down.

He had a moment to look around now. The men were talking amongst themselves, and the women were emptying the bundles of corn. A large group of children had gathered to stare at Hugh. Hugh looked around at the teepees and at the general layout of the village. Other than some of the markings and artwork he saw, this could almost *be* a Pawnee village. The biggest difference that he noticed was in the way the men wore their hair. Most Pawnee men shaved their heads, leaving only a scalplock. The Sioux warriors wore their hair long. This made the Sioux seem less ferocious, although only slightly so, and this, Hugh Glass knew, was an illusion. Some of the men wore buckskin shirts, but many were bare-chested. Those men who went shirtless all had thick scars on their chests. Hugh had heard that those scars came from enduring the Sioux rites of manhood.

The attention of the men suddenly turned to Hugh. They formed a circle around him, which he guessed consisted of their principal warriors and their chief. The chief was a proud, white-haired warrior with a powerful manner and sharp eyes. He said something to the man next to him, who spoke english to Hugh.

"You-fight with bear?"

"Yes," Hugh told them. "I fought with a bear."

The man related Hugh's words to the chief. The chief nodded and spoke again.

"Where bear now?" the man translated.

"The bear is dead," Hugh answered, not really knowing if it were true or not. "The men who were with me took the skin. They took my weapons and left me to die, alone. I am going to Fort Kiowa to get new weapons. Then I will find these men and kill them."

Again the interpreter told the chief what Hugh had said. Once more the chief spoke. The Sioux warrior relayed his words.

"You welcome here. Stay long—get better. You ready, we take to fort."

The men continued to stay with him for a few minutes longer, examining his wounds, shaking their heads in awe and appreciation. Then, one by one, they began to drift away. As the circle of men parted, the women were able to get in where they could see.

About fifteen feet away, one of the women stood idly looking on, holding a basket of corn at her waist. Something about her was familiar... Slowly, Hugh's mind accepted the fact that he was looking at Little Feather. Almost at the same instant, recognition showed in her eyes as well. Dropping the basket of corn, she pushed through the crowd of women and rushed to him, nearly knocking him to the ground in her excitement.

"Taka-Kuruks! Taka-Kuruks!" she cried. "You came! At last, you have come for me!"

The Sioux had pulled her from the river, more than a year earlier. She had been unconcious and close to death. Although they thought her their enemy, they nursed her back to health. It was only after she was awake and able to talk to them that they realized that Little Feather was one of their own. At that point they refused to let her return to the Pawnees. She explained that she had a husband— a white man *living* with the Pawnees, and that she had to get back, but they insisted she stay with her own people. Since that time she had waited for Hugh to find her, sensing and hoping that, somehow, he would do so. Over the past few months there had been pressure for her to choose a *new* husband Little Feather had been stubborn in her refusal, insisting that Taka-Kuruks would find her.

Ashamed and disappointed in himself for letting Little Feather down, Hugh found it nearly impossible to tell her that he had given up looking for her a year earlier. It was only his own sense of conscience, sharpened by contact with men who had no conscience at all, that would not let him keep silent.

It didn't matter to her. It pleased her that he had grieved for her for so long. What was important was that they were together again.

Hugh stayed with Little Feather for several days, growing stronger each day. They were happy, blissful days compared with those he had just been through. Under the care of the Sioux, his healing seemed to accelerate.

Both Hugh and Little Feather knew he couldn't stay. He had made a promise to himself to kill two men. Every scar he carried from his encounter with the grizzly, and every ache he endured from those wounds, was a reminder of that promise. Hugh knew he would never be at peace until he had confronted Bridger and Fitzgerald.

When it was over he would return to her.

PART THREE

"—And anger
in him...
was a still,
white Hell..."

—John G. Neihardt
"The Song of Hugh Glass"

CHAPTER FORTY-TWO

ON OCTOBER 8, 1823, Hugh Glass arrived at Fort Kiowa. Six Sioux braves were with him, having accompanied him from their village. The indians knew the fort, having gone there before to trade. Kiowa was the nickname of the man who had built the fort, a man named Brazeau, and had nothing at all to do with the indians of that nation. When Brazeau passed on, the nickname fell to his son, so it was Kiowa Junior that stood behind the counter at the general store, and looked in awe at the spectacle of a white man that entered, surrounded by six Sioux braves.

Hugh was wearing a new buckskin shirt and pants, so most of his wounds were hidden. He still limped, though. Little Feather had shaved him, so the wounds on his scalp and throat were visible. She had taken the stitches out for him, too. These had been in much too long. The scars would remain a permanent reminder of the hardships Hugh Glass had endured.

When Hugh told Kiowa what had happened to him, the storekeeper could only shake his head in wonder.

"My god," he told Hugh, "what an incredible story. What *trials* you have gone through! What did you say the names of the two men were?"

"I didn't. Don't worry, they know who they are. The others who were with them do, too."

"Well, I admire your discretion. If it were me they'd abandoned, *everyone* I came into contact with would hear of it!"

"After I deal with them. In the meantime, I'll need a new outfit. The bastards took everything I had."

"Take anything you need," Brazeau told him. "You're an Ashley man, so your credit's good. Just sign for whatever you take."

"I was hoping you'd say that." Then, indicating the indians who had brought him to the fort, he added, "In that case, I'd like to repay these gentlemen for helping me out."

"Of course. Take whatever you need."

Hugh gave each of the indians a new knife, blankets, and beads, thanking them for their kindness. Then he gave Bright Eagle, the man who spoke English, a bolt of blue cloth that had a red trim on it, and asked him to give it to Little Feather.

After the indians had gone, Hugh asked Brazeau how things were on the upper Missouri.

"Pretty much back to normal," the storekeeper said. "Some of the tribes started to go a little wild after the bad show that Leavenworth made, but after word got out about the burning of the Arikara village, things settled down again. In fact, Toussaint Charboneau is taking a party of men up to trade with the Mandans in a couple of days."

"I'll be going with them," Hugh told him.

Kiowa looked shocked.

"Are you sure you want to do that? I mean, so soon? Will you be in any shape to travel?"

"I made it here, didn't I"

As for the Arikaras, they appeared to have broken up into several groups, and no one seemed to know where any of the groups were. Two of those groups, though—one led by Elk's Tongue and another led by Bloody Hand, were known to be looking for trouble. Hugh Glass knew both of these warriors, and they knew him. He also knew that, since being recognized by Little Soldier during the fight at the Arikara village, Taka' Kur'uks would be considered an enemy to *all* Arikaras. It wouldn't matter that the Arikaras had attacked first. The fact that he had once been their "friend" and that he had slain one of their principal warriors would be enough to place him high on their tribal death list.

The barber at Fort Kiowa was also the doctor. In looking over Hugh's wounds, he could only shake his head.

"My friend," he told Hugh, "it is a miracle that you are alive."

"That seems to be the story of my life," Hugh answered tiredly.

On October 11th, three days after his arrival at Fort Kiowa, Hugh joined five other men and headed back upriver. The group was headed by Toussaint Charbonneau. Having helped lead Louis and Clark on their famous journey, nearly twenty years earlier, Charbonneau had spent more time exploring the American wilderness than probably any other white man. He was known by almost all the indian tribes and spoke many of their dialects.

The second in command of the group was named Antoine Citaliux, but everyone called him Langevin. The morning they left, he arrived at the boat looking worried.

"Something is wrong," He told one of the others.

"What is that?" the other man asked.

"I don't know—something about this just doesn't feel right. I think, perhaps, we should not be going on this trip."

The others chalked it up to a case of the jitters.

The party set sail. They were in a mackinaw boat, carrying a fair amount of sail. Fortunately, the wind was with them and they made good time. By evening, they had gained considerable distance from the fort. Shortly before sundown, they tied the boat up and made their camp next to the river.

The following morning, as they made ready to continue on their way, Langevin made nearly the same statement that he had before they left, the day before.

"I have a bad feeling," he told the others. "I don't know what it is, but I think this trip will not end well. I think maybe we should turn back."

"My friend," Charbonneau told him, laughing, "calm yourself. You'll make us all nervous!"

Langevin just looked worried.

The next day was no better, nor the day after that. They traveled upriver in the mackinaw, making good time, but Langevin's mood was starting to get on everyone's nerves. The small boat, loaded with supplies and goods to be traded with the Mandans, left little room for anyone to escape Langevins brooding pessimism. Each day he would start with the same litany, "I have a bad feeling…" —and would continue to express those sentiments throughout the day, whenever he opened his mouth to speak.

Hugh could see Langevin's words affecting the others. Langevin irritated them with his whining, but he was also starting to spook them. As for Hugh, he found it increasingly difficult to sit in the mackinaw, hour after hour, all day long. This was only in part because of Langevin. Hugh's wounds made it difficult to remain in one position for very long, and there wasn't a lot of room to move within the confines of the small boat.

On the morning of October 15th, Charbonneau suddenly told Langevin, "My friend, I think you have a good reason to have a bad feeling today."

"Why?" Langevin asked, suddenly alarmed.

"Because if I hear you say one word today about having a bad feeling, I am going to shoot you."

Langevin didn't find this amusing. Not knowing if Charbonneau was serious or not, he kept silent throughout the day.

That afternoon, they reached Simoneau Island. A small trading station had been set up there. The men in the mackinaw, accepting the hospitality of those who were stationed on the island, camped there for the night, then moved on the following morning. Langevin, true to form, spent the evening writing his last will and testament, which he left with the traders.

The next morning, as they were making ready to leave again, he started in once more.

"Oh," he began, "I wish I hadn't come on this trip!"

That did it. Taking his rifle, Charbonneau informed the others that he was walking the rest of the way to the Mandan village and would meet them there.

The weather had turned cool overnight, giving them the first hint of the coming of winter. Sitting in the boat, the chill added to Hugh's discomfort. He hated to see Charbonneau go like that. He had only known the Frenchman for a couple of days, but Charbonneau had a sureness in his manner and a sense of humor that Hugh liked. His decision to leave them and walk to the Mandan village made sitting in the boat and listening to Langevin even less tolerable than before.

They had reached a part of the river that he was familiar with. Shortly after noon, they approached a spot where the river made a long, narrow loop and doubled back upon itself. Knowing this, and feeling the need to stretch his legs, Hugh asked to be let out. He would walk across the narrow strip of land and meet them on the other side.

Before he was halfway across the strip he heard gunshots coming from the direction where the river made its loop. Moving as quickly as he could, Hugh went to investigate.

He arrived too late—not that he could have been of much help. Staring down from a rise that overlooked the river bend, it looked to him as though the entire Arikara nation had taken up residence in that spot. All four men in the mackinaw were dead and had already been scalped. Some of the squaws were desecrating the bodies. Others were busy taking the supplies from the boat. One of them looked up and saw Hugh Glass standing on the ridge.

Screaming, she raised the alarm. Rifle shots came in Hugh's direction, almost before he could turn and run. Scrambling as fast as he could, Hugh headed back in the direction he had come from. There was no way that he could hope to outdistance them, running on a broken leg that hadn't yet healed, but to wait for them would be worse than suicide. The Arikaras wouldn't just kill him—their torture would be slow and painful.

Long before he was safely away, he heard the Arikaras top the rise behind him. They came on, moving much more quickly than Hugh was able, yelling and shooting at him. Hugh felt the bullets whiz by, striking the brush and the earth around him. All he could do was keep running.

Crossing a low spot, he started up another long, slow rise. Bullets continued to strike near him. His injured leg felt as though it might break again at any moment.

Suddenly, over the top of the rise, two more indians appeared on horseback, rushing down toward him. Hugh's heart sank. They had him.

Continuing to run and angling away from the two horsemen, Hugh brought his rifle up. Just as he was about to shoot, he stopped himself. The two indians on horseback weren't Arikaras. They were Mandans.

Dropping his aim, Hugh kept running. The two Mandans rode down in a half-loop and came up behind him, one on either side. Working together, they managed to pick Hugh up without ever breaking stride. As the three men rode over the crest of the hill and out of range of the Arikara's gunfire, the two indians moved their horses together, helping Hugh into place behind the man on the right.

For the two Mandans this was quite a coup. For years they would be able to tell of how they had ridden into gunfire and taken the Arikaras quarry away from them, and how they had saved a white man named Hugh Glass from certain death.

This took on even more importance for them when they realized that Hugh Glass was actually White Bear of the Pawnees, and that this was the second time the Arikaras had had him in their sights only to lose him. On top of that, Hugh's encounter with the grizzly—which the Sioux had already begun to spread word of—made him seem, first to the Mandans and later to the other tribes of the plains, like a being that was half-man, half-magic.

CHAPTER FORTY-THREE

THERE WAS much celebrating on the part of the Mandans, with Hugh Glass and Toussaint Charbonneau as honored guests. The two white men were less than festive, though. Four of their party had been slain, and Charbonneau had lost all of his trade goods to the Arikaras.

On top of that, the weather had begun to turn cold. The morning after Hugh reached the Mandan village it snowed. It was a light snow and it melted quickly, but it was a portent of things to come. Winter was closing in, and Hugh Glass still had far to go.

Charbonneau told Hugh that his best chance for finding a boat that would take him up the Yellowstone was at Fort Tilton. Hugh didn't know where this fort was, but the Mandans did. They agreed to take him. This didn't happen right away, though. The Mandans were too busy celebrating their new guests to just stop and leave. Before they would leave the village, October would nearly be at an end. Hugh Glass didn't know it, but his story was starting to spread among the indians of the plains. The Mandans considered him to be something of a celebrity. They were in no hurry to let him go.

By the time Hugh Glass reached Fort Tilton, it was well into November. A foot of snow lay across the countryside. Fort Tilton was a small fort that belonged to the Columbia Fur Company. It had been built by William P. Tilton and boasted a garrison of only five men. As it sat near the site of another Mandan village, the Mandans who escorted Hugh dropped him off, then immediately went to visit their

175

cousins. Hugh went to see Tilton, where he learned right away that any hopes of finding a boat to continue his journey were in vain.

"Mr. Glass," Tilton told Hugh, "I'd like to help you but I can't. I've got five men here, besides myself. I can't spare any of them. We're under danger of attack here night and day by the Arikaras. I need every man I have to keep them away. Even if I *could* spare anyone, I doubt they would go. We're watched constantly. I had one man who left the fort for only a few minutes. From out of nowhere, that devil Stanapat rode up and killed him, practically on our doorstep. If you hadn't had the Mandans escorting you, don't think for a moment that you would have made it in here. Those damn Arikaras would have gotten you before you even came within sight of the fort."

Disappointed, Hugh exhaled heavily.

"Stanapat," he said ruefully. "—The Little Hawk With The Bloody Hand…" Tilton looked at him.

"You speak Arikara?" he asked Hugh.

"Pawnee," Hugh said absently. "The two languages are almost identical."

Tilton continued to stare at him. Slowly, a look of dread came over his features.

"Oh no," Tilton said. "Oh, Christ, I should have known by your scars—you're the one the indians call White Bear."

Hugh gave him a puzzled look.

"How did you know?"

"Mister, you're the talk of the plains. *Big* medicine. Went one on one with a grizzly, left for dead by two white men and still managed to crawl to Fort Kiowa. The Arikaras have tried to kill you and can't, that's what they say. Oh, I know about you. So does every tribe from here to the Rockies. As soon as Stanapat finds out you're here—and he will—he'll tear this place down to get to you. News travels real fast in these parts, mister, and the news here is that the Arikaras want you real bad."

Hugh was silent for awhile. He knew that what Tilton said about news traveling quickly between tribes was true. Like people everywhere, indians loved to gossip. They had no newspapers, nor did they need any. Their word of mouth was every bit as fast as the white man's convention, and at least as accurate. What he hadn't realized until now, though, was that he had made their version of the "front page". Far from helping him, this new development would hamper his efforts. Where the Arikaras were concerned, it made it infinitely more dangerous for him, or for anyone who tried to help him.

Finally, he spoke.

"Mr. Tilton, I didn't come here to bring you trouble. After it gets dark, if you could get a couple of your men to take me across the river, I'll move on."

"I think that would be good," Tilton told him.

At midnight, two of Tilton's men ferried Hugh across the river and let him out, and he began walking toward Fort Henry.

Despite the fact that his wounds had not yet completely healed, he carried a pack of nearly a hundred pounds. Although Hugh was a member of a rival fur company, William P. Tilton had given him some of the things he would need to survive the trip he was going on. Hugh would still have to hunt for most of his food, but Tilton provided him with blankets, tools, and some emergency stores for those times when he could not find game. Hugh had already gotten those items from Joseph Brazeau at Fort Kiowa, but had lost them to the Arikaras a month earlier. Tilton also gave Hugh a crude map of the area. According to Tilton, it would take Hugh about a month to get to Fort Henry.

Hugh consoled himself grimly with the fact that his wounds *would* heal, and that his pack would get lighter before he reached his destination. A lot lighter.

Actually, it wasn't too bad. It was cold, but not bitterly so. A crescent moon and a hundred thousand stars lit up the snow covered landscape. Hugh figured that as long as he had a star to follow, he could find anyplace.

There were no trees along this part of Hugh's journey, no timber of any kind. The wind blew from the north, almost directly into his face. Nor did the river offer any protection. It's bank sloped only on one side, while the other side dropped off straight into the water, so there were no cutaways or overhangs to crawl under for relief.

A week after Hugh left Fort Tilton, the weather turned bitterly cold, the sky dark and threatening. Hugh trudged on. There was nothing to do but keep moving.

After awhile it seemed to warm a little. Then snow began to fall—light at first, then heavier. The wind blew the snow into Hugh's eyes and made it nearly impossible to see where he was going.

Hugh knew he was in trouble. If he kept going he would almost undoubtedly get off his course. He might walk in circles, even stumble into the river if the snow blinded him enough. He had to stop.

There was still the problem of shelter. There were no trees, no brush of any kind, only snow-covered grass that stretched on for miles in every direction. The snow was a foot deep. For the first time, Hugh wished it was deeper.

Walking into the hollow between two low hills, he took off his pack. Then, using his pack-board, he began to push and pile the snow into the center of the hollow. In about an hours time he had a hill of snow that was about six feet high and a dozen feet across. Starting on the south side, the side that was away from the wind, he began to tunnel into it.

By the time his snow cave was finished, Hugh had to hunt for his pack, for it was buried under a blanket of white.

After facing the constant onslaught of the north wind for several days without relief, the little cave seemed incredibly warm. Hugh slept the night away, more comfortable than he had been for what seemed like a very long time.

When he awoke, it was still dark. Hugh lay for a while, listening to the storm. Then he drifted off again.

When he woke a second time, it was to a strange, eerie silence. A filtered twilight filled the tiny cave. Hugh realized the sun must be up. Snow had sealed the entrance to the cave. Hugh kicked it away and crawled, backward, out into the light. It was midday. The sky was gray, and it was a lot colder than he remembered it being before.

Disgusted with himself for having slept half the day away, he readied his pack and moved on.

Hugh had faced rough weather before. He had wintered on the plains with the Pawnees and had sailed around the horn of South America four times. On one of those voyages, it took six tries to make it around the horn. High winds and incredibly foul weather kept pushing the ship he was on back to their starting point. Each time they got close, the sails and lines, and the deck of the ship all turned to ice. As a sailor, he had been forced to work in those conditions. But there he had others to depend on for support and to help him with difficult jobs. He'd been able to go inside occasionally and catch a measure of warmth.

Here he was alone, with hundreds of miles of frozen wilderness stretching in every direction. And here there was no relief. There was only the bitter cold.

But the cold, like the pain he had endured before, only fueled the anger and hatred he felt for the two men whom he would kill.

And later, as Hugh Glass left the plains and began moving upward into the mountains, it grew colder still.

CHAPTER FORTY-FOUR

A WEEK AFTER Hugh Glass left Fort Tilton, a boat arrived from upriver, carrying three men. These were Black Harris, Jack Kellum, and John Fitzgerald. They were on their way to Fort Atkinson, having decided they'd had enough of winter in the high country.

William P. Tilton wasn't surprised that they had gotten past the Arikaras. The weather had turned cold again. When the temperature dropped, the indians, like most whites, remained in their lodges. He was, however, quite curious about them—when he learned where they were from.

"So," he said genially, "you men are down from Fort Henry. There was a Henry man through here several days ago, heading up. "I'm surprised you didn't see him. He was following the river. You must have passed each other by."

"Oh really?" Black Harris said. "Who was it?"

"Hugh Glass."

Harris and Kellum both looked at John Fitzgerald. Fitzgerald stared blankly at the floor, not meeting either man's gaze. Or Tilton's.

"He'd been tore up pretty good," Tilton went on, watching the three men. "He'd gone at it with a grizzly. Then he got left for dead by two men from your company, who took his fixin's. Ended up having to crawl three-hundred miles to Fort Kiowa without so much as a knife to protect himself with. He didn't say who the two men were, but he was headed to Fort Henry to even the score. I surely don't think I'd want to be *them* when he gets there!"

Harris and Kellum continued to stare at Fitzgerald. Fitzgerald looked down at the Hawken rifle he carried in his hands, and said nothing.

179

Two weeks after leaving Fort Tilton, Hugh reached the mouth of the Yellowstone. Here he was met with his first great obstacle—the Missouri River. His path lay beyond it and up into the hills that still sat in the distance. Tying two logs together, he made a raft and floated himself across. Then he continued onward.

He had begun to build snow caves almost on a daily basis, to use for shelter. Even with that, though, his life became a continuous, ongoing, freezing pain. After awhile, he and the pain became one. He could no longer imagine what it was like to be without it. As it had from the beginning, that pain continued to feed his anger, pushing him ever onward.

Hugh tried to think of other things—he thought of Little Feather, and of his two boys. The boys would be men by now, with their father only a memory long lost at sea. He even thought of Willie Brandt, the genial young pirate from the *Madalaine*. Hugh couldn't help wondering if Willie was still alive...

Always, his mind returned to the voices of two men, talking over a third who had not the strength to talk back to them. Two men, who had conspired to rob him of all his worldly goods, then to leave him to die, alone and helpless.

True it was, that Bridger had fought against that decision at first, and it was true that he *was* young. But in the end, he had gone along. He had made a man's decision, and he would pay a man's consequence. It was an unforgiving world they lived in. Bridger was old enough to know that a man lived and died by the decisions he made. He had done the deed. He would reap the reward.

Slowly, Hugh's trek began to incline upward.

Hugh Glass arrived at Fort Henry during the second week of December. It was midday when he suddenly came out of some trees and saw it lying ahead of him. He stopped for a moment and stared at it. Anticipation filled him. Before him lay warmth, hot food, and the two men he was going to kill.

Then he realized that he smelled no smoke, nor did he see any coming from the smokestacks at the fort. The gate in front of the fort hung loosely open.

Moving carefully, he began to circle the fort.

Almost two hours later, Hugh concluded that there was no life inside. Still careful, with his rifle at the ready, he walked up and entered the gate.

Nothing. Everything was gone. Hugh saw no signs that a battle had taken place. The men inside had just up and left.

One by one, he began to search the buildings. All were empty. On the wall of the last building Hugh looked in, he found the words written in red paint.

MOVED UPSTREAM TO MOUTH OF BIGHORN

With mixed feelings of disappointment and relief, Hugh leaned against the wall and read the words again. So they had moved upstream... He wondered how far the mouth of the Bighorn was, how many more days and nights he would have to spend marching through this frozen land. He felt suddenly very tired.

At least they hadn't all been wiped out by the Blackfeet. That had been his first fear upon seeing the fort empty. Two men from this company he wanted to see dead—but by Hugh's own hand, not by indians. For the rest of the company, he bore no ill will, and after walking alone for weeks, with only the icy wind for companionship, Hugh longed to hear the sound of a human voice.

The trappers had left a good supply of wood. Surprised that the indians hadn't come and hauled it away, Hugh set about making a fire. He would spend this night in no snow cave. Tonight he would be warm.

The next morning, leaving his pack at the fort, Hugh went hunting. His food supply was nearly gone and he had a journey of unknown length ahead of him. Hugh knew he would not get a chance like this again.

Luck was with him. Around noon he killed a small deer. Carrying it back to the fort, he spent the afternoon and evening smoking strips of meat over the fire.

The next day he moved on.

Two weeks after leaving the old fort, Hugh reached Fort Henry. It was late in the day. Hugh was about to make his camp for the night, when a shift in the wind brought him a whiff of smoke. Cautious as well as curious, he began to seek out its origin. Fully aware that it might be coming from the fort, he also knew there might be indians nearby.

It took him an hour to learn the truth, and this time there was no question that the fort was occupied. The gate was shut tight, and smoke came from every chimney. Hugh could see a lone figure standing inside the wall near the top of the gate, keeping guard.

It was nearly dark by the time he neared the entrance. The guard yelled down into the fort, "Man at the gate!"

Then, to Hugh, he yelled, "Who are you?"

Hugh hesitated for a second, then answered, "A member of the Company!"

"Can't be," the guard told him. "We're all here!"

"All but one. I'm Hugh Glass!"

The guard peered down at him for a moment. The man standing before him in the twilit gloom couldn't be Glass. Glass was dead.

Turning, the guard spoke to someone inside the fort. Then he turned back to Hugh.

"You can't be Hugh Glass," he said. "Glass was killed by a grizzly. Whoever you are, though, you're a white man. We'll allow you in."

The big gate opened.

They took him to the first building inside the fort, which was Major Henry's cabin and office. Henry rose to meet him as they entered.

"So," Henry began skeptically, "you're Hugh Glass?"

"That I am—and I'm here to kill two of your men. Look closely, Major. I can't have changed that much."

But he had. Scars, from where the bear's claws had torn his scalp, pulled the skin tight on one side of his face. He hadn't shaved for the six weeks he'd been walking through the wilderness. Still, there was something about the eyes...

"You don't sound like Glass," Henry told him.

"And how would *you* sound, Major, if your throat had been ripped out by a silvertip?"

Doubt began to show in Andrew Henry's eyes.

There were about ten men in the room, with more standing in the doorway. Suddenly they cleared to one side and Jim Bridger stepped in. He stood for a moment looking at Hugh. Then he went visibly pale. His mouth dropped open.

"Keep it away from me!" Jim's voice was barely more than a whisper. "Keep it away—it's a *ghost!*"

"No ghost, you little coward!" Hugh growled, "just the man you robbed and left to die out on the prairie!"

Without warning, Hugh rushed him. Jim tried to back away, but months of pent-up rage and endless pain drove Hugh Glass. He struck Bridger hard. The two men fell through the doorway and out into the snow, knocking two other men to the ground in their wake.

Glass came up on top. Jim didn't try to fight back, but attempted to protect himself as Hugh began raining blows on him. Most of Hugh's blows were deflected by Jim's heavy winter clothing. A few of them connected.

After what seemed an eternity to Jim, the others managed to pull the two men apart. Four trappers held on to Hugh as they moved back inside the building.

Major Andrew Henry was furious.

"All right!" he said loudly. "I'll have no more of that!" Looking at Hugh, he said, "You either control yourself, or I'll have you thrown out!" Then, breathing with disgust, he added, "Yes, you're Hugh Glass, all right! Too independent and too damn stubborn to be kept in line! You have yourself to blame for getting attacked by that grizzly—no one else! Your irresponsible actions could have gotten us *all* killed!"

"Still," he went on, "that doesn't excuse the fact that you were robbed and left to die..." As he spoke, Henry turned toward Jim Bridger. "Jim, you and John Fitzgerald both took extra money to take care of this man. What have you to say?"

Jim Bridger was a pathetic sight. For months guilt had plagued him, riding his conscience day and night. He stood, slump-shouldered, shaking visibly and watching Hugh Glass. Only now was his mind starting to accept the fact that Hugh was flesh and blood, and not a remnant.

Jim's mouth worked three or four times before he was able to get any words out.

"Mr. Glass," He began, "I'm sorry. Oh, God help me, I am. I'm really sorry!"

That was all he could say. Glass looked at him, waiting, but it was not Jim's way to pass the buck, or to make excuses, or to accept less than a full share of the blame.

Realizing this softened Hugh Glass. As much as he tried to keep the anger inside him, he felt it go out in a breath, leaving only mild disgust and, strangely, pity for the young man. If possible, Jim Bridger had let himself down in measures greater even than he had let down Hugh Glass.

"Pull yourself together, boy." Hugh said quietly. "I'll not harm you. I wanted to see if you would try to pass the blame. To your credit, you didn't. I was there, though, and I wasn't always unconscious. It was Fitzgerald that egged you on. He worked on you for days.

I will say this, though. In the future, if you give your duty to a man, you'd best stick to it. Otherwise, it'll come back on you."

Hugh turned to Major Henry.

"Now," he said, "where is John Fitzgerald, and where is my rifle?"

"Gone," Henry told him. "He and two other men left last month for Fort Atkinson. Your rifle went with him."

This was not something that Hugh Glass wanted to hear.

"Oh, Christ Almighty," he said under his breath. "How you test me…"

Andrew Henry was still watching him.

"So that's it, then?" Henry asked. "You're done with Bridger?"

"Yes, I'm done with him."

"And if I let you stay, you won't change your mind tomorrow or next week, and try to cause him harm?"

"Major," Hugh said, "I give you my word." He looked once more at Jim. "I'll leave you to your conscience, boy. I think it's already done more harm to you than I ever could."

Unable to look Hugh in the eye, Jim just nodded.

"In that case," Andrew Henry said, "let's get on with the celebrating!"

Hugh looked at him.

"Celebrating?"

"Yes," Henry told him. "Didn't you know? It's New Years Eve!"

CHAPTER FORTY-FIVE

March 27, 1824—

ONCE AGAIN, Hugh Glass was on the move. This time he wasn't alone, though. Four others were with him—Dutton, More, Chapman, and Marsh. They were headed for St. Louis. Hugh carried an important dispatch for General Ashley. That wasn't Hugh's main reason for going, though. He was after John Fitzgerald.

They had left Fort Henry nearly a month earlier, on February 29th—leap year. Foul weather had kept Hugh trapped at the fort for two months. It had done nothing to weaken his resolve to kill Fitzgerald. He also wanted his rifle back.

Shunning the still-frozen Missouri, the five men had followed the Powder River to its source, then worked their way over to the Platte. Here they stopped. The spring thaw had finally begun. The Platte was running. They would make much better time if they traveled by water. Working together, they built a bull-boat. This was done by cutting saplings and tying them together in the shape of a bowl, then covering the "bowl" with buffalo skins. When this was finished, they had only to pour tallow over the seams to make it watertight. Completely round, the boat was six feet in diameter, which made it plenty big enough for all five men and everything they carried.

Manuevering the boat was another matter. They were heading downstream. One man, using a pole, attempted to steer. The morning they set out was spent between hilarity and panic as the tiny boat whirled and dipped, rolled and rocketed through rapids and narrows, driven onward by the spring thaw, never quite under control. Hugh Glass could not remember the last time he had laughed so much or so hard.

By the end of the day, the scenery was starting to look familiar to him.

The following morning, just after they left, Hugh told the others:

"We're in my old stompin' grounds, boys. This is Pawnee country. I spent about four years in these parts, with a tribe of Pawnees. Don't be surprised if we see them camped along one of these riverbends."

In fact, Hugh was looking forward to it. Time had passed. Hugh's wounds had finally healed and he was no longer in pain, and he very much wanted to see his old friends again.

Around noon, on the next day, they saw the village. As Hugh had predicted, it sat just above a bend in the river. This would allow the people in the village access to the water from two different directions.

Seeing the men in the boat, the indians waved to them. Hugh and the others managed to manuever the ungainly little craft to the shore. Then, leaving their firearms in the boat, Marsh, Chapman, More, and Hugh Glass walked up to the village, leaving Dutton to stand guard over their belongings.

Hugh was a little disappointed that he saw no familiar faces among the people that greeted them. Even if this wasn't Old Knife's tribe, though, they were close enough neighbors that Hugh could probably get word of his friends, and would be able to send a message along to Big Axe and the others.

As they began to move into the village, Hugh felt a sudden sense of alarm. Two squaws were conversing alongside the four white men. One of them used a word that didn't sound quite right for Pawnee. It was more like an expression that the Arikaras might use...

Then he saw Elk's Tongue walking toward them.

"Run for it, boys!" he said suddenly. "These are Arikaras!"

In panic, the four white men ran back toward the boat. The Arikaras followed, whooping and yelling wildly. Having left their rifles with Dutton, Hugh and the others were almost defenseless. Hugh heard a gunshot from behind, but none of the whites fell. All four men kept running for their lives. Dutton, seeing their plight, picked up their rifles and began firing into the Arikaras, slowing them down and gaining precious seconds for the four white men.

Before they had covered half the distance back to the river, Marsh had gained a significant lead over the others. He reached the bull-boat nearly forty feet ahead of the others. In frantic effort to get into the boat, he pushed it away from the shore. Spinning out into the current, it was quickly carried away, with Dutton inside struggling to keep his balance and Marsh desperately clinging to the side. By the time Hugh and the other two men reached the water, the boat was already fifty feet away and moving fast. Hugh hit the water as, behind him, a hundred guns seemed to go off at once.

Staying under the surface, Hugh fought the current and swam hard for the opposite bank. The other two men, More and Chapman, entered the water at the same time and swam after the boat. Hugh wished he could have had time to warn them. The current carried the two men past the length of the village. Dozens of Arikara Warriors, some on horseback, raced out to meet them.

Not looking to see if he had been spotted, Hugh clambored out of the river, up the opposite bank, and disappeared over a small ridge. Out of sight of the village, he ran back upstream, to a point of rocks he had seen just before they had reached the village. There he hid himself, practicing every trick Big Axe had ever taught him on making himself invisible.

Later, the wind carried the sound of agonized screaming to him, and Hugh Glass knew that at least one of the others had been captured.

He stayed in his hiding place throughout the afternoon and well into the evening, and only well after it was dark did he slip away, unnoticed and unseen.

Once more he was alone in the wilderness, hundreds of miles from any white men and without a gun. This time, however, he had his knife and his tomahawk. He had his flint and steel, so he could make a fire. This time, too, he was no longer a cripple.

He also had a rough map of the land, and he still carried the dispatch for General Ashley. Looking at the map, Hugh noticed that Fort Kiowa and Fort Atkinson were equal distances from his position. He knew no one at Fort Atckinson, but the owner of Fort Kiowa, Joseph Brazeau, knew him. As a member of the Rocky Mountain Fur Company, Hugh would be able to get credit there once more.

Hugh headed for Fort Kiowa.

Hugh Glass reached Fort Kiowa for the second time in mid-June. Upon seeing him, Kiowa Brazeau simply stood behind the counter of his store, chuckling to himself and shaking his head.

"My friend," he said finally, "don't you ever stay dead?"

Hugh gave him a puzzled look.

"I've just been reading about you," Brazeau told him. He handed Hugh a newspaper.

The newspaper was the St. Louis Enquirer. It was dated June 7, 1824—more than a week old. Hugh read the story:

"—Mr. Vasquez, just from the upper Missouri, states that five men of Maj. Henry'sparty in descending the Platte, were attacked by a party of Aurikaree Indians—and that three, More, Chapman, and Glass were killed; that the others, Dutton and Marsh, made their escape and arrived at Council Bluffs."

Hugh put the newspaper down. So, Dutton and Marsh had escaped, and it had been Chapman and More that he had heard screaming afterward. Hugh said a silent prayer for them. He had no doubt that their capture had distracted the Arikaras and allowed him to escape unharmed.

Once more, Kiowa extended credit to him. This time, at Hugh's request, Brazeau included a horse. When Hugh casually asked if Brazeau had heard anything about a man named John Fitzgerald, Kiowa smiled.

"I wondered if you were going to get around to him," Brazeau said. "He's down at Fort Atkinson. He joined the Army back in April. Some say it's because someone was chasing him."

It was late in June before Hugh Glass finally reached Fort Atkinson. He had plenty of time to think about what he wanted to do, and plenty of time to reflect on all that had happened to him. Despite events at the time, he could find no excuse for Fitzgerald's actions; no reason to forgive the man. No reason not to kill him.

Atkinson wasn't at the fort. Nor was Colonel Leavenworth. The officer in charge was Captain Bennett Riley.

Something in Hugh's manner alerted Riley that something was wrong. He refused to let Hugh see Fitzgerald.

"Just tell me what the business is that you have with him," Riley told Hugh.

Unable to contain his emotions, Hugh fairly shook with anger and anticipation. He'd come so far, been through *so much*.

"I just…need to see him." Hugh fought to keep control.

"Mr. Glass," Riley said, "if this man has harmed you or your family, wronged you in any way—"

"Captain," Hugh interrupted, "look at me. Tell me what you see!"

Riley regarded him.

"I see a man who has been through…a lot."

"Yes…?"

Riley sighed.

"We've begun to hear stories," he said, "—from the indians—about a white man who was attacked by a grizzly. They say that two other white men, who were supposed to be his friends, left him to die, and that he had to crawl hundreds of miles, with wounds too numerous to mention—that wouldn't be you, would it?"

"THEY - *ROBBED* - ME!" Hugh exploded, unable to keep it in. "They left me…!"

"And now you're here to kill one of those men."

Hugh stared at the floor, blinking. A single tear ran down his nose and fell.

"What would *you* do, Captain?" he asked angrily. "If it were you, what would you do?" He looked at Riley. "What the *hell* would you do?"

"Well, in the first place, I probably would have died. I don't think there are many men who would have survived what you have. If I *did* survive, I'd probably feel just like you do. I'd want to kill them, too… But, as commander of this post, *I* can't allow you to do that."

Riley exhaled, then continued.

"I'll tell you what—I'll make sure he makes some kind of restitution, and that he returns to you any property of yours that he still has. If you harm one hair on his head, though, I'll throw you in prison. If you kill him, I'll see that you hang. Is that clear?"

After a moment, Hugh gave a slight nod. Riley left the room. A minute later he returned. They waited.

A little while later the door opened. Fitzgerald came in, carrying Hugh's Hawken rifle.

"Hello, Hugh," Fitzgerald said. "I brought your rifle. I took good care of it for you. It's all cleaned...and loaded."

Hugh took the rifle from him, remembering as he did, the old, familiar weight; the feel of it in his hands. Fitzgerald was right. He had taken good care of it. It was cleaned and oiled. And it was loaded.

"I'm sorry about what we done," Fitzgerald said. "I can't change it."

Hugh continued to look down at his rifle. Why had he brought it back loaded? Was he a fool as well as a coward?

"You know what it was like out there, Hugh," Fitzgerald continued. "We were all scared out of our wits. Hell, even the damn *Mandans* had declared war on us!"

I have only to point it and pull the trigger, Hugh thought, *but that would mean the end of me, too.*

"The indians were gettin' *real* close..."

—*Or, at least, one quick step in, and a butt stroke to the chin...*

"It didn't seem real smart to stay there an' get discovered." Fitzgerald kept talking. "Then we would have *all* been killed..."

...*He wouldn't be able to eat solid food for a month. I'd go to jail, but it would be worth it...*

But even as he considered it images began to appear in his mind, memories of Clint, of Potter and the other men of the *Gallant,* of the little girl that died after being brutalized aboard the *Madalaine,* of his two boys. All people that, at one time or another, Hugh had let down...

Hugh sighed heavily.

"Say somethin', will you?" Fitzgerald pleaded. "I'm tryin' to explain, to apologize, but...say somethin', all right? Or just shoot me..."

Hugh looked at him. Fitzgerald looked away.

Turning to Captain Riley, Hugh said, "Thank's for getting my rifle back." Then, without another word, he walked past Fitzgerald and over to the door. At the door he hesitated. Then he turned back to Fitzgerald.

"Don't ever leave the army." Hugh let the words hang there, with meaning. Then he went out the door.

Outside, the sergeant met Hugh and handed him a fairly good-sized leather pouch.

"Cap'n Riley had us take up a collection for you, Mr. Glass," the sergeant said. "For your trouble. There's about three-hundred dollars there."

Hugh accepted the money with a grunt. He nodded to the man. Then he got onto his horse and rode out of the fort. Somewhere, far to the north, Little Feather waited for him.

It was good to have his rifle back.

THE END

AFTERWORD

ANDREW HENRY: Tall, blue-eyed and self-assured, Andrew Henry epitomized what came to be the popular image of "The Mountain Man". Yet, before the summer of 1824 was to come to an end, he would leave the mountains forever and return to St. Louis, and to his books and his violin. Jedidiah Smith would take his place as William H. Ashley's partner.

JEAN LAFITTE and THE PIRATES OF CAMPECHE: About the time that Hugh Glass made his escape from them, the pirates' fortunes had begun to decline. Rumours of some of their unsavory practices began to float back to the U.S. Government. Pickings, for the pirates, became scarce. Shortly after Hugh and Clint escaped, a storm struck Campeche, destroying several of the ships that lay anchored in the channel and nearly destroying the town. Rallying, Lafitte took the entire black population of the island(which included free men of color who served aboard his ships)threw them into chains, and transported them to New Orleans to be sold as slaves. This allowed him to raise enough money to rebuild the stronghold. In 1822, after hearing numerous reports of piracy, the American Navy sailed to Galveston and ordered the pirates to leave. Lafitte and his band of men sailed away from the island. What happened to them after that remains a mystery to this day. Much is speculated. Little is known.

BIG AXE and BIG SOLDIER: In 1832, ten years after Hugh Glass left the Pawnees, an agent for the Bureau of Indian Affairs learned that a young indian girl was about to be sacrificed to the Pawnees' deity, Morning Star. The agent raced to the Pawnee village to try to intervene. He spoke with Big Axe, who said he didn't know if he could stop the sacrifice or not, but said he would try. The agent reported that, because of Big Axe's standing in the tribe and due to his indomitable will, the Pawnees gave the girl up. As they were leaving the village, winding their way through the maze of earth-dome lodges, they were forced to pass by the lodge that belonged to Big Soldier. An arrow flew from within the lodge, striking the girl and knocking her from her horse. As a group of indians began dragging the girl toward the east side of the village, the agent looked to see Big Axe and Big Soldier struggling together at the door of Big Soldier' lodge. Realizing that this development could put his own life at risk, the agent rushed to break up the fight, which he managed to do with the help of some other indians who were standing nearby. He then went to try to save the girl, but by the time he reached the edge of the village she had been literally "torn to pieces".

Big Axe continued to be a major force among the tribe. In the Spring of 1840 he died, reportedly killed by the Sioux. By 1844, Big Soldier was reported to be the Chief of the Skidi Pawnees.

JIM BRIDGER: The young man who tortured himself with the fact that he abandoned Hugh Glass and who actually believed that Glass was a ghost when he arrived at Fort Henry, was destined for greatness. Aside from this one episode, he was never known to let a man down. He became one of the most popular figures of the era, was the first white man to drink from the Great Salt Lake, and eventually became known as "The King of the Mountain Men". In 1868, he retired to his farm in Kansas City, Missouri, where he died in 1881. Bridger Mountains, Bridger Pass, and Bridger National Forest are all named for him.

HUGH GLASS: As Bridger's popularity grew, the story of Hugh Glass and the grizzly began to be played down. By the early 1900's there were those that contended that it never really happened. Others tried to say that Hugh Glass himself made the whole episode up. Letters, newspaper articles of the time, and personal accounts have proven that this was not the case, and that the story was true. In 1915, when John G. Neihardt ("Black Elk Speaks") wrote "The Song of Hugh Glass", he learned of the story—not only through newspaper articles and magazines, but from the indians of the plains, whom Niehardt knew quite well and among who, by that time, the story of Hugh Glass had become a tradition.

As for Glass himself, after retrieving his rifle from John Fitzgerald, he headed north for a bit, then went south for awhile. In 1825, while leading a trapping party up the Snake River for Etienne Provost, Hugh took a Shoshone arrow in the back. His friends were forced to transport him seven-hundred miles upriver before finding someone to remove it. Fortunately, it was a metal arrowhead, not one of the old stone heads that the indians were so fond of. Even with that, the wound had begun to fester by the time the arrowhead was removed. After he recovered, Hugh Glass headed once more for the high Missouri.

That same year—1825—William Henry Ashley held the first "Rendezvous". In doing so, he created a system that kept the trappers in the mountains and brought the "store" to them. The trappers could trade their pelts for a years' supply of goods, participate in games of skill and chance, and spend whatever was left on alcohol and women. At the end of each rendezvous, the time and place for the next one would be decided. It was a system that worked out well, for a time.

By 1828, change was in the air. The American Fur Company, or Amfurco, which was financed by John Jacob Astor and a few other investors, hired a man named Kenneth McKenzie to establish a post on the high Missouri, just west of the Yellowstone River. McKenzie hired Etienne Provost to take the message to the rendezvous—if the trappers brought their goods to Fort Floyd(where McKenzie was based)they might receive up to twice the dollar amount paid by the Rocky Mountain Fur Company.

This forced the trappers to make a decision. They could go on living with the monopoly created by the Rocky Mountain Fur Company, or they could take their wares down to Fort Floyd and get more money for them. The trouble was, none of the trappers wanted to leave the Rockies.

They decided to elect a delegate, someone they trusted, to go and talk to McKenzie and invite Amfurco to send some of their goods and supplies to the next rendezvous and break the monopoly of the Rocky Mountain Fur Company. The man the trappers elected for this job was Hugh Glass.

Making his way to Fort Floyd, Hugh presented McKenzie with their offer. McKenzie couldn't and wouldn't send a pack train into the mountains. He wanted Fort Floyd to become the clearing house for the fur trade. If the trappers wanted better than average prices for their furs, they would bring them to the fort. McKenzie did make one concession, though, which persuaded many a fur trapper to make the trek down out of the hills and trapped them into continueing to do so. In exchange for signing a contract to deliver all their furs to Fort Floyd, Amfurco would pay cash to the trappers—in advance. Enough of the trappers went for this deal that it weakened the monopoly held by Rocky Mountain Fur and, in time, would bring an end to the rendezvous system.

The Arikaras never forgot Hugh Glass—or their hatred of him. Early in 1833, Hugh was at Tulloch's Fort, which was also known as Fort Cass. The fort was located in Crow Country, who were at that time on friendly terms with the whites. One morning Hugh, Ed Rose (who had tried to warn Ashley of the impending attack by the Arikaras, ten years earlier) and a man named Menard left the fort to hunt beaver. A short while later, as they were crossing the frozen Yellowstone, a party of Arikaras who were waiting in ambush cut them down.

Days later, a friend of Hugh's, Johnson Gardner, encountered a group of Arikaras that were in possession of some of Glass' gear. Recognizing this, Gardner and his friends seized the indians. The Arikaras declared their innocence. Gardner let one of the indians go, on the condition that he return in twenty-four hours with Hugh Glass. When the Arikara didn't return, Gardner scalped the remaining indians and burned them alive. Within three weeks Gardner himself was captured by the Arikaras, scalped, and burned alive.

Hugh's rifle was never recovered.

BIBLIOGRAPHY

Alter, Cecil B. *Jim Bridger*. University of Oklahoma Press

Camp, Charles L. *The Chronicles of George C. Yount*. California Historical Quarterly, 1923. Vol. II. Berkeley, California

Celand, Robert G. *This Reckless Breed of Men*. University of Nebraska Press

Dale, H.C. *The Ashley-Smith Explorations: A History of the Rocky Mountain Fur Co*. Cleveland, 1918

Dana, Richard H. *Two Years Before the Mast*. Viking Penguin

Gosse, Philip. *The Pirates' Who's Who: Giving Particulars of the Lives and Deaths of the Pirates & Buccaneers*. Gordon Press

Grinnell, George B. *Pawnee Hero Stories and Folk Tales*. University of Nebraska Press

Hunter, John D. *Memoirs of a Captivity Among the Indians of North America*. Report Service, 1823

Hyde, George E. *The Pawnee Indians*. University of Oklahoma Press

Lewis, Meriwether. *History of the Expedition Under the Command of Captains Lewis and Clark To the Sources Of the Missouri; Thence Across the Rockies And Down to the Pacific Ocean*. Philidelphia, 1814

Manfred, Frederick. *Lord Grizzly*. University of Nebraska Press

Myers, John M. *The Saga of Hugh Glass: Pirate, Pawnee, and Mountain Man*. University of Nebraska Press.

Neihardt, John G. *The Song of Hugh Glass*. New York, 1915

Neihardt, John G. *Indian Tales & Others*. University of Nebraska Press

Oswalt, Wendall H. *This Land Was Theirs: A Study of North American Indians*. Mayfield Publishing.

Saxon, Lyle. *Lafitte the Pirate*. New York, 1930 Pelican

Camp, Charles L. *The D.T.P Letters: Essays for Henry Wagner*. San Francisco, California, 1947